About the author

Dr Mark Everard is an author, scientist and broadcaster with extensive involvement in the worlds of environment and sustainability, angling and music. Mark's work, books and other publications span these topics and others besides, all forming part of his personal mission to contribute to cleaner waters for all in a sustainable world. His books include *Common Ground* (Zed Books, 2011).

The hydropolitics of dams

Engineering or ecosystems?

MARK EVERARD

Zed Books
LONDON | NEW YORK

The hydropolitics of dams: Engineering or ecosystems? was first published in 2013 by Zed Books Ltd, 7 Cynthia Street, London N1 9JF, UK and Room 400, 175 Fifth Avenue, New York, NY 10010, USA

www.zedbooks.co.uk

Set in OurType Arnhem and Monotype Futura by Ewan Smith, London

Index: ed.emery@thefreeuniversity.net

Cover design: www.alice-marwick.co.uk

Printed and bound in Great Britain by CPI Group (UK) Ltd, Croydon, CRO 4YY

Distributed in the USA exclusively by Palgrave Macmillan, a division of St Martin's Press, LLC, 175 Fifth Avenue, New York, NY 10010, USA

A catalogue record for this book is available from the British Library
Library of Congress Cataloging in Publication Data available

ISBN 978 1 78032 541 5 hb
ISBN 978 1 78032 540 8 pb

Contents

Figures, table and boxes

Abbreviations

AMP	Accelerated Mahaweli Project (Sri Lanka)
AWRM	adaptive water resources management
CBD	Convention on Biological Diversity
CMA	Catchment Management Agency (Mpumalanga)
CRP	Conservation Reserve Program (US)
DAD	decide-announce-defend
DDP	Dams and Development Programme (UNEP)
DWAF	Department for Water Affairs and Forestry (South Africa)
EDD	engage-deliberate-decide
EU	European Union
ICOLD	International Commission on Large Dams
ICW	integrated constructed wetlands
IPCC	Intergovernmental Panel on Climate Change
IUCN	International Union for Conservation of Nature
IWRM	Integrated Water Resource Management
MA	Millennium Ecosystem Assessment
MUS	multiple use water services
NGO	non-governmental organization
NWA	National Water Act (South Africa)
OECD	Organisation for Economic Co-operation and Development
PES	paying for ecosystem services
PSA	Pagos por Servicios Ambientales (Costa Rica: Payments for Environmental Services)
SCaMP	Sustainable Catchment Management Programme (UK)
SLCP	Sloping Land Conversion Policy (China)
STEEP	Social, Technological, Economic, Environmental, Political
SuDS	sustainable drainage systems
TEEB	The Economics of Ecosystems and Biodiversity
TWP	Thukela Water Project (South Africa)
UNEP	United Nations Environment Programme
UNESCO	United Nations Educational, Scientific and Cultural Organization
UNICEF	United Nations Children's Fund
WCD	World Commission on Dams

WfW	Working for Water (Africa)
WHO	World Health Organization
WRT	Westcountry Rivers Trust (UK)
WSUD	Water Sensitive Urban Design (Sydney programme)
WWF	Worldwide Fund for Nature (formerly the World Wildlife Fund)
ZACPLAN	Zambezi Action Plan

Acknowledgements

This book arose from my practical work, at both policy and grassroots level in both the developing and developed worlds, engaging with people about developing water resources on a sustainable basis. It came about from a clash of cultures – the technocentric and the ecocentric – with no authoritative text to help me tread the tightrope between them. Dealing with the practical realities of our overpopulated, urban-centred world impressed upon me that we need both. Above all, we need to know how to work with people – all people who share catchment systems – to understand how their supportive ecosystems work and to respect each other's values and needs in planning for locally appropriate and truly sustainable development of water services.

Many people have given me insight and shared their wisdom. Some have done so knowingly, but many more simply by participating in this quest for sustainable outcomes. Were I to try to list them all, I would, I am sure, miss many. So I would like to name only a few who have made especially significant contributions, though thanking everyone whose paths I have crossed in the many initiatives I have had the good fortune to support.

These include the Department for Water Affairs and Forestry (DWAF), both nationally and in the provinces of KwaZulu-Natal and Mpumalanga. Thanks too to colleagues involved in the Mvoti Dialogue and the patient process entailed in setting up the Mvoti Water User Association (WUA) in KwaZulu-Natal, in the Inkomati Catchment Management Agency (CMA) in Mpumalanga, and the national science and policy team involved in the FETWater programme. Particular thanks to my colleagues John Colvin and Sam Chimbuya with whom I enjoyed working on all these South African water allocation reform projects. Myles Mander, Guy Preston, Chris Dickens and Mark Dent too have been constant friends and sources of wisdom about the economics and ecosystems of Africa. Turning to China, thanks to all those involved in the 2010 summer school and advisory visit in Beijing and Lanzhou. In India, many people have given me insight, particularly Gaurav Kataria, with whom I worked on the influential Pancheshwar Dam ecosystem services report and also established the 'paying for ecosystem services' market on the Western Ramganga river. A wide range of colleagues in Australia, the USA, the UK, South Korea, Ireland and across Europe have also collaborated in or applied my work to their own programmes.

Others deserving honourable mention include Steve Lockett, ever of inquiring mind and driving much of my early thinking about India's dam dilemma. Also Mairi Lee for her critique of the manuscript in various stages of its evolution. Thanks too to my colleagues at Zed Books for support, patience and editorial advice.

Apologies to all whom I have omitted to mention. This work truly stands on the shoulders of giants, pygmies and a wide array of other players of intermediate stature, all of whom have added immeasurably to the rich mix of ideas, even if they have not realized it.

But my main inspiration comes from those who will pick up this work and use it to improve the lot of people from all strata of society who drink from our common yet finite well. It is to you that this book is dedicated.

Introduction

Humanity's diverse activities are all ultimately buoyed by fresh waters and the water-yielding ecosystems with which we have co-evolved. Control of water flows was central to the settlement of humanity, forming not only the foundation of our first civilization but substantially shaping subsequent cultural and economic evolution. As a finite resource, fresh water and its management will inevitably also define much of our future relationships and potential.

Water is life. It is also power, opportunity, influence and status, particularly for those controlling it in arid and water-stressed lands. Access to and management of water are therefore inescapably political. And of course all politics are personal, never more so than for those with insufficient water to enable their families to drink, cook and wash, and whose crops are withering in the field.

The first of the three parts of this book, *Part 1: Development, water and dams*, is primarily concerned with the development of dams and other 'heavy engineering' approaches to manipulate ecosystems, significantly including water systems, at ever greater scales. The first chapter, 'Replumbing the modern world', addresses how we are re-plumbing entire subcontinents, but also how technology choice and implementation are not without profound consequences for ecosystems and the people who depend upon them. Chapter 2, 'Temples of the modern world', charts the evolution of large dams and their related heavy access, distribution and associated operational infrastructure. Some of the direct and indirect consequences of this technological pathway for people and ecosystems are addressed in Chapter 3, 'Stemming the flow', while measures undertaken to recognize and attempt to mitigate them are considered in Chapter 4, 'A changing mindset'. Chapter 5, 'The World Commission on Dams and beyond', addresses major international initiatives better to understand the consequences and potential future role of dams, with Chapter 6, 'The state of play with dams', then synthesizing what we now know. Chapter 7, 'Dams and ecosystem services', considers dams against the evolving framework of ecosystem services, before Part 1 concludes with Chapter 8, 'A new agenda for dams'.

1

But of course dams and related heavy technology are not the only way to manage water and the many benefits that water flows confer upon humanity. Other, often ecosystem-based means to manage water form the substance of *Part 2: Water in the postmodern world*. Its first chapter, 'Water in the postmodern world', considers our relationship with water and related aspects of hydropolitics. Different facets of ecosystem-based water management are then considered in Chapters 10, 'Managing water at landscape scale', and 11, 'Catchment production and storage'. We then turn to Chapters 12, 'Water flows through society', and 13, 'Markets for water services', before summing up some key considerations relating to Chapter 14, 'Nature's water infrastructure'.

My work throughout South Africa, India, Australia, East Africa, China, America and Europe has opened my eyes to the inconvenient truth that neither heavy engineering nor ecosystem-based management is a panacea if considered in isolation. Key considerations instead have to start with the needs and value systems of all people, the character and carrying capacity of the ecosystems that provide for them, and dialogic processes to connect them. This forms the substance of *Part 3: Rethinking water and people*. Chapter 15, 'Living within the water cycle', looks at some of the inconvenient realities with which we have to grapple in a heavily populated, water-stressed world, including the need to rise above an over-simplistic 'engineered versus green' dichotomy. Chapter 16, 'Governance of water systems', then turns to options for participatory decision-making and capacity-building necessary for planning management options to achieve sustainable, multi-benefit outcomes that address complex, often competing human demands. The concluding chapter, Chapter 17, 'Towards a new hydropolitics', together with its supporting annexe, 'Principles for sustainable water sharing', synthesizes lessons and principles from throughout the book into an integrated decision-making framework to guide complex, 'real world' decisions.

We do not have all the answers, and the challenges facing us are as massive as they are pressing and unavoidable. For it is an uncomfortable truth that humans, or at least the demands of contemporary resource-hungry lifestyles, place overbearing demands on the supportive capacities of the ecosystems that underwrite our well-being, wealth-creation activities and potential to live fulfilled lives.

While this book is educational, summarizing several complex fields with respect to what we are learning about integrated water management, it should also be viewed as a practical guide to working with people to better manage their water resources. After all, the reason I wrote it is precisely because I could not find an appropriate volume to help me achieve exactly that! It has been written to support and provoke tomorrow's water leaders and the people they serve; it is to these people and the heroic feats they will achieve that this book is dedicated.

ONE | **Development, water and dams**

1 | Replumbing the modern world

Manipulation of water flows to and from land is as old as settled agriculture. Irrigation and river management practices are found widely across the ancient human world, constituting one of the most fundamental technologies to enhance natural soil productivity and overcome limitations to survival and progress. Indeed, they were pivotal in the ascent of humanity from the moment *Homo sapiens* appeared in the fossil record in Africa about 130,000 years ago to eventually displace wider groups of hominids.

Settled agriculture in turn marked a revolution in human ingenuity, bringing into cultivation and domestication various species of plants and animals to provide staple foods. It signalled an evolution in human consciousness to the extent that farmers' decisions were premised upon future yields, rather than merely current availability, providing the need for the establishment of permanent communities, new levels of social structure and communication, and for the transfer of knowledge between individuals and generations. These innovations laid some of the foundations of modern culture. Writing systems were developed, empires were created often in the quest for more resources, and monumental buildings were constructed by a better-nourished populace less vulnerable to the vagaries of hunting and gathering. Many assign the origin of economic systems to the transition to settled agriculture as, released from the daily drudgery of pursuing food, societies were able to internally differentiate responsibilities and labour, and so to need a trading system for fair exchange between social groups.

The evolution of agricultural principles and applications, critically including the management of water, was followed by advances in the entrainment of water for defensive, industrial, municipal and other purposes. These broad and fascinating innovations have substantially shaped human history.

A brief history of dams

Dams were an early innovation in the rise of human civilizations. ICOLD,[1] the International Commission on Large Dams, defines a dam as a barrier or structure across a stream, river or waterway to confine and then control the flow of water. Dams vary in size from small slip dams built to intercept springs and small streams emerging from hillsides and gorges, generally for farm use, through to progressively larger engineered structures, generally used for water supply, hydro-power and irrigation and including some of the modern world's most massive civil engineering schemes.

Across the globe, major river systems have been progressively dammed over a period of centuries. The earliest unambiguous records of human agriculture appear in the 'fertile crescent' of Mesopotamia, between the rivers Tigris and Euphrates in land now covered by modern-day Iraq, with evidence of river engineering found in the ruins of irrigation canals over eight thousand years ago. At 104 metres (340 feet) long, 61 metres (200 feet) high at the crest and built of masonry blocks with a gravel and stone centre, Sadd el-Kafara, the Dam of the Pagans, is the world's oldest big dam built between 2950 and 2750 BC and today crumbling in the Egyptian desert.[2] The remains of water storage dams dating back to at least 3000 BC have also been found in Jordan, Egypt and other parts of the Middle East, though no more large permanent dams were built in Egypt until the twentieth century. In China, a system of dams and canals was constructed in 2280 BC, the Dujiang irrigation project once supplying 800,000 hectares in China. The 1,500-year-old Grand Canal, one of the wonders of ancient China, was once the largest artificial river of the pre-industrial world and was also the first to have lock gates. It was used to transport rice from the wet south of the country, primarily from the monsoon-fed Yangtze valley, to centres of population in the north. One of the oldest dams still in use today is an earth- and rock-fill embankment dam built around 1300 BC in what is now Syria. The building of the Marib Dam in Yemen began around 750 BC and took 100 years to complete, comprising an earth embankment 4 metres high with stone sluices to regulate discharges for irrigation and domestic use. In 1986, the existing Marib Dam was raised to a height of 38 metres, creating a reservoir of 398 million cubic metres of water. The famed though potentially mythical 'hanging gardens of Babylon', considered one of the Seven Wonders of the Ancient World and attributed to the neo-Babylonian king Nebuchadnezzar II, who ruled between 605 and 562 BC, were probably more miraculous for their water engineering than for the vegetation they supported.

In Sri Lanka, ancient chronicles and stone inscriptions state that numerous dams and reservoirs were built as early as the third century BC. Inter-basin canals built for irrigation augmented many of these large reservoirs. One of these large dams, the Minneriya dam, was constructed during the reign of King Mahasen (AD 276–303), and was still intact when it was rediscovered in 1900. It was restored in 1901 and is still in use today. More than fifty other ancient dams in Sri Lanka have been restored.

The Romans built an elaborate system of low dams for water supply. The most famous was the Cornalbo earth dam in southern Spain, which had a height of 24 metres (78 feet) and a length of 185 metres (606 feet). After the Roman era, very little development in dam construction took place until the end of the sixteenth century, when the Spanish began to build large dams for irrigation. European engineers refined their design and construction knowledge in the nineteenth century, giving rise to the capability to construct dams to a height of 45–60 metres (150–200 feet).

The first recorded dam in India was on the Cauvery river ('Kaveri' in the native tongue), the southernmost of the three great river catchments draining the Deccan peninsula. Here, the Grand Anicut (in Tamil, *anai* means 'to hold' and *katta* is 'something that is built') spanned the Cauvery near Tiruchirapalli in the time of King Karikala in the second century AD. The dam is still in use today, albeit massively altered and reinforced, and is just one of many ancient dams subsequently reconstructed throughout India, with a particularly pronounced period of dam-building as long ago as the thirteenth century AD, when the Hoysala Empire ruled much of modern-day Karnataka in the Deccan peninsula.

The Sayamaike dam, one of the oldest dams in Japan, was built early in the seventh century AD and, after several modifications and a raising of height, it is still in use today. Several ancient dams from the thirteenth to the sixteenth century in Iran are also still in use today.

In the 1950s, the German-American historian Karl A. Wittfogel coined the term 'hydraulic civilizations' to describe societies managing their use of water through technology rather than local access.[3] Today, much of the developed world constitutes hydraulic civilization, with many emerging nations aspiring to exploitation of technology rather than local access to natural resources to meet their water needs. Living with a significant legacy of engineering-dependent water management, we risk losing sight of other meanings of water, ranging from its cultural and spiritual importance to different people through to a respect for the ecosystems we depend on to maintain the quality and quantity of the basic resource of water that enters our ever more complex societal plumbing systems.

Different types of dam

Dams are classified by the material used to construct them. Embankment dams are constructed of either earth fill or a combination of earth and rock fill, while dams built of concrete, stone or other masonry are called gravity dams, arch dams or buttress dams. Engineers generally choose to build embankment dams in areas where large amounts of earth or rocks are available. Gravity dams depend entirely on their own weight to resist the tremendous force of the stored water. Some early gravity dams were constructed with masonry blocks and concrete, and are known as masonry dams. Today, gravity dams are constructed by mass concrete or roller-compacted concrete (concrete placed in layers and compacted by a roller) and are referred to as concrete gravity dams.

Arch dams are concrete dams that curve upstream towards the flow of water, built in narrow canyons such that water pushing against the dam transfers its force to the canyon wall. Arch dams require much less concrete than gravity dams of the same length, but need a solid rock foundation to support the weight of the dam. Conversely, buttress dams depend for support on a series of vertical supports (buttresses) running along their downstream face to transfer the force of the water downwards to the dam's foundation.

Topography, geology, foundation conditions, hydrology, likelihood of earthquakes and availability of construction materials are some of the factors affecting the selection of the type of dam. Narrow valleys with shallow sound rock favour a concrete dam, while wide valleys with varying rock depth and condition favour embankment dams. Earth embankment dams are the most common type encountered today, comprising 43.7 per cent of the global total, since they accommodate all the material from the required excavation. Gravity dams account for 10.6 per cent of the total, while rock-fill embankment dams total just 5.3 per cent.

Contested resources

It is not surprising that, with so much water collected and/or diverted by dams globally, there is a long history of conflict over potentially contested resources. As one striking example, approaching 100 per cent of the water needs of the South African province of Gauteng are diverted from outside its natural catchment, adding value to the recipient region while diverting the resource from donor catchments. But South Africa, formerly infamous for asymmetries in power under the apartheid regime, has been far from alone in the appropriation of water and other resources by a powerful elite to the detriment of other communities.

To this we can add the many international examples of often fiercely contested water rights. Examples of international tensions related to trans-boundary rivers, as well as some resolutions, are seen between India and Pakistan concerning sharing of the Indus river, between China and India contesting ownership of the waters of the upper Brahmaputra river, between Ethiopia and Egypt, regarding rights to the flow of the Blue Nile, and between the USA and Mexico regarding allocation of the Colorado river's water.

Contested rights also occur within nations. Former racial divisions in South Africa, including rights-related issues behind the diversion of water between regions, again serve as a classic example. However, the numerous dams, ancient and modern as well as periodically modified, that interrupt India's Cauvery river and its tributaries through Kerala, Karnataka and Tamil Nadu states are also a cause of ongoing tension. The river's waters are put to work throughout its course, including the headwaters in the state of Kerala and downstream in the union territory of Pondicherry, to irrigate crops and to water livestock, provide domestic and industrial supply, and to generate electricity. Many dams throughout the catchment store water during monsoon periods when around 100 hours of rain typically falls in just 100 days. This stored water is released during the drying months, though water reserves become very low in the driest months of February to May, and some riverbeds dry out entirely. Of the river's flow, some 60 per cent is thought to be used for irrigation, dwarfing but also potentially conflicting with other uses and the needs of ecosystems. Karnataka diverts water for irrigation and to provide virtually the entire water supply for the burgeoning cities of Mysore and Bangalore as well as many other towns and villages. Rights to this water are hotly contested by the downstream state of Tamil Nadu, through which the Cauvery river is also intensively dammed on its way to its delta as it enters the Bay of Bengal. Water sharing from the Cauvery has been a major issue of contention between the four states and a frequent cause of protests within them, with a central government agency – the Cauvery Tribunal – now set up to look into this issue. The Cauvery river, which has served as the lifeblood of ancient kingdoms, and continues to support modern cities throughout much of southern India, also absorbs the industrial, domestic, mining and diffuse wastes of an ever-larger human population, compounding the relative sharing of benefits and burdens.

The history of dam-building observed in the Deccan peninsula is mirrored elsewhere in India and around much of the rest of the world, from China and other Asian countries, throughout Africa, across North America, central Europe and Australia. In every case, the distribution of benefits and associated costs raise profound rights issues. With such large-scale and widespread rights issues associated with contested water resources, it is surprising that they have not been an even greater historic source of conflict.

The large dam revolution

Since 1900, the world has, on average, completed one large dam every day. The global economic recovery following the Second World War was accompanied by phenomenal growth in infrastructure systems that included the world's largest dam construction period. From the 1930s, dam-building reached a whole new scale, entering the era of 'large dams'. ICOLD, the International Commission on Large Dams established in 1928, defines large dams as those with a height of 15 metres or more (fifty or more feet) from the foundation, in addition to dams of 5–15 metres in height retaining a reservoir volume of 3 million cubic metres or more. The construction of large dams became, in the eyes of many, synonymous with development and economic progress. They were viewed as symbols of modernization and humanity's ability to harness or control nature, and construction accelerated dramatically. This trend peaked in the 1970s, during which decade 7,511 large dams were built: an average of two or three large dams commissioned each day somewhere in the world. A total estimated investment of $US2 trillion was ploughed into large dam construction worldwide during the twentieth century. Average height, resource volume and overall mass increased during the second half of the twentieth century.

Undoubtedly, large dams around the world have played an important role in helping communities and economies harness water resources for food production, energy generation, flood control and domestic and industrial use. However, the technology has been widely taken up around the world to serve many different purposes with varying degrees of success, unintended consequences and controversy. There are many oversights in planning, contributing to very many conflicts and disbenefits. The disadvantages include access to and sharing of water, energy, habitat impacts and viability of ecosystems, extinction of species, international allocation of water, displacement of people, spread of diseases, loss of river structure and many factors besides. Growing environmental awareness and the rise of the environment and human rights movements have been instrumental in this broadening of consciousness. All of this means that dams today are widely acknowledged as far from the panacea for water supply and other development needs that they were almost universally perceived to be up until the late 1970s.

Nevertheless, the 'big engineering' approach to development, of which dams are a dramatic manifestation, has attracted considerable support from political, engineering and economic institutions. Clearly, controlling water can deliver targeted benefits, meeting development agenda that may include food security and the supply of water and power. However, laudable though these aspirations may be, the wider ramifications of technology choice and implementation have often been overlooked in favour of immediate benefits for an advantaged minority of people, overlooking long-term consequences and the implications for historically marginalized communities, which often gain little or nothing yet shoulder the bulk of the disadvantages of dam creation and operation.

These unintended consequences, arising from narrow technical solutions to address the most noble of aspirations, can also be compounded by strongly vested interests as well as entrenched thinking. There is also something of a triumphal approach to big, emblematic solutions that demonstrate 'man's power over nature', including not only the building of great edifices but also a similar approach to the construction of large engineered solutions to 'tame' flooding, retain water, irrigate deserts and otherwise suppress natural processes in favour of technology-based advancements. Indeed, 'big technology' solutions including dam-building have often been conflated with nation-building, sometimes explicitly so, as we will see in the cases of India and Egypt, but often also implicitly. Problems, however, are inevitable when natural processes are so vigorously suppressed or overridden in pursuit of a narrowly framed set of benefits.

Many examples and case studies are used throughout this book, but we will focus below on five examples from three continents illustrating the diversity and increasing scale of modern large dams. These examples demonstrate the kinds of increasingly massive structures constructed for the management of water resources around the world, as well as some of their consequences. Today, there are thought to be around 800,000 dams globally, of which 45,000 were identified as large dams by the World Commission on Dams in 2000,[4] more than half of these in China and 8 per cent (3,600 dams) in India, with more than one hundred exceeding 152 metres (500 feet) in height. (The World

Commission on Dams, set up by the World Bank and the International Union for Conservation of Nature (IUCN) in 1997 to resolve contention about the pros and cons of dams, is discussed in detail later in this book.) It goes without saying, albeit that it has often been overlooked, that these massive interventions in the flows of water, energy, solutes, suspended and living matter have a proportionately huge impact upon the status and functioning of ecosystems and the livelihoods of people dependent upon them.

The Hoover Dam era

The 'big dam' era was unleashed by the Hoover Dam, the crowning glory of a massive dam-building programme driven by the US Bureau of Reclamation and the US Army Corps of Engineers. This programme was of course deeply political as part of a series of development-driven policies including supporting America's war effort by providing cheap electricity to smelt aluminium to construct aeroplanes and other machinery, as well as transforming the US west from desert into an agricultural centre.[5]

The Hoover Dam, also known as the Boulder Dam, was built across the Colorado river on the Arizona–Nevada border 48 kilometres south-east of Las Vegas in 1936. Constructed between April 1931 and March 1936 at a cost of $49 million, the Hoover Dam is a concrete arch-gravity dam in the Black Canyon of the Colorado river. Upon completion in 1935, ahead of its build schedule and official unveiling, it became both the largest concrete structure and the biggest electric power-producing facility on the planet.

The dimensions of the Hoover Dam are truly impressive. The dam stands 221.4 metres (726.4 feet) tall, still the second-highest dam in the USA after the Oroville Dam, while its width is a huge 379.2 metres (1,244 feet). The thickness of the dam base is 200 metres (660 feet) with a crest thickness of 15 metres (45 feet). The concrete in the dam comprises a volume of 3.33 million cubic metres (4.36 million cubic yards), enough to pave a two-lane highway stretching from San Francisco to New York. Behind the dam, Lake Mead covers an area of 639 square kilometres (157,900 acres) when full, backed up 177 kilometres (110 miles) and containing a volume of up to 35,200 cubic kilometres (28,537,000 acre feet) at an elevation of 372.3 metres (1,221.4 feet). Although eventually surpassed on both counts by the Grand Coulee Dam in 1945, the Hoover Dam still remains the world's thirty-fourth-largest hydroelectric generating station. The dam was scheduled on the US National Register of Historic Places in 1981, and designated a National Historic Landmark in 1985. The Lake Mead National Recreation Area, comprising all of the lake and the dam, significant reaches of river below and above it and some of the surrounding mountainous catchment, is the fifth-busiest US national park attracting 8–10 million visitors each year.

The dam was named after Herbert Hoover, who played a pivotal role in its construction, first in his role as Secretary of Commerce and then later as president of the United States. Lake Mead, the reservoir formed upstream of the dam, was named after Elwood Mead, who had overseen dam construction. Herbert Hoover had initially met with the state governors of Arizona, California, Colorado, Nevada, New Mexico, Utah and Wyoming under the aegis of a commission formed in 1922 to work out an equitable arrangement for apportioning the waters of the Colorado river. The ensuing Colorado River Compact was signed on 24 November 1922, providing a basis for the states to decide how the river's precious water should be divided, and clearing the way for the Boulder Dam Project. Part of the dam's design brief was to trap sediment, allowing water of reduced turbidity to run down the Colorado river.

Construction was a massive enterprise, not to mention hazardous, with 112 deaths associated with dam-building and many more, initially ascribed to 'pneumonia' and other causes, since attributed to carbon monoxide poisoning. Four concrete-lined tunnels, each 15.24 metres (50 feet) in diameter and with a combined length of more than 4,877 metres (3 miles), were driven through canyon walls adjacent to the dam site to divert the river's flow. After dam completion, the stream sections of the dam were plugged but the downstream portions were utilized as emergency spillways. The first concrete was poured into the dam structure itself on 6 June 1933, with the dam structure comprising a series of interlocking trapezoidal columns.

Seventeen hydroelectric turbine generators were installed in a power-house, producing a maximum of 2,074 megawatts of hydroelectric power at full flow. Electricity transmission to Los Angeles, some 428 kilometres away, commenced in October 1936 with additional generation capacity added through the early 1960s. Water, generally comprising the entire flow of the Colorado river, reaches these turbines at speeds of up to 137 kilometres (85 miles) per hour. These turbines can be 'throttled' to match electricity output to changing demand. Only rarely are the dam's spillways called into service following periods of intense rainfall.

The crown of the dam is so broad that it served as a crossing for US Highway 93, though the narrow, two-lane section of road approaching the dam is subject to rock slides. However, in the light of terrorism concerns following the infamous 9/11 attack of 2001 on the World Trade Center in New York, a Hoover Dam Bypass was constructed, opening in October 2010. So great were these concerns that, during construction of the bypass, some forms of traffic were excluded from the old road across the dam crown with inspection prior to crossing for all other vehicle types.

The Hoover Dam established a model of 'big engineering' progress subsequently adopted extensively throughout the world, a template exported by the US Bureau of Reclamation and the US Army Corps to other countries, including the riparian states of the Mekong.

The Vaal Dam

The sprawling conurbations of Johannesburg and Pretoria and the province of Gauteng in which they sit comprise the economic and industrial heartland of South Africa. Gauteng generates more than 50 per cent of South Africa's gross geographical product (GGP) and 80 per cent of the country's electricity, and also includes some of the largest gold, platinum and coal mines in the world. A report by the Department of Water Affairs and Forestry (DWAF) in 1997 emphasized its water dependency, with 'a staggering 100% of the gross geographic product (GGP) of Gauteng Province being dependent on inter-basin transfers involving the Orange system'.[6] The Vaal Dam forms the focal point of a wide range of water transfer and capture schemes spread across a broad geographical area. The dam forms the central storage reservoir for the Vaal River System (the VRS), which is therefore of huge economic and strategic importance to South Africa. Today, one quarter of all South Africans depend upon the water of the VRS.

The catchment area of the Vaal Dam is approximately 38,500 cubic kilometres, most of which is located in Free State province with the remainder in North West, Gauteng and Mpumalanga provinces. The predominant natural source of water filling the Vaal Dam reservoir, situated near Vereeniging about sixty kilometres south of Johannesburg, is the Vaal river, which rises in the eastern part of South Africa. The Vaal river is also contained upstream of the Vaal Dam by the Grootdraai and Sterkfontein dams. However, while flow in the Vaal river is generally large enough to meet water requirements, the region is subject to severe and often protracted droughts. For example, a particularly long drought in the 1980s almost caused the Vaal Dam reservoir to run dry, resulting in severe water restrictions. Furthermore, the legacy of mining and agriculture accounts for a recent history of water pollution including metals, salt, acidity, nutrients and other chemicals compromising the utility and ecological health of the reservoir and river system.

Against this backdrop of problems with intermittent and contaminated water in its primary source, new schemes have regularly been developed to augment this supply, tapping both the Vaal and Orange river systems and also catchments farther afield. The largest and most impressive such transfer scheme is the Lesotho Highlands Water Project, conceived in the 1970s with construction starting in phases from 1984 as a means to transfer fresh water flowing into the Orange system from the cool, moist uplands of the adjacent kingdom of Lesotho.

The Lesotho Highlands Water Project immediately drew controversy, ranging from a perception that the engineering was too complex and the costs prohibitive, to political criticism centred around the fact that the internationally ostracized 'white' government in Pretoria was going ahead with a project that would use the resources of a neighbouring 'black' country to sustain the industrial engine of the apartheid regime. Today, project benefits are still perceived as asymmetric, providing vital water supplies to South Africa with few tangible benefits for the people of Lesotho. In terms of the original plans, Lesotho was to receive cash payments for the water diverted into the Vaal system. While funds have been forthcoming, the money has not benefited all those affected by the new dams. The local population has been unhappy about the number of professional and manual workers brought into Lesotho during the construction phases, with villagers saying they were bypassed even for relatively unskilled jobs. Many more complaints relate to the uneven distribution of payments to Lesotho. But there are also benefits to Lesotho beyond payment for water. One of the fringe benefits of the construction of Lesotho's Katse Dam, for example, was the creation of a recreational area. Local entrepreneurs were told to prepare for a massive influx of tourists wishing to enjoy water sports on the dam, although, while Katse has attracted some recreational visitors, numbers have fallen far short of expectations.

Construction of the Vaal Dam, a concrete gravity structure with an earth-fill section on the right flank, was started under a private/public partnership venture during the depression of the early 1930s. The dam was completed in 1938 with a wall height of 54.2 metres above the lowest foundation, giving the reservoir a full supply capacity of 994 million cubic metres. It was subsequently raised in the early 1950s to a height of 60.3 metres, increasing reservoir capacity to 2,188 million cubic metres, with a second raising to 63.4 metres above the lowest foundation in 1985. The current capacity of the dam is 2,536 million cubic metres, with the facility for a further 663 million cubic metres (or 26 per cent by volume) to be stored temporarily for flood attenuation. These flood attenuation properties of the dam were severely tested in February 1996 during the largest flood recorded at the Vaal Dam site.

Formerly South Africa's largest impoundment, the vast reservoir behind the Vaal Dam has a perimeter of over 800 kilometres fronted by three provinces. The Free State is the largest by area, Mpumalanga has a beautiful but rural riparian area, and the most active by far is the Gauteng coast, though it is the smallest. The reservoir behind the dam even encompasses an island almost five kilometres in length that was reportedly used for secret meetings during the apartheid era. Many world-class sporting events take place on the reservoir.

The Aswan High Dam

Egypt has a venerable history of 7,000 years of continuous civilization, the longest in the world in what is a largely rainless land wholly dependent upon the River Nile. Construction of the Aswan High Dam between 1964 and 1970 was intimately linked to Egypt's political aspirations. It formed a key objective of the Egyptian government following the Egyptian revolution of 1952, in which King Farouk had been overthrown, shortly to be followed by abolition of the former class structure and the constitutional monarchy and an ending of British occupation. The staunchly nationalist, non-aligned political agenda adopted by the revolutionary government included wholesale agrarian reform and industrialization programmes, supported by massive infrastructure-building. The Aswan High Dam was championed by Egypt's revolutionary leader, General Gamal Abdel Nasser, whose name is given to Lake Nasser behind the dam. Aswan was praised as a saviour of Egypt from famine and major environmental disaster in the delta. The USA and the UK vetoed funding for Aswan from the World Bank, which was at the time just branching out into supporting dam construction. Meanwhile, Russia was keen to increase political control in Africa and so bankrolled the scheme. In May 1964, Soviet engineers began construction.

Lake Nasser is huge. The dam retaining it is 4.8 kilometres (3 miles) wide and 100 metres (330 feet) high and, until construction of the Three Gorges Dam, retained the world's largest reservoir at up to 563 kilometres (350 miles) long and 64 kilometres (40 miles) wide. The intent was to store up to two years of river flow, supplying reliable power and water and securing food production throughout the irrigation command area. Perhaps the archaeological damage inflicted by the dam was symbolic, as various significant sites were inundated and the famous Abu Simbel monument was moved. The removal of 130,000 Nubian people gained less publicity.

A number of significant omissions and oversights were evident almost immediately. For example, 2 metres (6 feet) of water are evaporated each year by the heat of the Saharan sun, a massive volume more or less equating to the entire water demand of England. Worse still was the entrapment of a huge proportion of the sediment flow down the Nile, building up at approximately one metre a year in Lake Nasser, massively compromising the anticipated reservoir volume and lifetime of the dam. The loss of this sediment and its associated nutrients to the river system is disastrous for Egypt, starving downstream floodplains and deltas of fertility, habitat structure and landscape. The unforeseen reality is that the Nile's silt is as important to Egypt as its water, so the planned boost in water availability unintentionally undermined a range of critically important ecosystem services. Whereas Egypt once relied on annual floods to nourish soils with nutrients and trace elements for agriculture and brick-making, it is today one of the world's largest users of artificial fertilizers and now also imports clay for the making of bricks. One of several ironies is that the manufacture of fertilizer now consumes much of the hydroelectric power generated by the Aswan High Dam. Although the dam and Egypt's concerns about food security for its increasing population have opened up substantial new areas of agriculture, a significant proportion of fertilizer production offsets that formerly provided freely by natural nutrient flows associated with seasonal flooding of the Nile, partially defeating the potential benefits of energy generation. While some lesser impacts of dams can be mitigated at least to some extent, there is no effective way to offset these negative silt-associated impacts through modification of design or management once a dam is operational. Salt accumulation in soils is also a huge problem, with new irrigated desert lands becoming waterlogged and then subject to high evaporation rates. Drainage to flush this salt now costs more than the original cost of the dam.

Egypt has also experienced substantial riparian erosion. Farther downstream, huge areas of the Nile Delta have eroded owing to a lack of recharge of river silt. Many of the small dams in the delta operated to divert water to fields have been lost, along with the delta's natural storm defence services, leading to the flooding and loss of villages and land. Some predict that the delta will be lost entirely in a matter of decades. The overall ecological consequences are unknown but undoubtedly huge, including the disappearance from the eastern Mediterranean of sardines that formerly bred in the delta.

The Three Gorges Dam

The Three Gorges Dam,[7] a concrete-walled hydroelectric river dam spanning the Yangtze river at Sandouping, is massive, ranging from its sheer size to its potential benefits and impacts, political and economic pronouncements, and associated controversies. The Three Gorges Dam directly displaced some 1.4 million people, with up to four million advised to move to create the world's largest man-made reservoir and housing the biggest hydroelectric power station potentially generating up to 22,500 megawatts. The Three Gorges Dam was initially planned to serve 10 per cent of China's electricity requirement, though energy demands in China have spiralled since the planning phase and so it is more likely to support a more modest 3 per cent of the country's total electricity consumption.

The dam was envisioned as long ago as 1919 by Sun Yat-sen, with planning starting in 1932 under the Nationalist government of Chiang Kai-shek. Plans were advanced in 1939 when the area was occupied by Japan, though the planned overthrow of Chinese control did not materialize. Following the communist victory of 1949, the project had the support of Mao Zedong, but plans were not revived until the 1980s. Final approval of the dam was to follow in 1992, though reportedly with a record number of abstentions and dissenting votes. Construction commenced in December 1994. The dam body was completed in 2006, and all initially planned elements with the exception of the ship lift were completed in 2008. Full operation was attained by mid-2011 following initial plans for completion by 2009. The first hydroelectric generator started to produce power in July 2003.

The dam wall comprises 27,200,000 cubic metres (35,600,000 cubic yards) of concrete, with a total length of 2,309 metres (7,575 feet) and a height of 101 metres (331 feet). The dam is 115 metres (377.3 feet) thick at its base and 40 metres (131.2 feet) at the crown, holding back a water depth of up to 91 metres (299 feet) above river level and forming a reservoir of about 660 kilometres (410 miles) in length, containing 39.3 cubic kilometres (9.43 cubic miles) of water with a total surface area of 1,045 square kilometres (403 square miles).

Many environmental benefits are claimed for the dam. Notably, these include reduction of emissions of air pollutant and greenhouse gases relative to traditional (often coal-fired in China) forms of energy generation. There is also a claimed reduction in greenhouse gas emissions due to navigation by ships through the locks of the Three Gorges Dam, which is planned to increase the freight capacity of the river sixfold. However, some critics claim that heavy siltation will clog ports such as Chongqing within a few years, based on evidence from other dam projects.

Although the dam's official website claims that the first target of the Three Gorges Project is flood control, the hydrological benefits of the dam are less clear. The project is intended to moderate flows of the Yangtze river by intercepting seasonal rains with its 20-million-cubic-metre capacity for floodwater detention, elevating flood protection in the downstream Jingjiang section of the river from ten-year to 100-year events. It is claimed that the dam will also help control the consequences of rare (but increasing under climate-change scenarios) 1,000-year flood events. However, once filled, reservoir surfaces lack buffering capacity, potentially exacerbating the effects of extreme flooding previously buffered by interaction with wetland habitats and floodplains across the catchment. The July 2010 floods that saw the Three Gorges Dam overtop, contributing to loss of life, are a horrific reminder of impacts that may intensify in an increasingly less stable climate. Recognizing the value of ecosystems to catchment hydrology, China is now investing substantially in reforestation to reverse a history of tree loss heavily implicated in damage caused by flooding in 1998,[8] including the loss of 4,150 human lives, forced relocation of 18.4 million people and a cost of 255 billion yuan (equivalent to $US37 billion).

Wetlands lost by dam filling may be crucial for some scarce species, such as the critically endangered Siberian crane. The dam is also implicated in the functional extinction of the Baiji (the Yangtze river dolphin). Populations of the Yangtze sturgeon, classified by the IUCN as Critically Endangered,[9] are noted as 'negatively affected' by the dam. Silt flows too are likely to have negative impacts, with silt accumulation in the reservoir potentially compromising the effectiveness of power generation but also reducing sediment feed, nourishing of the floodplain and rebuilding of soil fertility, and habitat maintenance downstream on the Yangtze river through to the Yangtze Delta, which may contribute to erosion and sinking of coastal areas. Conversely, it is claimed that the dam will relieve the invasion of saline tides in the river's mouth to the East China Sea, though it is hard to see how reducing river flows will achieve this, and furthermore these saline tides are presumably natural phenomena with associated dependent and valuable ecosystems and livelihoods.

An estimated 1,300 archaeological sites have been lost under the reservoir, which is over one hundred metres deep in places, together with the irreplaceable homelands of indigenous peoples such as the Ba.

The sheer mass of the Three Gorges Dam, which sits on a geological fault, gives cause for concerns about dam-induced seismicity. Some scientists also claim that the weight of the water from the reservoir will be so great that it will tilt the Earth on its rotational axis to a slight degree. Already, filling of the dam has been implicated as a possible cause of earthquakes in the area. There is also concern that the Three Gorges Dam may represent a potently symbolic target for anti-Chinese terrorists.

There are claims that the dam will contribute to prevention and cure of schistosomiasis (bilharzia) epidemics formerly blighting downstream lakes. However, it remains unclear how this conclusion is derived given the proliferation of waterborne diseases elsewhere in the world resulting from the damming and flow buffering of river systems. There are indeed rising concerns about this likely consequence in the lower Yangtze river.[10]

The Nagarjunasagar Dam

The Nagarjunasagar Dam is one of the largest dams built in Asia and one of the earliest hydroelectric projects in India. The Nagarjunasagar project, the first to be executed in the Indian state of Andhra Pradesh, was designed to divert water from the Krishna river into massive irrigation plants across the five districts of Guntur, Prakasam, Khammam, Nalgonda and parts of West Godavari.

The dam was symbolic in more than one way. It was the first time that this much money, hundreds of crores (crore are tens of millions) of rupees, had been marshalled by independent India for such a major engineering project. It was also a massive undertaking with some 55,000 people labouring to move mountains of cement and earth. And, at the laying of the foundation stone between the cities of Guntur and Hyderabad in 1955, Jawaharlal Nehru asked, 'Would my people be poor after the completion of the Nagarjunasagar dam?', expressing the view that the dam would be the answer to the extreme poverty of the local tribes.

The dam was completed in 1969, with a crown height of 124 metres (407 feet), a length of 1 kilometre (0.6 miles) and equipped with twenty-six crest gates. This makes it both the tallest and the most massive masonry dam in the world, creating the third-largest reservoir in the world. Flows from the dam were diverted into a dam command area of 21 lakh (2,100,000) acres.

The impacts of the Nagarjunasagar project certainly changed the lives of millions of people. Irrigation water has transformed the formerly drought-prone, rain-fed agricultural systems with positive implications for food security and wealth creation through large-scale paddy and water-intensive cash crops such as cotton, chillies and tobacco. This has changed the livelihoods of farmers but also the staple diet of local people, stimulating a dairy industry through availability of fodder crops, access to education and consumption of consumer goods. Many have benefited, often substantially, from the dam, which has made many millionaires within the state of Andhra Pradesh. Contractors hired to organize labour and the officials transacting the works were major beneficiaries, as were the lawyers who negotiated land acquisition and the farmers who benefited from flows diverted into the dam's irrigation command area.

However, the spread of benefits was far from even. Displaced tribal people simply did not figure in the planning or evaluation, with many still reportedly living in extreme poverty. The dam also displaced significant heritage, built on the site of the birth of one of the early river valley civilizations and inundating an area rich in both Buddhist and Hindu history dating back to the third century AD.[11]

Although the extension of irrigation from the Nagarjunasagar Dam has been hailed as a major developmental project, there is compelling evidence that this and other dams can bring about changes in subsoil water levels and soil chemistry, contributing to various human diseases. Following construction of the Nagarjunasagar Dam, the rising water table and water alkalinity influenced the concentration of trace elements in food grains grown in that area. In particular, rising concentrations of molybdenum contribute antagonistically to copper deficiencies, leading to local bone deformities. More importantly, there has been a significant increase in fluoride content in subsoil water and foods grown in the region, promoting *genu valgum* (knock-knees) among young adults. These geochemical transformations are also likely to have unforeseen ecological repercussions.

The Nagarjunasagar geochemical experience has been repeated in other parts of the country, in connection both with other dams and the proliferation of tube wells, for example in the increase of fluorosis in fluorine-rich geologies. The same phenomenon has been observed for arsenicosis in some other districts such as the Malda district of West Bengal. There is also substantial and growing civil opposition to the mining of uranium close to the Nagarjunasagar Dam, which many feel will affect health across the wide irrigated command area.

Meanwhile, waterborne diseases have continued increasing in spite of government control initiatives for this and other dams across India. Malaria has now become endemic in Punjab, Haryana, Andhra Pradesh and Uttar Pradesh states owing to expanses of open water and slowed river flows, elevation of the water table, waterlogging and seepage in canals, and there are also numerous and rising cases of filariasis (an infectious tropical disease caused by nematodes).

Now that the Krishna river is dammed at a dozen other points upstream, has the anticipated miracle of the Nagarjunasagar Dam run its course? Nehru's question about consequences for the poor has a less than resoundingly positive answer sixty years down the line. Many of the planned beneficiaries are doing rather well, but there are many less advantageous consequences for huge numbers of people whose needs were simply not considered.

'Megawater'

Early human civilizations had largely built their cities in proximity to natural sources of water. This situation remained mostly unaltered until the first half of the twentieth century. Early instances of large dams, such as Hoover and Aswan High, served the primary purpose of controlling flows rather than redirecting water over long distances.

Major change is seen today in many large dam schemes in China, including the Three Gorges Dam, where numbers of large dams form part of a massive infrastructure to redirect water northwards across not only drainage basins but almost the entire country. This was viewed as a political necessity, as demands from farming and industry in the north of the country had drained the Yellow River dry, converting part of its bed into little more than unproductive desert during dry seasons. China's capital city, Beijing, had relied on aquifers recharged from the Yellow River, yet these too had receded by 61 metres (200 feet) over the last four decades of the twentieth century, with 90 per cent of underground water depleted around the city as part of a cycle of aridification, also leading to some land subsidence. Saline intrusion into depleted aquifers compounds threats to water supply in the North China Plain. Yet the north of China constitutes its breadbasket and industrial heartland, comprising two-thirds of the nation's croplands, even though it receives only one fifth of national rainfall. The political view of the solution was to tap into the monsoon-fed rivers to the south of the country, diverting them northwards to change the nation's hydrology on an epic scale.

In April 2003, water started flowing into Beijing along a canal 61 metres (200 feet) wide and as long as France. This water had begun its journey in a tributary of the Yangtze river (the world's fourth-largest river system) nearly a thousand kilometres (600 miles) to the south, diverted into the translocation system by the massive Danjiangkou Reservoir, which is being raised to 168 metres (550 feet), displacing an estimated quarter of a million people. China proudly claims that this water translocation scheme is the largest engineering project undertaken anywhere on the planet, echoing the pride of early Western dam pioneers in humanity's dominance over nature. It was planned for completion in time for the 2008 Beijing Olympic Games. Amazingly, it is just one of three huge diversion projects designed to replumb the nation, diverting water from the south into the arid north. The four diversions comprising the total south-to-north water transfer project are due for completion by 2050, and will reroute some 45 million cubic metres of water per year. The target recipients of this expensive water are the cities of the north, with little or no provision for the poor people that the channels will bypass, nor for the people of the lower Yangtze now deprived of 'their' water. Recognizing the ever-tightening water crisis, China is also driving a range of water-saving measures on farmland which include water deficit irrigation, use of straw mulch to reduce evaporation, changing crop structure and water-saving education for farmers, although this policy change is not, at least yet, implemented nationally.

Worryingly, the sheer scale of aspirations to replumb China is not without precedent elsewhere in the world. There is top-level political support and momentum behind an ambitious River Interlinking Project to solve the perceived problem of regional imbalance of water access across India.[12] Under this scheme, which has huge associated costs approximating 1 per cent of India's gross national product over twenty-five years and an implementation timescale to match, engineering solutions will enable the transfer of vast volumes of water between major drainage basins. While in theory it will help overcome the devastating effects of seasonal floods and ensure energy security, the main benefit is perceived to be a more even sharing of water across the country to stimulate food and commodity production as well as other economic activities. This project builds upon a project first mooted in 1972 to interlink the Ganga (Ganges) river, the huge glacial-fed system to the north of the country, and the Cauvery river, which is monsoon-fed and is the southernmost of the three drainage basins of the Deccan peninsula. The concept of the River Interlinking Project builds from this basis, joining up other great river systems such as the Godavari, Narmada and Krishna rivers into a form of 'national grid'. The project is unprecedented in scale and ambition, joining rivers across climatic zones, and results are highly unpredictable in terms of ecological impacts on whole catchments, deltas and the coastal zones, the spread of disease and organisms, human consequences and overall efficacy.

Fred Pearce coined the term 'megawater' to describe the stages beyond merely controlling flows, including the engineering of large dams and associated infrastructure on a pharaonic scale.[13] This mega-scale engineering approach may demonstrate our ingenuity, boost economic prospects for targeted beneficiaries in the immediate term, and become emblematic of 'man's power over nature'. However, it also raises huge questions about sustainability and equity in terms of dependence upon engineering structures, substantial energy inputs and political stability, not to mention the consequences for regions from which water is drained in a climate-changing world. Irrigation may be essential to feed today's substantial and tomorrow's escalating human populations. However, if most irrigation-based civilizations have failed throughout human history,[14] it is clearly essential that we call into question the sustainability of our future technological approach rather than assume that the lessons of history no longer apply.

The extent to which dams as well as other water diversion schemes modify river flows around the world is staggering. Israel has long been a pioneer of water diversion for its agricultural and urban needs, with similar schemes across Pakistan, Egypt, India and elsewhere in the world. This includes Libya, at least until the revolution of 2011 hardly the world's most democratic or equitable regime, which is now 'mining' the vast fossil groundwater reserves beneath the Sahara Desert to serve its burgeoning demands. Libya's Great Manmade River, the world's largest underground network of pipes and ducts, moves 6.5 million cubic metres per day from an ancient aquifer beneath the Sahara Desert, fuelling the nation's aspiration to export crops. And, as we have seen, the hydrology of South Africa has been massively re-engineered to the advantage of those living in the arid interior of the country. Spain's large dams regulate 40 per cent of the country's river flow. Current estimates suggest that some 30–40 per cent of irrigated land worldwide now relies on dams, and that dams generate 19 per cent of world electricity. However, there is today a declining pace of large dam construction as optimal sites are used up and societal opposition intensifies.

Dams and the future

The demand for water is spiralling across the world in response to booming population, industrialization and shifting lifestyles. There are also mounting concerns about how society is providing for these needs, in technical terms but also in addressing the needs of all people on an equitable basis. The 'hydrological amplifier' of climate change is likely only to compound concerns about adequate supply of water.

Dams offer some solutions. However, like all technological innovations, they bring with them both benefits and costs, many of which are poorly evaluated if considered at all. Yet, even in the light of what we know today, as many as 250 new dams are being built each year,[15] and over half of the world's major river systems are seriously affected by fragmentation and flow regulation resulting from the construction of dams.[16] Yesterday's innovations need to be re-examined in the 'modern world', including optimization of benefits for all and assessment of broader costs which it may or may not be possible to mitigate.

Also, in considering large dams, we have to be cognizant that there is no one type of 'large dam'. There are different designs which interact differentially with ecosystems and people depending upon geography, climate, population density and the decision-making process. Furthermore, dams of different scales – from giant structures such as China's Three Gorges Dam to small hillside 'slip dams' such as those common at farm scale across South Africa and Australia, and run-of-river small dam schemes through to tidal barrages – offer a different scale and scope of benefits, beneficiaries and negative implications.

It is timely to reappraise the contribution of dams to our quest for a world in which the needs of all are met equitably and sustainably.

2 | Temples of the modern world

In India, as indeed in many developing and arid countries, dam-building was once seen as a means of deliverance from hunger and poverty, providing hydroelectric power as well as irrigating dry lands throughout the year and not merely in the wet months of the monsoon. The most famous advocate of India's dam-building programme was Jawaharlal Nehru, India's first prime minister, who famously described dams as the 'temples of modern India'. Nehru's famous and oft-repeated utterance related substantially to their symbolic role to an increasingly technologically capable nation taking its place among 'developed world' powers by equating science with progress, with examples such as the 'big engineering' of cities, weapon systems, power plants, steel mills and other massive schemes. These words are still widely quoted in Indian school textbooks, despite the fact that Nehru came to regret his statement within his own lifetime.

It is undoubtedly true that dams have delivered a great deal of benefit to many people around the world, particularly in drier regions where water is a more immediate limiting factor. It is also true that dams have brought with them many environmental, social and economic problems, and significantly a redistribution of benefits across different strata of society. We will look at the benefits in this chapter, turning to the generally unintended and unforeseen negative consequences in the next.

Watering the drylands

Half of the world's dams have been built exclusively or primarily for irrigation, contributing to the one fifth of the world's agricultural land that is irrigated. Generally, irrigation water is more economically valuable than rainwater because it is secure and dependable. Consequently, irrigated agriculture uses two to three times the volume of water of rainfed agriculture but the profits may be as much as fifteen times higher.[1] Irrigation represents the world's biggest use of water, accounting for about two-thirds of all water abstracted. In many hot countries, as much as 90 per cent of water withdrawals go to irrigate fields. The benefits of irrigation are particularly felt in arid countries for food production and food security. However, this high dependence upon irrigation occurs not merely across the developing world but also in the developed world. In America, for example, 10 per cent of croplands are irrigated using water stored behind dams.[2] This, in turn, contributes to global food security as well as employment, with substantial numbers of jobs tied to producing crops grown with irrigated water.

Water storage also serves many other uses, often simultaneously with irrigation. Throughout the United States and other areas of the world with significant cities and industrial demand, dams are used also to supply water for many people, including industrial and municipal consumption. Damming of rivers with seasonal or intermittent flow may further provide security between dry and wet seasons and years – for example, in monsoon regions.

A number of global initiatives and reports, significantly including the work of the International Commission on Large Dams (ICOLD),[3] the World Commission on Dams (WCD)[4] and the United Nations Environment Programme (UNEP) Dams and Development Programme (DDP),[5] all discussed in more detail later in this book, have documented the dramatic impact of human-induced water withdrawals from the world's lakes, rivers and aquifers (groundwater resources). In 2000, total annual freshwater withdrawals were estimated at 3,800 cubic kilometres, a quantity almost double that estimated for the middle of the twentieth century.

Power to the people

Water has been used as a form of power since Roman times. It was first used to drive waterwheels for various mechanical processes, such as grinding corn, sawing timber or driving textile mills. In the early nineteenth century, the water turbine was developed as a much more efficient machine than the waterwheel. By the mid-nineteenth century, water power was used to produce electricity for the first time. The concept of using moving water to turn a turbine connected by a shaft to a generator to create electricity is known as hydropower, a potentially renewable and now widely installed source of electricity.

There are now hundreds of thousands of hydropower stations worldwide, the largest of them China's Three Gorges Dam and the second largest the Itaipu, built on the Rio Paraná between Brazil and Paraguay with a power capacity of more than 14,000 megawatts. Some of the first countries to develop hydroelectricity on a large scale were Norway, Sweden and Switzerland in Europe, Canada, the USA, Australia and New Zealand. The successes of these early schemes, from the

1890s in the USA, led to a rapid expansion of the technology. India's first hydropower plant was constructed in 1902 on the left falls of the Cauvery river at Shivasamudram, supplying power to the city of Bangalore. When connected in 1906, Bangalore became the first city in Asia to be electrified and to have electric street lights.

Today, hydroelectric energy accounts for approximately 18 per cent of the world's electricity supply,[6] with a remaining economically exploitable potential estimated by the International Energy Agency at 5,400 TWh/y (terawatt hours/year) in 2006, of which about 90 per cent was in low-income regions.[7] Globally, hydroelectric reservoirs cover an area of 3.4×10^5 square kilometres, comprising about 20 per cent of all reservoirs.[8] The world's largest contemporary generator of hydroelectric power is Canada, closely followed by the United States, where dams produce over 103,800 megawatts of hydropower, meeting 8–12 per cent of the nation's power demand. Brazil produces more than 90 per cent of its electricity from hydropower projects. While hydroelectric power is renewable, plugging into natural fluxes of energy within the water cycle, it is not, however, automatically sustainable, owing to wider environmental and social impacts reviewed in the following chapter. But, compared to traditional fossil-fuel-based generation, it undoubtedly has a different profile of contribution to climate change, air pollution, acid rain and ozone depletion.

The benefits of reliable power supply to industry and large cities are undeniable, albeit that often, as we will see in the following chapter, more serious questions are raised about who has access to this power. Power supplied to the poorest sectors of society can make huge improvements to their lives and livelihoods, though it is often the already wealthy who benefit disproportionately.

Inland fisheries

Dams of all sizes, retaining the smallest farm pools to the largest of reservoirs, can support fisheries of value for recreation, subsistence or commercial purposes. In paddy fields across India and Bangladesh, stocking of rice paddy with fingerlings of medaka or other smaller carp species is a commonplace practice, yielding an additional protein source for domestic or commercial use when rice is harvested at the onset of the dry season.

At the opposite end of the scale, major commercial fisheries thrive in some of the world's largest reservoirs, such as that fed by the Zambezi river and contained behind the 128 metre (420 feet) high, 579 metre (1,900 feet) long hydroelectric Kariba Dam in Zambia.

Stemming the floods

In addition to water and power supply, dams are also thought to help prevent the loss of life and property caused by flooding by storing peak flows after dry seasons. For centuries, people have built dams in part to help control devastating floods. These flood control dams impound floodwaters, either releasing them under controlled conditions or else storing or diverting the water for other uses. For example, South Africa's Vaal Dam has 26 per cent headroom for temporary flood attenuation, while flood control is one of the primary stated purposes of China's gigantic Three Gorges Dam.

It has long been known that reservoirs may have a role to play in floodwater control. However, they achieve this goal not by providing a consistent brake to flows but by absorbing peaks up to the capacity of the reservoir. Beyond this peak capacity, downstream flood risks may be increased as open reservoir surfaces lack buffering capacity, unlike the wetlands, river habitat and floodplains that they displace. Beyond design thresholds, the potential for damaging floods may therefore be exacerbated rather than mitigated. Ultimately, the impacts of many major dams under extreme flood events are untested, with the potential for disaster not merely omnipresent but intensified under climate change scenarios.

Other beneficial uses of dams

Dams are associated with a wide range of additional benefits. Navigation is a potential benefit in some large river systems where river-borne transport is significant. A practical example here is in the USA, where a system of dams, locks and navigation channels provide for a stable system of inland river transportation throughout the heartland without adding to road congestion.

Dams also serve a variety of secondary recreational benefits, providing a major recreational resource in some advanced economies. They support boating and water-skiing, camping, picnic and other amenity areas, as well as sport fishing and wildlife-watching opportunities. As noted for the Hoover Dam, the Lake Mead National Recreation Area is the fifth-busiest US national park, attracting between 8 and 10 million visitors annually. The Rietvlei, as another example, is popular as an angling, boating, wildlife, birdwatching and vacation destination for the residents of Pretoria, South Africa. Reservoirs can also form a centrepiece of major nature reserves, as in the case of the Kalagarh Dam on the Ramganga river in Corbett National Park in northern India.

Other dams serve a pollution detention function by, for example, intercepting mine tailings. There are reported to be 1,300 such mine tailings impoundments in the United States alone, allowing the mining and processing of coal and other minerals while holding back waste materials from the wider environment. Dams may also be used to retain other hazardous materials and abate detrimental sedimentation. Clearly, questions remain as to the ultimate fate of these contaminants, but their temporary abatement potential provides a short-term benefit.

Multiple uses, multiple benefits

Most modern dams are designed to serve a range of purposes simultaneously, and it is generally these dams that deliver the greatest cumulative public value. The range of potential benefits may include water storage for distribution in agriculture, industry and/or municipalities, pumped storage to meet peak demand, secondary tourism, recreation and aquaculture opportunities, job creation and regional development, and stimulation of an industry base on the back of more reliable water and power supplies (particularly energy-hungry industries such as aluminium refining).

The most common arguments advanced in favour of dams are that they generate power, retain and direct water for direct uses and irrigation, tame flooding, provide recreational opportunities, and 'green the deserts', fitting the ideology of a technological age 'improving upon nature'. However, this sense of dams providing environmental benefits needs careful scrutiny, for in the creation of one type of environment there is a displacement of the pre-dam environment and the people resident in and benefiting from the processes performed by those ecosystems. This will concern us throughout the following chapter and subsequent parts of this book. We also have to be conscious that approximately two-thirds of the world's existing large dams are in developing countries, where developed-world perspectives do not automatically apply.

3 | Stemming the flow

We have been guilty of a cavalier disregard for rivers and their eco-systems. From the Home Counties of England to the Yellow River of China, America's Mississippi, the formerly blue Danube of central Europe, the Nile's course from East Africa through to Egypt, and even India's sacred Ganges, Narmada or Cauvery rivers, our rivers are in precipitous decline.[1] This is due to pressures ranging from the demands of thirsty cities, croplands and industries, siltation and agrochemical run-off from farmlands, loss of habitat with its many natural regulatory functions, direct pollution, and impoundments of all scales.

Our freshwater systems are essential natural capital providing many services, many taken for granted, supporting a broad sweep of needs ranging from subsistence to commercial uses, recreation, education and 'quality of life'. River degradation automatically compromises their capacities to supply clean water, control the transmission of diseases, dilute or metabolize liquid waste, fertilize land, maintain habitat and landscapes, and regenerate fisheries, wildfowl and other natural resources. Mass drainage schemes and constraints on the free flow of water in channels and across floodplains and wetlands further increase the risk of flooding downstream, blocking exchange of water with underground aquifers which absorb heavy rainfall and eke out flows throughout drier periods of the year.

The tragedy of iconic fishes

The 'tragedy of the hilsa' – not a parable but a real ecological dis-aster with significant ramifications – exemplifies river management undertaken with the best of intentions but within a narrow perspective. The hilsa, or hilsa shad (*Tenualosa ilisha*), is a member of the herring family that normally grows to around 60 centimetres (2 feet) and a little over half a kilogramme in weight. The hilsa is sometimes described as India's favourite fish as it is a familiar and popular food fish found in many of the larger river systems of southern Asia. Like European and American shad species, the hilsa is anadromous, running rivers from the sea to spawn in fresh waters. For most of the year, schools of hilsa assemble around the coasts of Iran and Iraq, the western and eastern coasts of India, and eastwards through to Vietnam. During the south-west monsoon, hilsa run Indian and other Asian rivers for prodigious distances of up to 1,200 kilometres to inland spawning sites. Though they are prolific, this migratory habit makes the hilsa particularly vulnerable to obstructions such as dams, which have been implicated in the extinction of whole populations.

Owing to their popularity as an oil-rich food fish, hilsa are the basis of some of India's most commercially valuable freshwater and estuarine fisheries. However, an entire population of hilsa was wiped out on the Cauvery river, the lifeblood of much of the Deccan peninsula, upon the completion of the Mettur Dam retaining the massive Stanley Reservoir at the upstream end of Tamil Nadu state. As a consequence of this river 'improvement', the formerly thriving river population crashed to virtually nothing; hilsa are found today only in the Cauvery's estuarine delta and limited zones of the lower river, and it is not clear if these are Cauvery-spawned fish or stray fish spawned in other Asian river systems. Hilsa prosper still in other major Indian rivers but increasing numbers of impoundments, particularly major dams, are imposing a serious threat to some populations.

Blockage to fish migration in the river systems of India and neighbouring countries has already proved disastrous to various species of mahseer, large members of the carp family of the genus *Tor* reaching as much as 1.5 metres (4.9 feet) long and weighing up to 90 kilogrammes (200lb). Mahseer too rely upon a variety of river habitats throughout their lives, including deep, lowland reaches in which to feed and survive the drier months, from where they surge upstream to spawn in fast-flowing and often intermittent upland jungle headwater streams and rivers as the monsoon rains swell their flows. As the fish hatch from eggs, grow on as fry and then develop from fingerlings to maturity, they require a diversity of habitats and need to be able to move freely within the river system. This need to access and exploit whole river systems renders mahseer uniquely vulnerable to over-exploitation, pollution, habitat degradation and obstructions of all kinds. Notwithstanding their high social value, as a source of food, as spiritual icons and as economically valuable sport fishing quarry, mahseer populations are in precipitous decline owing to a range of development pressures on Asian rivers. Whole mahseer populations have followed the hilsa to extinction through dam construction, compounded by a range of other pressures ranging from poaching to pollution, over-abstraction and habitat replacement or degradation. The elimination of the humpback mahseer (*Tor mussullah*) from the once globally renowned and record-breaking fishery in the Kabbini river, a major tributary of the Cauvery, is widely accepted as being due to impoundment of the river and blockage of spawning habitat. Meanwhile, to the north, the extinction of *Tor neilli* (admittedly a species of disputed taxonomic status) on the Thungabhadra, a tributary of the Godavari river, is seen as resulting from completion of a major dam. The impacts of dams on mahseer are widely seen as representing major threats,[2] not only physically obstructing fish movement but also causing a chain of alterations to rivers, including to regimes of oxygen, temperature and hydrology, and interruptions of habitat-forming processes, all of which modify ecosystems and the well-being of wildlife and people dependent upon them.

The story of the hilsa and the mahseer is echoed by other examples of India's iconic migratory fishes, and in the decline of northern Europe's Atlantic salmon, the sturgeons of the Caspian and Black Seas, the Yangtze paddlefish, various endemic fishes of American rivers and a number of other charismatic and conspicuous migratory fishes worldwide. It also mirrors the decline or demise of river dolphins and other significant and iconic components of Asian river ecosystems. The global decline of large fish and other aquatic species is indicative of the plight of rivers resulting from damming, changes in land use, poaching and over-exploitation, pollution and a host of other threats.

A river system's fish population serves as a primary indicator of overall health, integrating diverse pressures across catchments. However, it is also a charismatic part of the ecosystem with associated economic, cultural and subsistence values for communities across catchments which may be overlooked by the frequently narrower focus of dam proponents and designers. Nevertheless, despite all evidence to the contrary, India, China and some other regions still retain a political presumption that dams offer a better and more secure future for all. And, of course, among the main proponents of this belief are the major power and engineering companies, supported by many engineers, contractors and consultants, that stand to reap substantial profit from dam construction and generation capacity.

Thinking more broadly

The tragedy of these various migratory fishes across the globe illustrates Garrett Hardin's metaphor of 'the tragedy of the commons',[3] a now well-used term describing the consequences of over-exploitation of commonly shared goods. Under this metaphor, unconstrained exploitation of common resources in the absence of common stewardship agreements ultimately dooms the resource owing to the uneven sharing of benefits and burdens. In the cases of overgrazed common meadowland (from which the metaphor gains its name), international marine fisheries or any of a host of other environmental 'commons' such as air or fresh water or catchment systems, individual (or state or national) benefits stemming from exploitation create an incentive for an increased 'take' of benefits by all players, since they do not wholly incur the associated costs of exploitation which are distributed between all those sharing the resource. Individuals then compete to maximize their take from the 'common' before others beat them to it. In the simple telling of the metaphor, if no one owns the common good, it inevitably withers away under aggressive competition since all overlook its natural regeneration rate. The metaphor of the 'tragedy of the commons' has as many strong advocates as it has critics, who argue that it ignores politics and economics, which often are the real drivers of exploitation. The metaphor certainly often holds true for many unmanaged commons lacking some form of strong governance, as for example in open-seas fisheries or freshwater resources which are inadequately valued. However, in many places, it is an over-simplistic representation when governance structures, ranging from international treaties and protocols to more local communal governance arrange- ments, permit more sustainable exploitation and sharing of common resources to which people may have rights if not ownership.[4] Never- theless, the 'tragedy of the commons' is a parable that graphically illustrates the consequences of inequitable sharing, whether intentional or uninformed, of the costs and benefits associated with a resource.

If we need further practical illustration of this phenomenon in action, we need look no farther than the generally unintended drying of catchments and aquifers, the collapse of forest ecosystems and marine fisheries, or the decline in structure and quality of soils ob- served worldwide. The collapse of fisheries, marine or riverine, is just the metaphorical 'tip of the iceberg' of potential blights to human well-being associated with ecosystem over-exploitation and misman- agement. For example, the collapse in the 1990s of Canada's Grand Banks cod fishery, formerly the world's most prolific fishing ground, has tipped tens of thousands of people into long-term unemployment and social decline.[5]

Staunching the flow

Dams, designed as they are to hold back water, inevitably also stem associated flows of silt and sediment, nutrients and other chemicals, energy and biota, interrupting their free passage through riverine, riparian and linked ecosystems and human beneficiaries. Wider consequences for river systems inevitably arise from staunching these flows. Water held in one place is no longer free to continue its journey downstream where it interacts with other living and non-living elements of ecosystems, and this has consequences which are often poorly considered, if considered at all, in dam design. As Graham Harris notes, 'building new dams does increase the total water supply for human use, but only by the amount harvested from catchments and diverted from their component ecosystems', observing that 'The imposition of constancy on natural systems that require variability causes particular problems for systems that are naturally non-linear, non-equilibrium CAS [Complex Adaptive Systems].'[6] Dams thereby fragment and transform the world's rivers, changing flows of water, associated solutes and suspended matter, biota and the balance of human benefits including a wealth of cultural meanings and values. Many elements of this 'common' are lost to people, particularly to the least powerful members of society whose livelihoods depend upon them.

Furthermore, a range of transformation processes occur in dams relative to the habitats that they displace. One regionally important example here is evaporation. Water may be rapidly lost again to the atmosphere from water surfaces exposed to sun and wind, accounting, as we have seen, for more than two metres (six feet) of water each year from Lake Nasser. While Egypt has consistently opposed the construction of dams in Ethiopia, refusing to renegotiate a 1959 treaty that grants Egypt the lion's share of the Nile's flow, it has interests in deeper, cooler dams on the upper Blue Nile to improve water security. However, these additional dams would have their own set of consequences for the river system.

Commonly, in tree- or scrub-lined channels and wetlands, vegetated land and permeable soils, water may instead be conserved in subsurface aquifers, in biological matter and organic soils, and by tight recirculation within habitats such as valley forests, where evaporated water is efficiently recaptured as mist, dew and other forms of precipitation in complex vegetation communities and associated ecosystems. Direct evaporation from reservoir surfaces is compounded by a huge loss of water commonly observed in distribution and conveyance infrastructure; India's canals are said to lose 70 per cent of their water to leakage and evaporation before it can reach the intended consumer.[7] The net effect on water balance may be locally significant, with additional consequences felt more broadly.

Changes in the quality of reservoir water

It is often unsafe to assume that water stored behind large dams will remain a high-quality resource. Because large dams act as sinks for sediment, organic matter and nutrients, many have experienced problems with enrichment which have compromised the quality of water as well as its value to wildlife and water-contact uses. South Africa's Hartebeespoort Dam in North West province and also the Roodeplaat Dam near Pretoria are just two of many examples of dams across the tropical world which have experienced substantial blooms of blue-green algae, which are not only capable of depleting the oxygen concentration of the water as blooms collapse but which may also liberate a range of toxins into the water, implicated in various harmful biological effects for people and animals.[8]

Dams can also suffer dramatic localized or widespread deoxygenation. A dramatic example was seen in the invasion by Kariba weed of Lake Kariba, detained by the Kariba Dam on the Zambesi river and forming a border between Zambia and Zimbabwe. Kariba weed (*Salvinia molesta*), a floating fern native to south-eastern Brazil, has been a problematic invasive species occurring now across much of the tropical and subtropical world. On part of Lake Kariba, as is often the case in other smaller water bodies where still or slow-moving conditions suit the species, dense mats may form at the surface, impeding the exchange of gases with the air, blocking sunlight, clogging water intakes and impeding access for wildlife, boats and other human uses such as fishing. Drastic changes to ecosystems and the quality and utility of water are frequent consequences of invasion by not only Kariba weed but also a range of invasive floating plants that include water hyacinth (*Eichhornia crassipes*), another invasive species originally from tropical and subtropical South America, and water lettuce (*Pistia stratiotes*), which is of uncertain origin but now has a pervasive pan-tropical distribution across which it is frequently problematic.

Destratification of reservoirs, entailing mechanically breaking down distinct layers of water, helps prevent nutrient releases by oxygenating the surface sediment layers that hold these chemicals in an inert state. An example here is on Roadford Reservoir in Devon (England), where a curtain of bubbled air breaks down stratification, and has overcome former problems with algal contamination of water. Other destratification systems include water jets – for example, as used in the Farmoor Reservoir water supply systems in Oxfordshire, southern England. However, this approach is ineffective in large reservoirs owing mainly to their size but also to the prohibitive energy costs.

Unaccounted costs

Dams fundamentally alter rivers and the pattern of access to, and exploitation of, their associated suite of natural resources. Frequently, this entails a reallocation of benefits from local riparian users to new groups of beneficiaries at a regional or national level. Both costs and benefits change in response to the design and operation of dams and their associated canals, generation and other infrastructure, changing ecological functioning and the structure of economies and local society.

In *Silenced Rivers*[9] and *The Algebra of Infinite Justice*,[10] Patrick McCully and Arundati Roy respectively summarize a broad swathe of adverse effects of the dams of India and those of some of the rest of the world, cataloguing their seemingly inevitable failure to deliver upon the brash promises of their proponents but instead leaving a trail of environmental degradation and human misery. As McCully states, 'A reservoir is the antithesis of a river – the essence of a river is that it flows, the essence of a reservoir is that it is still.' Stream flow is renewable, but the resource contained by a dam cannot automatically be assumed to be so, and the full life-cycle costs and consequences, including 'collateral damage' and decommissioning, are all too commonly ignored. McCully's and Roy's writings are, admittedly, anti-dam polemics. However, the authoritative 2000 *Dams and Development* report of the World Commission on Dams,[11] considered in detail in subsequent chapters, is no less damning in its judgement of the wide range of negative factors associated with many large dams worldwide. It also balances these observations with as rigorous an analysis of benefits. Further analyses of broader social and environmental impacts are available.[12]

Conflicts over access to water

Conflicts over shares of water within catchment systems are probably as ancient as dam-building itself. Not just large dams either, but even relatively small-scale weirs and mills used to abstract water or to harness motive power for irrigation, milling, generation or other machinery. Even as relatively benign an innovation as the post-medieval water meadow systems of southern England caused such conflicts.[13] References in the manorial Court Book of Affpuddle, Dorset, dating back to 1605, relate to ditches and channels being constructed in the meadows along the River Piddle in the very earliest days of water meadow creation. By 1607 and 1608, complaints were made about the use of the water and disturbance to the ancient watercourse. In 1610, the Affpuddle manorial court agreed that three men should be appointed to oversee the watering of the meadows with tenants paying for the work in proportion to their holdings of meadowland, and issued an order that no one should interrupt the work or interfere with the channels. Over the following centuries, the now long-defunct manorial courts across the UK provided rich case histories of conflicts over allocation of water between mills, navigation interests, water meadow operators and other users of water during this largely feudal era of English history.[14]

In other parts of the world, the history of water impoundment and extraction is no less ancient or contested. For example, today's conflicts over allocation of water from India's Cauvery river between the neighbouring Indian states of Karnataka and Tamil Nadu echo those going back centuries between the Madras Residency of the British Raj and the princely State of Mysore in the early twentieth century. The state of Kerala and the union territory of Pondicherry are also parties in the quarrel about allocation of the Cauvery's water. Current uneasy agreements between the four states affected by water allocation from the Cauvery are now established under the aegis of the Cauvery Tribunal, set up as a central government agency. The state government of Karnataka has committed since 1982 to seek the prior consent of the Chennai (Madras) government before embarking on new irrigation projects lest these ventures compromise the extensive canal network engineered in the Thanjavur delta region, which has turned the district into the 'rice bowl' of Tamil Nadu. During conditions of limited rainfall, the state government of Tamil Nadu has to request that of Karnataka to release water downstream from its major reservoirs and dams to enable farmers in the delta region to meet their irrigation needs. All such agreements are contentious, for example stimulating anti-Tamil riots in Bangalore in 1991, frequent representations from the Tamil Nadu government to India's Supreme Court and ongoing civil protests throughout the first decade of the twenty-first century. Such conflicts have been exacerbated over recent years by delayed and frequently insufficient rains, changing land use, including the felling of rain-trapping and soil-stabilizing tree cover, and the belligerent stances of politicians and farmers.

Somehow, amid the noisy conflict over allocation of resources to different sectors of Indian society, the needs of the Cauvery river itself have had no voice. Yet it is the functioning of the ecosystem of the Cauvery which captures rainfall, stores it through the 'sponge effect' of interconnected wetlands, forests and groundwater, buffers flows to reduce flood peaks and eke out water in drier months, and feeds sediment, nutrients, young fish and other living resources to provide for the needs of people along the whole river system. The Cauvery is consequently a river facing a wide range of problems, including low flows in dry summers, declining fish stocks, wetland loss, the construction of large dams and pollution. People are the inevitable victims. Through excessive, inappropriate use of the Cauvery, society is ultimately compromising the river's capacity to sustain it into the future. The long-term integrity of the magnificent, ancient and holy Cauvery River and the many people who depend upon it are today in a fine state of balance.

Sadly, the Cauvery is just another example of a global pattern of ecological decline compromising human security. Elsewhere in the world, in the absence of political agreements, the 'first come, first served' riparian principle has held sway with net negative consequences for the equitable distribution of the benefits and costs of disturbance of a host of ecosystem services. Larger-scale dams bring with them increasing sets of problems of ecosystem perturbation and redistribution of associated costs and benefits, generally rising in proportion to their size.

Changing biodiversity, changing ecosystems

The impacts of dams on river and wetland ecosystems can be severe, ranging from the primary physical, chemical and geomorphological consequences of blocking a river, through to blockage of species movement and reproduction, displacement by alien species, effects on biological productivity, or fundamental alterations to river form and biochemical cycles. Reservoirs displace former ecological communities of river systems, with often quite different assemblages of fish, birds, trees, vegetation and invertebrates both in and beside the water. They can also affect regional ecosystems in diverse ways, including disruption of the migration routes of larger organisms and a fundamental alteration of food webs. The impoundment of water does, of course, create areas of still-water habitat that may have been absent before, and these can be attractive for amenity, commercial or recreational fisheries, and/or nature conservation. However, reservoir habitat is relatively uniform, supporting sparser and less rare biota than the river corridors that it displaces. Furthermore, the dam can attract species not representative of the regions in which they are sited. Examples of this are the attraction of wetland birds into predominantly arid areas with their associated predation and competitive pressures and potential burden of parasites.

Changing hydrological regimes downstream of major impoundments are known to exert substantial ecological impacts over long distances. Flooding and other aspects of flow variability throughout the year have multiple consequences for ecosystems and habitats. Fish are particularly vulnerable to any change in hydrology, their annual and life cycles (migration, spawning, fry nurseries, food sources, etc.) adapted to specific hydrological regimes and habitats. Consequences for invertebrates, plants and other groups of organisms are less well studied but they are likely to be no less significantly perturbed by alterations in characteristics. Secondary consequences arising from geomorphological effects, such as siltation or scouring out of river gravels, erosion of floodplains, chemical changes in water released from dams, and loss of complexity in river channel habitat, can also have significant consequences for ecosystems. The lateral connection between the river channel and its connected floodplain during flooding periods, as summarized, for example, by the widely accepted Flood Pulse Concept,[15] may be a major driving variable for ecological processes in large tropical and temperate river floodplain systems. A positive relationship is also often observed between the diversity of different groups of organisms and the connection of river channels with diverse floodplain habitats.

All of these multiple changes potentially perturb the integrity of ecosystems and the viability of livelihoods dependent upon them. By a large majority, mitigation of habitat lost by development of large dams has historically been seen as expensive and unimportant.[16] Where mitigation does occur, it is often ineffective and at best addresses only a small part of the most directly affected habitat taken by dam development, ignoring wider ecosystem impacts and their many consequences for catchment functioning and dependent human livelihoods. In extreme cases, habitat created to mitigate some of the impacts of dam filling may itself displace habitat of a different character which may have been of no lesser importance.

We are now accustomed to seeing fish passes associated with dams and weirs of all sizes, including installation of 'fish-friendly' turbines. Fish passes are commonly, but wrongly, assumed to enable various fish species to actively migrate upstream and passively pass back down again. However, detailed study of fish passes demonstrates that there is no 'one size fits all' solution. The particular characteristics of fish species, location and local hydrology are all germane to whether fish populations can successfully use these passes, passage through which also often requires from them considerable energy expenditure and also may create concentration points which predators may target. Nor is it safe to assume that fish will be attracted to fish pass outflows related to the tail races of hydropower or other dam outfalls. Furthermore, the downstream movement of fishes has generally been assumed to be passive and readily achieved at high flows, although more recent study demonstrates that downstream migration is also active and relies on a range of environmental clues generally not influencing fish pass design. The effectiveness of fish passes and 'wildlife-friendly' turbines remains fiercely contested.[17] And this, of course, is just considering the larger and more charismatic fish species. Overall ecosystem balance would depend upon 'minor' species of fish, invertebrates and other groups of organisms also traversing freely up and down rivers; this manifestly does not occur, although it is hard to prove conclusively as the migratory behaviour and needs of most species and groups of organisms have simply not been studied. This swathe of pressures cumulatively renders fish less resilient to disease, competitive predation and other stresses.

Dams have impacts both upstream and downstream, with obstructions in the movement and, often, reproductive success of fish, invertebrates, heptiles and many other groups of organisms. Successful lake fishes and other alien organisms can invade and dominate native catchment communities, including, for example, common carp (*Cyprinus carpio*), to which many adverse ecological effects are attributed where introduced worldwide,[18] and also the zebra mussel (*Dreissena polymorpha*), which is also a troublesome colonizer of waterways and water infrastructure around the world. Disruption of native ecosystems can be particularly severe where spawning or nursery sites, or access to them, are compromised by impoundments, habitat change and competitor species. Ecosystems are further perturbed by simplification of habitat hydrology, often permitting dominance by 'weedy' vegetation at the water margin, or aiding colonization of riparian zones by invasive species that further perturb the ecosystem. Various studies around the world have demonstrated how the simpler habitat structure and changed hydrology of man-made impoundments make them more vulnerable to alien invasive species than natural lakes.[19] Starvation of sediment fluxes, compounded by changed hydrology, can radically alter riparian habitat and linked wetlands downstream, together with the vitality of their associated ecosystems. Floodplain area and fertility are both likely to decline under sediment starvation, affecting biodiversity and the potential utility and value of land and other natural resources.

Below dam outfalls, water flowing from deeper layers may contain a lower concentration of oxygen while, conversely, that overtopping from the top of the dam or released through turbines may become super-saturated with oxygen. Each of these extremes has its own lethal and sub-lethal impacts. All of this compounds with changes in river temperature regimes, timing of hydrology, alteration of food webs through factors such as release of algal-rich reservoir water, habitat modification and a host of other impacts that can not only fundamentally alter ecosystem structure and functioning but also facilitate invasion by non-native and further disruptive species.

There may be significant socio-economic implications from changing populations of important species, particularly for indigenous people with locally adapted livelihoods and lifestyles. For example, although various dams and reservoirs of the James Bay hydropower complex in Canada did not provide any specific compensation for indigenous populations when commissioned in 1970, significant social issues, particularly those arising from reduced incomes from hunting and fishing due to hindrances to the free migration of fish and loss of breeding grounds of geese and caribou, proved a basis for subsequent litigation. The indigenous people initiated legal action on the basis of unsettled land claims, leading to the James Bay and Northern Quebec Agreement, signed in 1975, which provided compensation in the form of a 'remedy fund', including a comprehensive lump sum and an annual payment to address outstanding social issues.

The breadth and magnitude of ecosystem impacts have historically been poorly predicted in dam design, if they have been predicted at all. Furthermore, where they have been predicted, the World Commission on Dams is extremely critical of the quality of prediction, including both certainty of magnitude and of likely direction.[20]

Displacement of people

The marginalization of people by 'development' decisions advantageous to a politically and economically powerful oligarchy found its apotheosis in the age of slavery, a practice far from abandoned around the world albeit often now more cryptic under the guise of bonded and other iniquitous labour practices concealed down long supply chains. However, dam construction too has had, and in many places continues to have, its own implications for poor and politically impotent people. The scale of historic dam-induced displacement of people has been staggering: Thayer Scudder, one of the twelve commissioners of the World Commission on Dams, dedicated his 2005 book *The Future of Large Dams*[21] 'to the tens of millions of river basin residents who have been unfairly impoverished by large dams'. And, of course, the mass displacement of predominantly black people in apartheid South Africa and during other imperial African regimes has left a scar on the global conscience.

The commonplace displacement and disenfranchisement of people resulting from the construction and filling of large dams is widely reported,[22] cataloguing an inglorious history of appropriation of considerable benefits by advantaged sectors of society at substantial and often permanent costs to people less advantaged or able to participate in negotiations.

Somewhere between 40 and 80 million people, by overwhelming majority already marginalized, have been physically displaced by dams worldwide.[23] There are many documented cases of displacement by violent means, including the shooting and killing of protesters by officials; 10.2 million of this mass of people were displaced in China between 1950 and 1990 based on official figures, and this of course pre-dates the construction of the massive Three Gorges Dam. In fact, official figures often wildly and perhaps deliberately underestimate the true numbers of people displaced by large dam schemes. As one of several examples, the 1979 Narmada Water Disputes Tribunal provided an estimate of the people displaced by the Sardar Sarovar project in Gujarat, India, as 6,147 families (about 39,700 people). Subsequently, in 1987, the World Bank mission placed the total at 12,000 families (60,000 people). By 1991, the estimate of displaced families had risen to 27,000 families and, by 2000, the estimate of three state governments was of 41,000 displaced families (205,000 people). All figures are confidently expected to continue increasing since, thirteen years after full-scale construction started on the Sardar Sarvovar dam, resettlement surveys had still not been completed.

The misery did not stop with the displacement of people from the Sardar Sarovar dam site itself. None of these estimates included the 57,000 people (at least) displaced by canals, those moved to make space for the creation of compensatory wildlife sanctuaries to mitigate some of the ecological harm from areas inundated behind dams, or those resettled to clear the way for people displaced by the dam, nor those displaced by construction site infrastructure, including the 'construction village', as well as generation and transformer plant. More people yet are subsequently displaced by new industries and large agricultural concerns. More worrying still, the Sardar Sarovar is just one of numerous examples of such underestimates and oversights of often substantial secondary and tertiary effects of dam construction.

Life for displaced people is, with generally minor exceptions, harsh. Often, only those with well-established legal title to land are compensated, which is at best a small minority among the largely landless or tenant populations living resource-dependent lifestyles. Indigenous peoples, in particular women and children, suffer disproportionately from these consequences, which destroy or damage lives, livelihoods, cultures and heritage, and spiritual existence.[24] A number of studies reveal increased ill health and mortality related to the effects of displacement for dam, oil and other major development schemes owing to factors such as poor access to food and water, many of which have a disproportionately negative impact on women.[25] Some populations have been subject to multiple displacements, exacerbating their already serious problems. Women, who produce between 60 and 80 per cent of the food in most developing countries, are major stakeholders in all development issues related to water, yet they often remain on the periphery of management decisions and planning for water resources.

Resettlement programmes, where operated, have historically focused on the process of physical translocation. However, it is rather more important to think in terms of 'livelihood displacement', including opportunities for the economic and social development of negatively affected people together with the social networks that define them and provide them with the necessary resilience to cope with change. The best land is already in the hands of those who can afford to buy or control it. In most cases, these factors exacerbate food shortages and other factors stemming from inadequate clean water, sanitation and nourishment. All too often, the net result is the creation of permanent poor camps, resulting in mass unemployment, loss of traditional ways of life, spread of disease and of hopelessness, and the creation of tensions between host communities and 'displacement slums'. Even in the rare cases where displacement surveys have been undertaken, official figures tend to overlook these secondary but major consequences of displacement as the poor lack political or economic power. Wider human costs, it seems, are all too frequently trivialized or wholly overlooked in the calculation of benefits to the already advantaged.

This is, of course, even before we take into account changes in the behaviour of river and wider water systems downstream of the dam, and its tertiary impacts upon the livelihoods and traditions of the many people dependent upon the diversity of ecosystem services through, as just a few examples, subsistence fishing, seasonal grazing, floodplain agriculture, harvesting of thatch, timber and other construction and craft materials, or dependency upon characteristic landscapes supporting traditional lifestyles and spiritual values. Whether local to the dam or distant, resilience of human populations is frequently, and often profoundly, undermined by degradation of the catchment resource base.

By and large, the consequences for the vast and, under closer scrutiny, increasingly diverse and geographically dispersed body of disadvantaged people do not appear on the balance sheet of costs and benefits. Were they to do so, the case for many dams would most likely be weakened. And yet the further marginalization of these people is short sighted as, if care were taken with their resettlement such that a capacity for productive and fulfilled lives was assured, they could contribute to the overall package of benefits derived from dam schemes rather than being forgotten or overlooked victims of a blinkered model of 'progress'.

Alteration of water and energy use

Large dams also to tend to influence the water and energy use habits of communities benefiting from them. The siting of energy-intensive industries, such as aluminium smelting and associated processing and manufacturing industries, close to sources of cheap and reliable hydroelectric power is just one instance of a change in the balance of socio-economics of a region. The availability of more reliable sources of irrigation water can also stimulate a shift in agriculture from region-ally adapted crops to more water-intensive varieties, particularly such water-hungry crops as cotton, rice, sugar cane, wheat or commercial forestry, of greater value to large-scale commercial growers. This pattern of water inefficiency is commonly exacerbated by inappropriate charging mechanisms for water, often founded on irrigated area rather than abstracted volume, which, though substantially easier to calculate and police, creates a significant incentive for inefficient water use that maximizes individual profit with unaccounted costs borne by those sharing the water or dependent upon environments starved of it. The 'tragedy of the commons' is manifest once again, in this instance favoured by perverse economic incentives.

Frequently, perhaps even generally, local people may benefit least from more lucrative changes rewarding incoming investors and already influential figures and corporations with greater negotiating powers. This appropriation of water by the economically influential can increase the hydrological and food poverty and depress livelihoods of diverse water-dependent communities. Where water is available, greater reliance on intensive farm technologies can not only reduce the resource base available for traditional subsistence and cash crop farmers, but may also erode skills in locally adapted land and water management and water-harvesting traditions.

The net result is that both water-intensive crops and industries tend to displace those that formerly fulfilled local needs, again with a shift in beneficiaries and the balance of ecosystem-mediated costs and benefits incurred across society. As an almost uniform generality, the net result is a skew of benefits from water management towards the already rich and powerful in a model of Western-style industrialization and capitalization, effectively subsidized by the livelihood expectations of many who live closest to subsistence. Often, as we will see, this is driven by a technocentric political perspective on development that overlooks the needs of many in society.

Soils gone sour

Another well-known but, for reasons that are hard to fathom, poorly heeded consequence of intensive irrigation of agricultural land in hot climates is the waterlogging of soils and salinization due to excessive surface evaporation.[26] This is sometimes compounded by corruption of quality in water distribution and by degradation of the natural purification processes of catchments in which dams are constructed. Another significant contributor to the problem as flows decline, particularly in coastal and delta regions, is the intrusion of saline water, which may be compounded by over-pumping of groundwater in coastal regions.

Waterlogging is a huge global problem, generally caused by a failure to match the irrigation of land with commensurate drainage. Globally, the area affected by waterlogging is increasing at a rate faster than that of reclamation of land.[27] As observed previously, the annual costs of drainage of land irrigated by the Aswan High Dam in Egypt now exceed the cost of initial dam-building. This is yet another interesting instance of unaccounted costs exceeding the net perceived benefits yielded by dams and associated infrastructure.

Rather better known and as serious are the effects of salinization due to elevated evaporation rates in hotter climates, resulting in accumulation of salts at the soil surface often compounded by poor-quality water. These lessons go back to the fall of the first irrigation-based civilization of the modern world in Mesopotamia. Over centuries, accumulations of salt leached from the mountains of Turkey and Iran gradually ran down to accumulate under evaporation in the irrigated soils, leading the Sumerians to abandon wheat for the more salt-tolerant barley until that too inevitably failed as salt levels rose. By the nineteenth century, when Europeans started visiting what is now modern-day Iraq, the population had already declined to around one tenth of what it had been at the peak of the hydraulic civilization. Likewise, in the Harappa 'Civilization in the Sands' in the Indus Valley, build-up of salt caused the soils and crops to fail around four thousand years ago, reversing the fortunes of a society built on the newly discovered miracles of irrigation.

The knowledge base supporting the work of the World Commission on Dams[28] demonstrates the pervasive global extent of salinization and its serious and frequently permanent impacts on livelihoods. Excessive soil salinity resulting from irrigation affects approximately 20 per cent of irrigated land worldwide,[29] reminding us again of the question: if a key lesson from history is that most irrigation-based civilizations have failed, will ours be any different as we enter the third millennium AD? From the available global evidence, the answer appears far from positive if we continue to rest upon inherited technologies, assumptions and oversight of likely consequences.

Siltation

Siltation of dams is a further major problem worldwide. Dams without low-level out-takes typically trap 90–100 per cent of the sediment flowing into them from tributary rivers, some such as the Hoover Dam intentionally so as to reduce the turbidity of the Colorado river. Even those with low-level outflows tend to accrete significant volumes of silt throughout the stilled, marginal and deeper waters of the reservoir behind the dam, with progressive siltation around inflowing deltas a common sight in impoundments. This impact is all too often woefully underestimated in dam design and calculation of lifetime performance, particularly where changing upstream land use and climate exacerbate erosion rates.

The World Commission on Dams found that the majority of dams fill up with sediment released from their catchments far more quickly than projected.[30] The loss of dam volume and implications of sediment build-up for turbines can significantly reduce both the economic return and the longevity of dams, from which no one benefits. Not only are design projections often optimistic, perhaps to increase their appeal to investors, but changes in land use and other aspects of catchment management and development can increase pressures on river systems relative to baseline conditions at the time of design. When dams silt up, be they big or small, their benefits to society decline in proportion. For example, land use changes exacerbated by sand mining in the Krokodil river catchment in Mpumalanga province, to the east of South Africa, have resulted in the complete siltation of a number of dams built to benefit small-scale farmers and other low-intensity water users; the net result has been to negate all of the benefits for which the dams were built. This pattern is not uncommon, nor is it restricted just to South Africa or to smaller dams. Another example already cited is the excessive silt trapping in Egypt's Aswan High Dam, which has massively compromised the anticipated volume, lifetime, utility and economic returns of Lake Nasser, let alone the fortunes of rural Egyptians dependent upon the Nile.

Sediment fall-out in dams also produces 'hungry' erosive water downstream, able neither to fertilize floodplains nor maintain the habitat of rivers and their associated wetlands, deltas or coasts. Loss of sediment feed is a particular problem in some localities, perhaps most famously in terms of the degradation of Egypt's Nile Delta. Degradation of the Mississippi delta in the USA and the loss of storm buffering were thought to have had a significant effect on worsening the impact of Hurricane Katrina as it hit the Louisiana coast in 2005, inundating the city of New Orleans. Delta loss also has substantial implications for loss of habitat, fisheries and farmland, reduced regulation of storm and tidal damage, loss of valued and culturally important landscapes, damage to biodiversity and erosion of a range of other benefits derived from ecosystems.

Dealing with accumulated sediment can also be a serious issue, for which solutions remain to be found. Nor can they generally be mitigated in dam design and operation. The problem of disposal of the massive tonnage of silt that accumulates in dams is one currently without solution, compromising the potential for dam decommissioning or the appraisal of full life-cycle benefits and costs. This is particularly the case where the silt is contaminated by accumulation of pollutants and problematic substances running down rivers. For the 1,300 or so mine tailings dams in the USA noted in the previous chapter, as well as the attenuation of pollutants by dams around the world, the lack of an 'exit strategy' to permanently manage pollutants represents a problematic legacy for the future for which we currently lack solutions.

Draining the land

During the 1960s, fisheries on the Aral Sea, then the world's fourth-largest inland sea, supported a huge Soviet cannery industry on the shoreline. At the same time, Soviet engineers were tapping into the Syr Darya and Amu Darya rivers that fed the Aral Sea to increase the productivity of a cotton industry that had been present for decades. The two initiatives were not mutually compatible; the last trawler was abandoned with the canneries in 1984 as the Aral Sea receded, starved of fresh water and dried up by the tropical sun. By 2003, continuing declines in the water level saw the Aral Sea not only shrink to a quarter of its former area but separate into two small hyper-saline seas.

Today, Aralsk city stands not as it once did on the seashore, but instead 64 kilometres (40 miles) north of it, separated by a huge and unproductive salt pan. The decline continues, with every likelihood of this formerly vast and productive inland expanse of water vanishing entirely in a few short years. The fate of land irrigated with water that once fed the Aral Sea is no better, the massive scale of damming and water transfer resulting in the waterlogging and salt panning of fields. Now, winds whip up a dangerous cargo of salt and pesticide residues from their arid surfaces, destroying the ecology, economy and health of central Asia. The 'big engineering' ideology that was once perceived to prove humanity's dominion over nature has ultimately proved only our folly, with profound and enduring consequences.

The Aral Sea is a far from isolated example of major hydrological disruption delivering not the intended uplift of people but instead a legacy of unintended problems. Africa is rife with dam schemes controlling flows for intended benefit but which, in reality, dry up wetlands and other habitat crucial for the livelihoods of the wider population. One such major scheme is Nigeria's Hadejia-Nguru wetlands, which were tapped to 'green the desert' but which, in fact, have achieved the reverse by starving formerly productive lands, waterlogging other irrigated areas with consequent salt accumulation, have prevented natural flooding regimes with their benefits of restoring soil fertility and moisture, and have even resulted in civil conflict in which protesters have been shot and killed. The story is repeated many times elsewhere across Africa, as in the case of the Maga dam in northern Cameroon on the Logone river, where drainage of a natural, productive floodplain has eliminated subsistence agriculture, natural disease control and groundwater recharge, and depleted fish and wildlife populations, creating a desert in its wake. The positive news from Cameroon is that this area of wetland has been reflooded since the mid-1980s. However, loss or degradation of wetlands with their critical services to humanity through well-intentioned but ill-conceived development schemes has been a blight from Uganda to Botswana and many African countries besides.

The Earth moves

There is now a sizeable body of science demonstrating with certainty that large dams are weighty enough to induce seismic effects. Studies were taking place in the USA at least as long ago as the 1940s,[31] more recent studies concluding that large dams contribute to earthquakes across the world, in New Zealand, Canada, India, the USA, Egypt, Venezuela, the eastern Alps of Europe, Pakistan, China, Thailand, Brazil, Africa, Albania, Japan, Greece, Vietnam, Mexico and Turkey.[32] As many as a quarter of the world's superdams have triggered some earth tremors as their reservoirs filled.[33] Earthquake activity has been found to be most strongly correlated with the size of the dam and the time lag since reservoir filling, although the height of the reservoir is also germane to hazard assessment.

Aside from dam failure, the harm associated with greater seismic activity is widely recognized as potentially disastrous. India's Koyna Dam initiated an earthquake that seriously damaged the dam and killed 200 people in an area that had not previously been seismically active. Another significant, albeit not conclusively proven, case is that of China's huge Three Gorges Dam, generally considered as contributory to the disastrous Chinese earthquake of 2008, which was the biggest such event in China in over thirty years, affecting an enormous area of Chinese territory.

Flood control

Many dams have been effective in controlling some flooding, including those designed explicitly to intercept and store seasonal rains. However, widespread evidence suggests that larger dams may also generally increase the vulnerability of floodplain communities. This is due to the fact that, when a dam has been completely filled by floodwater, it contains no buffering for further rainfall, which overtops the spillways in a spate unabated by riparian habitat lost on dam filling. The quantum of damage downstream can be exacerbated where settlement of land is encouraged in floodplains which, though protected for much of the time, remain subject to flooding when dam levels exceed maximum design capacity.

Modern approaches to flood risk management, informed in the early 2000s by the increasing conflict between altered hydrology and development pressure, emphasize the protection of ecosystems critical to storing floodwater, detaining flooding peaks and permitting percolation into groundwater. Engineered flood banks are giving way once more to functional habitat. This ecosystem-based ethos is counter to the ways that dams themselves function, but is highly germane to better management of upstream catchment areas that compensate for the mechanical limitations of dams in absorbing flood conditions. As we have observed for the Three Gorges Dam (and will return to in Parts 2 and 3 of this book), Chinese authorities are promoting tree-planting in the upper catchment of the Yangtze river to restore some of its natural water storage and erosion control services. Not only was removal of 85 per cent of the original tree cover recognized as contributing to direct flood damage but the surge of storm water, no longer slowed and stored by mature forests, carried with it huge quantities of topsoil, depleting the primary resource of agriculture and silting the dam.

We also have to be mindful that flooding has natural advantages, such as the redistribution of sediment and nutrients and the maintenance of biological diversity, which may be lost, together with community and ecological benefits, when natural hydrology is perturbed. We have already cited Egypt's Aswan High Dam as a prominent example, but the principle applies generically.

Dams and the atmosphere

The simplistic notion that hydropower, whether marine or freshwater, is carbon neutral is often implicit in political pronouncements. Worryingly, this seems often to lead to a broader assumption that hydropower is environmentally benign. This is a far from logical extrapolation. It is certain that hydroelectric power, such as that now often harnessed from large dams, may have a role to play in a mix of renewable forms of energy. However, this potential contribution should be approached critically, and explored on a case-by-case basis.

In the early years following large dam completion, the decay of inundated vegetation can make a significant contribution to greenhouse gas emissions. This process cannot be assumed to cease on continued dam operation as organic matter washed into the dam or growing within the reservoir will also rot down with a release of various gases, particularly of methane, which has a far higher climate change potential than carbon dioxide. Anoxic habitat of all types on the reservoir bed or walls also liberates methane into the atmosphere in substantial quantities, particularly where the standing waters, throughout the complex contours, bays and backwaters of larger dams, result in an accumulation of algal or other higher plant material that subsequently decays.

Generally, this impact has been overlooked or assumed to be trivial, but peer-reviewed research suggests that it may be highly significant. A paper published in 2007 by Ivan Lima and colleagues[34] has stimulated vociferous global debate on the contribution of large dams to climate change. The Lima study suggests that, although largely ignored to date, huge amounts of methane, a gas seventy-two times more potent as a greenhouse gas than carbon dioxide although removed from the atmosphere rather more quickly, is generated through degradation of organic matter in the reservoirs behind dams and released both from dam surfaces and also on depressurization of water in turbine spillways. So large and dependable is this production, estimated at a massive 104 +/− 7.2 Tg (million metric tonnes) of methane each year based on ICOLD inventories, that Lima and co-authors proposed capturing methane in reservoirs before it reaches the turbines, using it to fuel power plants as a Clean Development Mechanism under the Kyoto Protocol. These authors note that, 'If we can generate electricity from the huge amounts of methane produced by existing tropical dams we can avoid the need to build new dams with their associated human and environmental costs.' In a May 2007 press release, the international NGO International Rivers extrapolated Lima's calculations, concluding that large dams around the world may be one of the single most important contributors to global warming, accounting for more than 4 per cent of the total global warming impact of human activities.[35] A 2007 press release by the South Asian Network on Dams, Rivers and People concurs with these conclusions, and considers on this basis that large dams in India are responsible for 19 per cent of the country's total global warming impact, with Indian dams the largest global warming contributors compared to those of all other nations, accounting for 27.86 per cent of the methane emission from all the large dams of the world.[36] Brazil's reservoirs come second in the world by this calculation, emitting 18.13 per cent of the global figure.

A 2011 study found that carbon emissions (carbon dioxide and methane) from hydroelectric reservoirs are linked to reservoir age and latitude.[37] Using this more nuanced finding and extrapolating from data for a subset of reservoirs, the study estimated that hydroelectric reservoirs globally emit about 48 teragrams of carbon (TgC) as carbon dioxide with an additional 3TgC methane annually: 51 TgC in all, corresponding to 4 per cent of global carbon emissions from inland waters. This downgrade of estimates from the Lima et al. study nevertheless points to a substantial mass of climate-active gases.

These implications have yet to factor into Intergovernmental Panel on Climate Change (IPCC) calculations, and more science is required to confirm the implications. However, the International Rivers press release speculates that the massive amounts of methane produced by hydropower reservoirs in the tropics mean that these dams can have a much higher warming impact than even the dirtiest fossil fuel plants generating similar quantities of electricity, shattering the myth that power from large hydropower projects can be assumed to be 'clean' from a climate change perspective.

Furthermore, as former wetlands dry in response to changed hydrology throughout the catchment, they too will tend to oxidize and liberate their often substantial stores of sequestered carbon. Concerns also arise from the largely unquantified biological processing of nitrogen-containing organic matter, which, under certain conditions, can result in the release into the atmosphere of nitrous oxide, a gas with a 'greenhouse potential' about three hundred times greater than carbon dioxide. Rates of production of nitrous oxide are incompletely understood at present, with many questions remaining unanswered. All of this amounts to a far from straightforward assumption about the carbon neutrality, or otherwise, of dam-based power generation.

Two of the world's largest energy companies, Électricité de France (EDF) and GDF-Suez, pledged in 2012 to explore the broader impacts of dams using the Hydropower Sustainability Assessment Protocol (HSAP) to produce a scorecard of social and environmental impacts of at least one hydropower project each, though critics suggest that this assessment framework serves dam builders and not local communities.[38] The extent to which contentious climate-active gas issues will be assessed remains moot.

Dams and disease

With their multiple consequences for ecosystems, it is unsurprising to observe that dams can result in the spread of water-associated and other human diseases. The proliferation of Rift Valley fever across Africa is generally ascribed to the spread of dams and the success of the mosquito vectors that transmit the disease. The same principle is accepted for the spread of malaria more widely across the world. Also, in India, a causal link has been proved between the devastating incidence and spread of Japanese encephalitis and the proliferation of dam schemes in the Narmada and Upper Krishna rivers.

Mollusc-mediated diseases such as schistomsomiasis (bilharzia) are also facilitated by creation of large bodies of standing water and the stilling of rivers downstream. These impacts, as well as those of other waterborne diseases, including the spread of diarrhoeal diseases due to reduced dilution effects, may also be felt more widely across the catchment. For example, Myles Mander's elegant 2003 socio-economic study *Thukela Water Project: Reserve Determination Module* (reviewed in greater detail in Part 2 of this book) provides evidence of the potential boost in incidence of bilharzia and its associated economic impacts in the Thukela (Tugela) river system of KwaZulu-Natal in South Africa under a range of scenarios for dam development and water transfer.[39]

Other direct effects commonly encountered in dams of all sizes include toxicity from blooms of blue-green algae (cyanobacteria) in reservoir waters, which can be lethal or harmful for riparian communities and animals as well as poisoning wider communities through distribution of contaminated lake water. Reduced dilution in downstream river reaches can also exacerbate the spread of cholera and diarrhoeal diseases.

The introduction and rapid spread of HIV-AIDS from construction camps into local communities is another well-documented secondary impact of dam-building. A parallel but relevant example here is the spread of HIV-AIDS in Kenya through routes such as socially influential fishermen and middleman fish dealers (almost exclusively male) requiring sexual favours of unempowered (almost exclusively female) household consumers. It is probable that these secondary health effects may also be prevalent wherever dams exacerbate a polarization in access to money, fish, water, power or other vital resources. The transmission of HIV-AIDS and other related diseases from construction camps during dam-building is well recorded by authoritative studies such as those of the World Commission on Dams.[40]

We can assume that similar principles will apply to the transmission of animal diseases. However, these have not been studied to anywhere near as great an extent.

Further concerns arise from the propensity for the formation of methylmercury in dams due to bacterial action in the organic and anoxic conditions frequently found in deeper water. The organic nature of mercury in methyl form makes it particularly dangerous as it is readily taken up by and bioaccumulated in living cells and ecosystems, and biomagnified up food chains.[41] This means that even relatively low concentrations of methylmercury in the environment can result in potentially toxic levels in larger fish and the land animals or birds that eat them. This of course includes humans, in which high levels of organic methylmercury are known to be destructive to the central nervous system in adults as well as stimulating birth defects and causing developmental problems in children.[42] Newly formed reservoirs appear to be at a greater risk of organic methylmercury production than natural lakes, their fish accumulating higher methylmercury concentrations than those inhabiting surrounding waters.[43] Studies of the James Bay region of northern Quebec revealed that methylmercury concentrations in all species of fish increased six times after impoundments were constructed.[44] Although carbon levels decline in reservoirs over time with a consequent lowering of methylmercury production, any adjustments to the reservoir's water level can once again increase the percentage of carbon with consequences for mercury transformation.[45] In the James Bay region, the elevation of mercury levels in fish beyond safe limits has had profound effects on the economy and nutrition but also on the cultural identity of the Innu, the local indigenous peoples, for whom 'hunting and fishing not only feeds the stomach but also nourishes the soul'.[46] The occurrence and often severe impacts of methylmercury formation and bioaccumulation are widely reported in connection with large dams globally.

Strategic targets

We live in a world that is far from politically secure. Particularly in regions of greater instability, though perhaps now more all pervasively given the global reach of terrorism, dams represent strategic targets. We have known this for many years, of course, with the targeting of dams by all sides throughout the Second World War (particularly as made famous by the 'Dambusters') and other military campaigns, although control of water for warfare is far longer established than this.

In this modern era, the pollution or disturbance of supply of water and hydroelectric power, and the carnage caused by flooding when dams are destroyed, represents both a powerful terror target and a potent weapon to any aggressor. As a direct consequence, it is now an offence to photograph large dams in India, Zimbabwe, South Africa and many other nations. When considering the Hoover Dam, we also noted that the USA too has heightened its security around large dams in the post-9/11 era, with US Highway 93 across the dam crown now replaced by the Hoover Dam Bypass.

Not only are the services provided by large dams critical and the potential for harm substantial, but there is also great political importance in the seamless functioning of critical hydrological infrastructure. Dams, then, are fiercely guarded assets, ever more expense to secure in the light of escalating terrorism threats.

The economics of large dams

On the basis of the above catalogue of potential and actual impacts, it is unsurprising to learn that the average cost overrun of large dams (according to the knowledge base compiled by the World Commission on Dams[47]) was 56 per cent, though individual cases were as high as 235 per cent. Almost three-quarters of all dams assessed exhibited capital cost overruns. For their irrigation benefits, generally the primary design purpose of large dams, almost half fell short of target performance for irrigated area within the first five years of operation. This shortfall was often significant, with one quarter of dams delivering less than 35 per cent of target irrigation area.

Direct economic influence from dam construction may start even at the pre-design stage, with planning through to construction imposing a blight on the value of adjacent land and property. At design and construction phases, many of the benefits may accrue to foreign con-sultants and contractors. This is particularly so in developing countries lacking their own technical capacity and where dam-building remains most prevalent owing to both a current greater social acceptance of dams and the exhaustion of suitable sites elsewhere in the world. And, as we have observed, transition to more water- and energy-hungry crops and industry can further centralize profit to relatively few commercial beneficiaries, leaving broader, generally marginalized rural commun-ities suffering even more from the hardships that large dam projects are often billed as solving.

Repeatedly throughout this chapter, we have highlighted costs to people, ecosystems, long-term viability, future liabilities, disease and other parameters that rarely if ever feature in traditional cost–benefit analyses. Many implications for livelihoods, health, social systems and cultures are commonly overlooked by the kinds of traditional eco-nomic accounting applied to dam evaluation. The World Commission on Dams study, covered extensively later in this book and providing substantial input to this chapter, concluded that there is commonplace economic failure in large dam projects across the world. This is even more worrying when one considers that many of the factors addressed in this chapter are largely externalized from economic systems, and hence from detailed consideration within cost–benefit assessment.

However, even based upon the narrow direct benefit criteria con-sidered for many large dams, their value is often equivocal at best. More searching questions still remain to be addressed if we begin to include into a final ledger the balance of broader ecosystem and socio-economic factors and legacies for the future.

Whose dam?

The above economic discussion is presented, of course, before we begin to ask questions about corruption, which is generally accepted to be endemic in many developing countries. There is, indeed, a large body of evidence that self-benefit has been a powerful motive in decisions about large development projects across the world, including dams. This can take many forms, including the choice of site, design, selection of contractors and consultants, and the channelling of aid, associated fees, compensation payments and other funds.

Dams also, as stated in the previous chapter, have a huge symbolic value in terms of national and state pride, emblems of human and corporate prowess, and political statements. It is not coincidental that many large dams and dam-associated schemes – for example, the Indira Gandhi Canal, Lake Nasser or the Hoover Dam and Lake Mead – have the names of influential people associated with them. Likewise, planning for the Akosombo Dam (formerly the Volta Dam) on the Volta river in Ghana commenced shortly after Ghana became the first country in Africa to gain independence from Britain in 1957, completed in 1961 and launched in 1966 by President Kwame Nkrumah, who promoted it as a symbol of the industrialization of the new Ghana. Also, Turkey's Ataturk Dam, which began filling and appropriating the waters of the Euphrates river flowing into Syria and Iraq downstream in 1989, was seen as a monument to Turkish innovation and pride about which, at its launch in 1992, President Turgut Ozal proclaimed that 'The twenty-first century will belong to Turkey'.

We need not look just to the tropics, the distant past or even the homelands of mega-dams to see real political upheaval caused by dams. Infamously, construction of the Llyn Celyn reservoir in Gwynedd, North Wales, between 1960 and 1965, in the valley of the River Tryweryn, was a major factor fuelling the rise of Welsh nationalism, leading eventually to the devolution of Wales from the UK and the establishment of a quasi-autonomous Welsh government by 2012. At roughly 4 kilometres long by 1.6 kilometres wide (2½ miles long by a mile wide), with a maximum depth of 43 metres (140 feet) and a capacity of 71.2 megalitres[48] held back by a rock gravity dam, Llyn Celyn reservoir is small by global standards. However, its construction entailed inundating the village of Capel Celyn, outlying fertile farmland and a railway line. The purpose of the dam, to maintain the flows of the River Dee to provide water for the distant industrial city of Liverpool and the Wirral peninsula over the border in England, caused deep controversy that is still strongly felt today in this centre of the Welsh language and Welsh culture. Driven through by national legislation notwithstanding the opposition of thirty-five out of thirty-six Welsh Members of the UK Parliament, the backlash led to the rise of the Welsh nationalist party

Plaid Cymru, establishing a powerful momentum towards eventual Welsh devolution.[49] Notwithstanding a public apology by Liverpool City Council in October 2005,[50] tangible animosity remains with fresh Welsh nationalist graffiti still regularly daubed on buildings adjacent to the dam.

For all of these dam schemes, both huge and small, a key question remains far from resolved: who really benefits?

The sins of omission

It would be unjust and disingenuous to accuse dam pioneers of seeking to undermine human well-being. Indeed, quite the converse is true, with dams perceived as beacons of hope for delivery from poverty and the ravages of drought, famine and energy deficits. On the face of it, the positive contribution of dams to enduring public well-being and the national economy seems compelling when one takes account only of the basket of planned benefits such as controlled supply of water or assumptions about the reliability and carbon neutrality of hydroelectric dams in tropical countries.

Portrayal of dams throughout much of the twentieth century as icons of hope and prosperity has been due to consideration of river systems as merely flows of water to be exploited without wider consequences for ecosystems and the many people who benefit from them. However, it is generally not what is planned or perceived which causes problems. Rather, the devil lies in what is overlooked. The water and energy that dams can supply do not magically appear; rather they are diverted from natural flows of water, energy, solutes, sediments and organisms taking place within often radically modified systems. And, when we change the nature of a system, we alter its inherent properties, including its capacities to support diverse livelihoods.

On those occasions when broader constituencies have been considered, there might have been an assumption of the 'trickle down effect', whereby benefits to some people percolate out to local constituencies through, for example, local trade and other opportunities. However, in practice, the 'trickle down effect' has been largely discredited, particularly in a developing world context, where a powerful oligarchy and/or foreign investment results in returns to sectors of society that are more likely to keep them to themselves. Again, the sins of omission are committed in the voicing of this empty hope.

The list of knock-on consequences in this chapter is both substantial and substantially incomplete. Large dams are evidently no cost-free means of deliverance from hunger and poverty. Indeed, the very notion of dams as 'temples of modern India' is particularly ironic when the temples and ancestral lands, viewed by many local and native people as inhabited by their gods, disappeared under floodwaters as dams filled. Many lives have been lost in protests against this perceived cultural and spiritual vandalism, and in the refusal of some to submit to enforced relocation to make way for a different model of 'progress' enjoyed by other strata of society. Consequences for displaced and disenfranchised peoples, loss of habitat and natural hydrology of rivers, silting up of dams well short of design life, erosion of downstream floodplains, salination of soils resulting from irrigation in a hot climate, and many other devastating factors besides evoke even fewer of the implications of the term 'temple'. Realization of some of these costly consequences provided adequate reason for Nehru to regret his statement within his own lifetime.

4 | A changing mindset

Particularly in the last two decades of the twentieth century, societal attitudes towards large dams started to change rapidly, challenging their previously uncontested status as emblems of modern human progress. Unsurprisingly, it was in areas of the already developed world, wherein dams had the longest legacy, where these seeds of disquiet first took root.

Mitigating the problems of large dams

The scale at which large dams modify catchments and their associated human livelihoods and rights means that even their most bullish proponents acknowledge that the benefits of large dams cannot be realized without adverse consequences. ICOLD, the International Commission on Large Dams, was established in 1928 as an international non-governmental organization (NGO) providing a forum for the exchange of knowledge and experience in dam engineering. Today, ICOLD has National Committees from eighty-eight countries with approximately ten thousand individual members, predominantly comprising practising engineers, geologists and scientists from government and private organizations, consulting firms, universities, laboratories and construction companies. ICOLD is, in effect, a cross-sectoral body comprising people with an interest in promoting large dams.

ICOLD aims to lead the profession by ensuring that dams are built safely, efficiently, economically and without detrimental effects on the environment. Its original aim was to encourage advances in the planning, design, construction, operation and maintenance of large dams and their associated civil works, by collecting and disseminating relevant information and by studying related technical questions. Since the late 1960s, ICOLD's focus has shifted from predominantly engineering issues – dam safety, monitoring of performance, reanalysis of older dams and spillways, the effects of ageing and so on – towards broader concern for impact on the environment, costs and financing, the harnessing of international rivers, and information for the public at large.

ICOLD's 1981 report *Dam Projects and Environmental Success*[1] made a more concerted appraisal of the environmental impacts of large dams, concluding that these impacts were generally negative albeit that performance varied substantially from dam to dam. The need for new ways of thinking about the benefits and the largely unintended negative impacts was becoming apparent through the changing awareness of the age. In 1997, ICOLD published a *Position Paper on Dams and the Environment* which presented guidance for environmental consideration, assessment and mitigation. It concludes by stating that 'Increased awareness of the natural environment and its endangered situation is one of the most important developments of the late 20th century'.

ICOLD recognizes that there are complex environmental issues associated with dams. Most reservoirs trap nearly 100 per cent of the river sediment loads that enter them. Consequently, sedimentation typically becomes a significant problem only fifty or more years after construction of a dam, since dams are designed with extra storage to allow for sediment deposition, though this is hardly the most far sighted of long-term planning. Owing to the rapid growth in dam development during the 1960s and 1970s, about 45 per cent of the current storage capacity in reservoirs would be seriously affected by reservoir sedimentation over the coming two decades. Most existing dams would be seriously affected by lost storage due to sedimentation by the year 2065. This threat is exacerbated by increasing erosion driven by changing land use methods and intensity, and compounded by a changing climate.

However, today ICOLD claims to be 'mitigating the environmental impacts of dams',[2] using measures including clearing of vegetation in the area to be flooded, multilevel outlet structures to optimize downstream water temperature and quality, provisions for the migration of fish and other aquatic organisms, and operational rules for regulating downstream flows at critical times to protect habitat for reproduction or migratory routes. ICOLD also recognizes that, since the peak of dam construction in the 1970s, the world population has become aware of the environmental price being paid for its historic 'big engineering' path of development, acknowledging the need for a better balance between the economic benefits and impacts on the environment as well as distribution of benefits among the population in affected regions. Somewhat inconsistently, the ICOLD website[3] notes that ecosystem restoration is one of the primary environmental objectives of a dam project.

This naturally shifts the focus from discrete dam schemes towards planning at entire watershed level, and ICOLD has recognized that the watershed must become the basic element for managing water resources and the environment. The organization also states its agreement with the UN's analysis that the resource of water is an essential ingredient in achieving Millennium Development Goals to eliminate poverty and hunger, improve health, and combat disease by 2015. ICOLD's formula for helping the international community is, unsurprisingly, that dams have a major role to play, albeit that they must implement emerging protocols for public involvement and coordination, management of socio-economic issues such as resettlement and equal distribution of project benefits, and environmental mitigation. This, says ICOLD, will mean that dams of a proper size and location can be designed and constructed in the watershed, with a particularly important role in developing nations.

Clearly, ICOLD represents a strongly pro-dam lobby, and sees the world in terms of opportunities for its membership. It does, however, acknowledge the evolving need to address sustainability and has been taking reactive measures for a matter of decades.

Movement for change

The theory of democratic government is that the will of the people is expressed through the political machine. We might question the transparency of this process in practice and its freedom from influence by the economically powerful, but the basic premise that the task of government is to reflect the best interests of its people nevertheless applies across a range of different political models.[4] However, the dominant task of government is largely to maintain the status quo of the operation of civil society. Consequently, the best place to scan for the emergent concerns of society is not in government messages but in the NGO sector.

Indeed, the history of environmental awareness and subsequent progressive response by government across the world has been most effectively driven by campaigning NGOs. The NGO sector has often been at the forefront of championing the interests of less influential people in the face of the interests of the more economically and politically powerful. This influence is evident in growing awareness and progressive culture change related to such issues as whaling, acid rain, logging, the rights of indigenous peoples, river protection and many more spheres across the globe. NGOs are not of course value free, often having their own vested interests and agendas. Nevertheless, though the messages emanating from NGOs are frequently uncomfortable, and sometimes even misinformed, the world owes a huge debt to its diverse campaigning pressure groups and other environmental and sustainability NGOs for persistently pushing back the barriers of ignorance and hegemony on the journey to a sustainable future.

In the 1960s and 1970s, environmental NGO activism across the world was largely confrontational. Issues as diverse as acid rainfall and other forms of pollution, human health and the ecological effects of unrestricted use of dangerous chemicals, erosion of wetlands, rainforest and other habitats, species extinctions and inhumane exploitation were indeed so far from public and political consciousness that these guerrilla tactics were essential. Since that time, there has been a metamorphosis of NGO activity and professionalism effectively paralleling society's evolving understanding of how ecosystems function and what constitutes an effective conservation strategy. As the interconnections between ecosystem functioning and the resources underwriting social and economic progress have become better understood, precipitating modern concepts of sustainability founded upon the indivisibility of ecology, economy and society, so too the NGO sector has by majority made a transition from opposing economic and government direction towards working in synergy to help guide it towards sustainable outcomes. A reactionary element in the environmental and sustainability NGO movement remains loud and strong today, continuing its traditional function of raising to public awareness issues that are currently off the general 'radar of perception'. However, much of the mainstream NGO movement has made a progressive transition towards becoming 'solutions oriented'.

We see both faces of the NGO movement expressed in relation to concerns about large dams.

A turning tide

Anti-dam campaigns in the USA commenced from 1950, with shifting social attitudes influencing environmental legislation from the 1969 National Environment Protection Act (NEPA) and the 1974 Endangered Species Act. In 1966, the Committee on Water of the US National Academy of Sciences–National Research Council produced a report entitled *Alternatives in Water Management*, which noted 'the possibility that there may be alternatives to water development for promoting regional growth'.[5] To balance the argument, it should also be recorded that there were pro-dam protests in the USA, largely led by farming interests intent on receiving a share of the much-touted benefits of the 'big dam' era. Other pro-dam protests persist today in India and South Africa where there is an automatic, if often flawed, assumption on the part of some sectors of society that the only way to boost and secure water supply is to construct more dams.

Across India, there is a growing non-governmental movement focusing public concern on many issues ranging from indigenous people's rights to protection of cultural relics, and of course spanning a breadth of environmental issues. Some of these are already focused upon rivers, covering diverse aspects of wildlife, public health, angling and other special interests. Given the connectedness of rivers, all of these issues are ultimately interdependent. Dams have become a flagship, as well as the emblem of spoiled rivers. Of all the mounting number of anti-dam campaigns in India, that of the Sardar Sarovar Dam on the Narmada river in the state of Gujarat is the most well known around the globe owing to the effectiveness of campaigning by the Narmada Bachao Andolan[6] (Save the Narmada Movement) and other similar grassroots struggles. The active involvement of such prominent figures as the award-winning author Arundati Roy[7] has been a major contributory factor in the global visibility of the campaign. The Narmada river valley has been home to an uninterrupted flow of human civilization since prehistoric times, and the river is one of the seven most sacred rivers in ancient Indian texts. It was the prospect of massive environmental destruction and social disruption on the Narmada which engendered the setting up of the Narmada Bachao Andolan; up to one million people are likely to be affected if the dam is constructed and completed, with 320,000 risking being displaced and many likely to suffer the permanent effects of disenfranchisement. While dam proponents proclaim the benefits of reliable supplies of water and electricity, opponents and a wider and growing Indian and global consensus question the basic assumptions of the whole Narmada Valley Development Plan, which is intended to dam the Narmada river throughout its course.

This activism on the Narmada is the tip of a substantive iceberg of public concern over a range of issues associated with dams, with growing unrest and opposition expressed across India. Some of it is confrontational, but some solutions-based. A prime example of the solutions approach is taken by the Swatcha Ganga Abhiyan[8] (Clean Ganga Campaign), launched in 1982 as a not-for-profit, apolitical and secular non-governmental organization to expose to public awareness the extent of damage to the river and its environs at a time when all of the cities along the river were discharging untreated sewage and industrial effluents directly into the water. At this time, there was a complete lack of any action plan at either national, state or local levels to clean any of India's rivers, nor was there any widespread public appreciation of the extent of damage already inflicted upon the Ganges. Indeed, much of the populace had an unshakeable faith that this great holy river possessed an infinite power to wash away the sins of the people, and was beyond mankind's capacity to pollute. Owing largely to the special significance of the River Ganga to the diaspora of Hindu communities scattered throughout all countries, the campaign claims support from every corner of the world. It takes an overview of the river, tackling problems of pollution at local level and challenging government centrally through activities ranging from design and petitioning for implementation of sewage interception, setting up of a laboratory to generate a scientific database of water quality, support for various branches of activism, and the establishment of the Friends of the Ganges network. In part driven by the successes of the Swatcha Ganga Abhiyan, the government of India created the Central Ganga Authority and Ganga Project Directorate and launched its famous Ganga Action Plan when Shri Rajiv Gandhi became prime minister. The Swatcha Ganga Abhiyan has found it necessary to act as public watchdog with respect to these state bodies.

The growing evidence of unintended harm to wider society stemming from large dams was not lost on the donor community, particularly the World Bank, which had been a prominent global proponent and financier of large infrastructure projects since its inception in the reconstruction of post-Second World War Europe. Publication of the Bank-sponsored 'Morse Report' in 1992[9] on the increasingly contentious Sardar Sarovar dam project on the Narmada river highlighted issues of displacement and resettlement of people and broader environmental consequences. The Morse Report was instrumental not only in withdrawal of World Bank support from the Sardar Sarovar in 1993, but also in a wider change in attitude to sponsorship of large dams. On 1 September 1994, 326 signatories from forty-four countries signed the Manibeli Declaration, named after the first village in Maharashtra state submerged by dam filling in that year, calling for a moratorium on World Bank funding of large dams.[10] The Bank undertook another relevant review in the shape of *Resettlement and Development: The Bank-wide Review of Projects Involving Involuntary Resettlement 1986–1993*,[11] also co-sponsoring the World Commission on Dams. While the World Bank retains a positive attitude to the value of irrigation in arid environments, it notes in its 2007 *World Development Report: Agriculture for Development*[12] that both positive and negative implications can arise for environmental services, including vulnerability to climate change. The report recognises that,

Access to water and irrigation is a major determinant of land productivity and the stability of yields. Irrigated land productivity is more than double that of rainfed land ... With climate change leading to rising uncertainties in rainfed agriculture and reduced glacial runoff, investment in water storage will be increasingly critical. Even with growing water scarcity and rising costs of large-scale irrigation schemes, there are many opportunities to enhance productivity by revamping existing schemes and expanding small-scale schemes and water harvesting.

In South America, a similar groundswell of activism is growing in opposition to the 'Belo Monte Monster Dam' in Brazil, a scheme on the Xingu river that aims to build the third-largest dam in the world and which is being progressed by the Brazilian government seemingly at any cost.[13] Belo Monte is one of the Amazon's most controversial development projects, dating back to the days of Brazil's former military dictatorship. Diverting up to 80 per cent of the Xingu river, the scheme will create drought in some currently naturally watered areas, flooding others via a system of channels bigger than the Panama Canal and fundamentally changing the character of the region and livelihoods of its endemic people.

Since the 'glory days' of dam-building across the world, large dams have fallen strongly out of favour with the international community for the simple reason that many fail to meet their often extravagant promises. Instead, or at the very least in addition, they degrade or substantially perturb ecosystems, displace people, risk producing saline rather than fertile agricultural land, block the migration of fish and other wildlife even when passes are integrated, silt up more quickly than anticipated while denying fertility to lower river reaches and their floodplains, and also often deepen rather than relieve the cycle of poverty. When the balance of benefits versus costs is considered, the overall advantages of large dams are substantially less rosy than when considering planned benefits to target communities alone, which often accrue only to narrow sectors of society. The cumulative value – economic, social and environmental – of allowing catchment ecosystems to function more naturally with their range of associated human benefits has almost exclusively been omitted from consideration.

Today, attitudes to dams diverge across the world. The USA now leads the way in decommissioning dams, blowing up its major dams to let rivers run freely once more, having realized that the benefits of restoring more natural flows to rivers substantially exceed those of many older dams. In the USA, the rate of decommissioning exceeds that of dam-building. Significantly, this includes removal of two dams on the Elwha river, part of the largest river restoration project ever undertaken in the world, which it is hoped will restore the character and ecology of the river eliminated by dam construction. This includes restoring runs of five species of Pacific salmon which were reduced a thousandfold, severely impacting animals such as black bears and bald eagles that rely on them.[14]

Removal of the upper dam, the 64-metre (210-foot) high concrete-built Glines Canyon Dam, built in 1927 with no fish pass whatsoever, presented the greatest challenge as it is the tallest dam ever to be taken down. Handling the huge volumes of sediment built up behind both dams presented a particular challenge. However, allowing sediment to run free again will eventually help restore not only the natural geomorphology of the river but also see the return of sandy beaches at the Elwha delta. Removal of these dams cost a total of $27 million but, after scheme completion, salmon are returning as the river slowly regains some of its natural character.[15]

Continuing momentum

However, more large dams, many of them very large indeed, are still being built in India, China and a number of other countries in which the primacy of the economy and short-term thinking continue to blind planners to the lessons of history and even the opprobrium of neighbouring countries and the global community. China, for example, has already constructed a number of major dams and is planning to build more on the upper Mekong river. These schemes will have inevitable and profound impacts on the flows and other characteristics of one of the last big untamed rivers in the world, with potentially serious consequences for the downstream countries of Laos, Thailand, Cambodia and Vietnam. A string of further dams is being considered in the lower Mekong which would convert nearly 55 per cent of the river to slow-flowing reservoirs, inflicting harm on the nearly sixty million people who rely on its rich fisheries and who farm and live on its fertile floodplains.[16]

China is also planning to dam the Yarlung Tsangpo river on the Tibetan Plateau to retain its flows for distribution eastwards across the country and to harvest power in what would be the world's largest hydroelectricity scheme.[17] The Yarlung Tsangpo is known downstream as the Brahmaputra (and also the Dihang), a wellspring of water, nutrients, organisms and spiritual significance to Arunachal Pradesh and Assam states in India and subsequently Bangladesh, and also a major source of sediment that maintains the structure and fertility of the delta that comprises so much of Bangladesh's fertile land. The proposed Yarlung Tsangpo dam is a major source of international conflict.

Meanwhile, Ethiopia is planning Africa's tallest dam, the 243-metre-high Gibe III dam on the Omo river. At the time of writing, Ethiopia is also constructing the Grand Renaissance Dam, formerly known as the Millennium Dam or Hidase Dam, a gravity dam on the Blue Nile that will on completion become the largest hydroelectric power plant in Africa. Gibe III is planned to be taller, and threatens at least eight tribes in Ethiopia and about 300,000 people living around the internationally important Lake Turkana in Kenya. Almost four hundred organizations have signed a petition against construction of the Gibe III dam, which was delivered to Ethiopian embassies in France, Germany, Italy, Belgium, the UK and the USA to mark World Water Day on Tuesday, 22 March 2011.[18] At the time of writing, the Gibe III dam is nearly half completed, funded by a consortium of private interests including technology and technical input from Italy, China and the USA and finance from Chinese banks and indirectly also from the UK, as Ethiopia was the largest single recipient of British development aid. The European Investment Bank and the African Development Bank had decided against funding the dam. Gibe III will inevitably remove the natural flood patterns of the river upon which the lifestyles and agricultural practices of tribes in the Omo depend, and will as inevitably perturb fish stocks that are currently an important protein source for local people as well as part of their lifestyles. Despite Ethiopian government claims that 'artificial floods' will solve the problem, and also plans by the dam's constructors for the tribes to switch to more modern forms of agriculture, local tribes have not been consulted about this national lurch towards industrialization and the associated radical switch in their livelihoods, or the lease of their land to foreign investors, in violation of Ethiopia's own Constitution. The Gibe III Hydroelectric Project Official Website[19] states that 'The interest behind the adverse comment against Gibe III Dam is ignorance', that 'Gibe III Hydroelectric Project is a gift of God for the Dawro People' and that 'The Gibe III HEP implementation is very much in line with the local communities', though none of these statements is substantiated. Implications for the already water-stressed north of Kenya, including the character, ecology and livelihoods of Lake Turkana, the world's largest permanent desert lake and also the world's largest alkaline lake, as well as for international relationships, have yet to be considered in any detail, although Kenya has signed a Memorandum of Understanding regarding receiving some of the electricity output from Gibe III.

So too on the other side of the planet, Brazil's energy planners are viewing the Madeira river, the largest tributary of the Amazon, as a vital resource for hydropower.[20] Giant dams are slated for construction at Jirau and San Antonio, planned to deliver in excess of 3,000 megawatts each by 2013. Notwithstanding substantial opposition, the Brazilian government has described them as a top priority. The opposition is not without just cause as, even with mitigation measures, largely powerless indigenous forest dwellers will be displaced, flooding could be greatly aggravated, and the neighbouring government of Bolivia has lodged a complaint about the interception of the huge sediment load normally carried down the Madeira river. Add to this the spiralling cost, way above the original $US55.3 billion budget and still increasing before construction has even started. Environmental disruption during the construction phase of the Madeira river scheme will be substantial, with contractors already having triggered penalty fines for illegal forest destruction and fish kills due to the use of dynamite. However, this is just a foretaste of a range of likely impacts post-construction, including, for example, disruption of the breeding cycles of catfish and other species, the progress upriver of which will be halted. Fears have also been raised that converting this wild river into a massive internal waterway may prove a cost-effective way of transporting lucrative crops, such as soybeans, out to export markets, substantially escalating development pressures on the surrounding forests and tropical savannah. Continued degradation of the substantial carbon sink of Amazonia is also a likely outcome.

Some proposals remain even in countries that, evidence suggests, are beginning to see the light about the longer-term and wider consequences of dam construction and massive water transfer schemes. In a provocative article entitled 'Zombie water projects (just when you thought they were really dead ...)',[21] Peter Gleick highlights four kinds of 'zombie water projects' that 'have been repeatedly beaten down for a variety of reasons but that keep rearing their ugly heads'. These include various proposals for massive water transfer from the Great Lakes or the Mississippi River or Alaska and Canada to the arid south-western USA, including California, Arizona, Las Vegas and even into northern Mexico. Though the proposals are technically feasible, some promoted by powerful players such as the NAWAPA (the North American Water and Power Alliance) and the Million Conservation Research Group, there are clearly massive associated political, economic, energy and environmental costs. Despite these obstacles, the proposals are revived periodically, as if we had learned nothing about the environmental and associated human consequences of such massive transfers. Other highlighted 'zombie water projects' include through-ocean transfers to Asia or the Middle East from Alaska, Norway, the Arctic or the Antarctic, and the proposed Cadiz Valley Water Conservation, Recovery and Storage Project, which hopes to mine fossil groundwater from an aquifer located in the eastern Mojave Desert in San Bernardino County, USA, which will inevitably dry up surface springs and ephemeral water in desert lake beds as groundwater recedes.

Trust in increasingly wise governance

These are just some of a range of schemes with likely major impacts. Owing to their placement on international rivers, they are also sources of dispute and potential conflict. And yet, in each case, the perceived self-benefits are driving the interests of host nations regardless of potential consequences for their neighbours or pressure from the international community. This may be a significant issue globally when approximately 60 per cent of the world's fresh water is drawn from international rivers, the supply from which increases in uncertainty when several nations rely on the same river as a source.[22]

One has to have faith in science, and the hope that the politics and economics of what we now know about the human and environmental consequences of such major interventions with natural systems will ensure that some rational perspective is brought to bear on future scheme design, funding and approval.

5 | The World Commission on Dams and beyond

The World Commission on Dams (WCD) was established against a background of contention about the pros and cons of dams, large dams in particular. It was set up by the World Bank and the IUCN in 1997 following a meeting involving 800 participants from governments, agencies and NGOs from across the world. The WCD was established as an independent body in 1998 under the chairmanship of Professor Kader Asmal, then the first post-apartheid Minister of Water Affairs and Forestry and later Minister of Education in South Africa. The twelve members of the Commission were selected to address diversity in geopolitical region, expertise and stakeholder perspectives, each serving in an individual capacity with no partisan representation. The WCD's two operational principles were: to review the development effectiveness of large dams and assess alternatives for water resources and energy development; and to develop internationally acceptable criteria, guidelines and standards, where appropriate, for the planning, design, appraisal, construction, operation, monitoring and decommissioning of dams.

The starting point of the WCD was acknowledgement that all sides of the debate deserved to be heard and respected. The ensuing process of hearing all voices entailed over two years of intense study, dialogue and reflection by the Commission, its Secretariat and Stakeholders' Forum, and representations from many experts as well as people affected by dams. Diverse perspectives were heard, ranging from those of technical experts to those of marginalized communities displaced, impoverished and unheard in the face of major dam projects.

The WCD produced its weighty 404-page *Dams and Development*[1] report in 2000, also published electronically on the WCD's website,[2] reflecting the complexity of the challenge.

The efficacy of dams

As part of fulfilling the first of its two operational principles, the WCD undertook a broad and independent review of the experience of large dams. This resulted in the WCD Knowledge Base,[3] which included eight detailed case studies of large dams (three of them huge projects costing over $US6 billion each) as well as country reviews for India and China, a briefing paper for Russia and the Newly Independent States (countries that until 1991 were constituent republics of the USSR, including Armenia, Azerbaijan, Belarus, Georgia, Kazakhstan, Kyrgyzstan, Moldova, Tajikistan, Turkmenistan, Ukraine and Uzbekistan), a cross-check survey of 125 existing dams, seventeen thematic review papers, and the results of public regional consultations (one each in South Asia, Africa and the Middle East, Latin America, East and South-East Asia). More than nine hundred submissions were made to the Commission from external interests to further extend the Knowledge Base, enabling informed assessment of the technical, financial, economic, environmental and social performance of large dams, and a review of alternatives to established dam models.

Both positive and negative outcomes were assessed and analysed, including the substantial benefits derived from dams but also questions relating to why some dams achieved their goals while others failed so to do. The Commission's analysis gave particular attention to understanding the reasons why, how and where dams did not achieve their intended outcomes, or indeed produced unanticipated outcomes precipitating the issues underlying the dams debate. Many submissions and findings within the Knowledge Base highlighted common shortfalls in technical, financial and economic performance. Frequently, these were compounded by significant social and environmental impacts, with the resulting costs borne disproportionately by poor and indigenous peoples and other vulnerable groups.

One of the alarming, albeit not entirely surprising, findings of this review of large dam performance was the almost complete lack of substantive evaluation once dam projects were completed. Those evaluations that had taken place were narrow in scope and poorly integrated across impact categories and scales, usually based on targets set by their proponents, leading them to lack objectivity. Furthermore, evaluation findings were poorly fed back, if at all, into dam operation. This is disturbing given the substantial capital investment in large dams as well as the scale of detrimental effects.

The WCD also found wide variability in the delivery of predicted water and electricity services, leading to broader disparities in social benefits. A considerable proportion of large dams fell well short of physical and economic targets. In particular, large dams designed for irrigation typically failed to meet their service targets or to recover costs, while there was widespread economic underperformance relative to projected benefits. These findings were, however, far from ubiquitous, as some other dams continued to deliver benefits thirty or forty years after commissioning.

Although closer to their intended outputs, large hydropower dams still tend to operate below their design targets for power generation. They generally meet their financial targets but demonstrate variable economic performance, including a number of notable under- and over-performers. Overruns in construction schedules and estimated costs were also a commonplace trend in large dam construction.

The impacts of large dams on ecosystems

Inevitably, construction and operation of large dams in drainage basins were found to introduce a broad range of impacts on river systems, their connected wetlands and the wider catchment. The WCD found these impacts to be, by overwhelming majority, more negative than positive, frequently also leading to irreversible loss of both species and ecosystems.

The WCD concluded that mitigation of many of the ecosystem impacts of large dams has, by and large, met with only limited success. The major contributory factor to this failure was a general lack of forethought about likely impacts, backed up by low quality and certainty of forecasts where produced, collectively leading to a pervasive and systematic failure to assess the range of potential negative impacts and to implement adequate mitigation.

The impacts of large dams on people

The WCD also observed a wholesale failure to address resettlement and development programmes for the displaced, or to account for the consequences of large dams for downstream livelihoods. People bearing the greatest social and environmental costs and risks associated with large dams comprise overwhelmingly the poor, vulnerable and future generations. This is markedly different to the profile of people enjoying dam-derived benefits such as water and electricity services. Continuing inequities in the sharing of benefits and costs is at best equivocal and at worst infringes stated commitments to human rights and sustainable development. Cumulatively, these oversights have contributed to the impoverishment and suffering of millions, giving rise to growing opposition to dams by affected communities worldwide.

Dams and Development noted the growing opposition arising from dam impacts on people, river basins and economies. While recognizing many benefits that had flowed from dams, it called for new directions in energy and water resource policy and a reversal of presumptions in favour of large dams. The report also found that, while the debate over dams often centred on national needs set against local or regional social and environmental impacts, examples of ecosystem impacts and their implications for human development provided damning evidence from across the world.

Where implemented – relatively rarely – the success of mitigation measures was further compromised by partial implementation. Furthermore, the WCD found a systemic failure to account for the broader environmental and social costs of large dams, skewing and confounding objective appraisal of the true value of these schemes.

Broadening the debate

Issues associated with dams, often reduced previously to technical arguments by a decision-making elite, were instead broadened beyond technicalities of design, construction and operation to embrace a wider range of associated social, environmental and political choices. These wider choices are fundamental to the success of schemes in meeting human aspirations to development and improved well-being. *Dams and Development* clarified how, at the very heart of the debate, a basic and familiar set of principles of equity, governance, justice and sharing of power were key, albeit commonly overlooked issues. The WCD concluded that the strategic decisions relate not to dams themselves but to options for freshwater (and in some cases energy) resource development, a pressing challenge in an increasingly water-stressed and climate-affected world.

All sectors of society – governments, the private sector, academics, civil society and affected peoples – have a role to play in shaping better decisions in the future about dams, water, power and the many other aspects of human development. Following exhaustive studies, the Commission felt that there were five key issues about which there were no longer any grounds for doubt:

- Dams have made important and significant contributions to human development.
- Too frequently, unacceptable and unnecessary social, environmental and economic costs have been paid to achieve those benefits.
- Relative to alternatives, the value of dams has often been questionable owing to a lack of equity in the distribution of benefits.
- Positive resolution of competing interests and conflicts is enabled by dialogue among all those whose rights are involved and who

bear the risks associated with different options for water and energy resource development.

- Unfavourable water and energy projects may be eliminated at an early stage by debating options with key stakeholders.

The WCD proposed an approach to decision-making on water and energy development that: integrates social, environmental and economic dimensions; creates greater transparency and certainty for all involved; and increases the capability of nations and communities to meet their future needs.

Although this requires a more painstaking and consensual process, *Dams and Development* illustrates how 'business as usual' is neither feasible nor desirable. The challenge is to find ways of sharing water resources equitably and sustainably, addressing the interlinked needs of all people as well as those of the environment and economic development. This highlights the importance of the nature of decision-making. Recommendations for improving the way such decisions are made form an essential element of *Dams and Development*, which states that

> The World Commission on Dams considers that the end of any dam project must be the sustainable improvement of human welfare. This means a significant advance of human development on the basis that is economically viable, socially equitable, and environmentally sustainable. If a large dam is the best way to achieve this goal it deserves our support. Where other options offer the best solutions we should favour them over large dams. Thus the debate around dams challenges a view of how we develop and manage our water resources.

Alternatives to delivery of water and electricity services

There are, of course, many means, some of them very ancient indeed, by which water and/or energy services may be delivered as alternatives to large dams. Review by the WCD found that the feasibility and relative benefits of some of these alternative sources vary considerably with the local natural resource base and site location. Others, such as demand management measures, are primarily behavioural and economic but have much to offer in improving and expanding water and energy services to meet evolving development needs in all sectors of society and in all countries and regions of the world. (A wide review of these and other alternatives constitutes much of Part 2 of this book.)

For energy, small and decentralized options (micro-hydroelectric schemes, home-scale solar electric systems, wind and biomass systems, and so forth) based on local renewable sources offer an important near-term, and possibly longer-term, potential, particularly in rural areas far away from centralized supply networks. For both water and energy, novel distributed supply-side options operating at a range of scales, from distributed generation sources or localized water collection and water recovery systems to regional interconnection of power and water grids, may improve or expand the delivery of water and energy services in a timely, cost-effective and publicly acceptable manner. There is, however, a variety of market, institutional, intellectual and financial obstacles to the broader adoption of these novel options.

The decision-making process

The WCD found that a decision to build a dam is influenced by many variables beyond immediate technical considerations. Frequently, the interests and aspirations of politicians, centralized government agencies, international aid donors and the dam-building industry blinker options in favour of large dams, excluding consideration and evaluation of alternatives, all contributory to frequent failure to recognize affected people and empower them to participate in the process. The WCD Knowledge Base contained indications that opportunities for corruption exerted a major influence on decisions. Then, once the preliminary technical and economic assessment of a dam has been undertaken and support gleaned from financing agencies and political interests, the momentum behind the project often becomes unstoppable, frequently marginalizing evaluation of social and environmental impacts that compromise the balance of benefits and costs of dam schemes and so fuelling conflicts.

The WCD identified five principal sets of values – equity, efficiency, participatory decision-making, sustainability and accountability – that can collectively provide essential tests to be applied to water and energy development decisions as a basis for improving delivery of outcomes for all stakeholders.

The debate about dams, the Commission asserts, is a debate about meaning, purpose and pathways for achieving development. The single most important factor in understanding the conflicts associated with development projects and programmes, particularly large-scale interventions such as dams, lies in reconciling competing needs and entitlements. Recognizing rights and assessing risks (particularly rights at risk) in the planning and project cycles offers a means to apply these core values to decision-making about water and energy resource management. This helps identify stakeholder groups entitled to a role within the consultative process, and in negotiation of benefit-sharing, resettlement and compensation. The decision-making framework must also address the environment as a public good.

Strategic priorities

The WCD sets the emergence of large dams within a broader history of water resource management, demanding a decision-making framework that recognizes human rights, including the right to development and the right to a healthy environment. The Commission developed seven strategic priorities, each supported by a set of Policy Principles, within its decision framework:

1 *Gaining public acceptance.* Public acceptance of key decisions is essential for equitable and sustainable water and energy resource development, recognizing rights, addressing risks and safeguarding the entitlements of all affected people.

2 *Comprehensive options assessment.* This entails assessing all available options, including alternatives to dams, in addressing clearly defined water, food and energy objectives. This requires a comprehensive and participatory assessment of needs and options, within which social and environmental factors have the same weight as economic and financial factors.

3 *Addressing existing dams.* Opportunities are not limited to new dams but extend to the design and operation of existing stock, which may be revised to better address social issues, environmental mitigation and restoration, evolving technology, and changes in land and water use in the river basin.

4 *Sustaining rivers and livelihoods.* The integrity, resilience and functioning of catchment water systems provide the basis for life and the livelihoods of local communities, so ecosystem protection and/or restoration is central to equitable human development. Avoidance, minimization and mitigation of harm through dam site, design and operation can safeguard elements of ecosystems and resource-dependent livelihoods.

5 *Recognizing entitlements and sharing benefits.* The needs of and implications for dam-affected people need to be included at all stages, with a presumption in favour of improving the livelihoods of all as the basis for 'development'.

6 *Ensuring compliance.* All commitments made for the planning, implementation and operation of dams must be adhered to in order to ensure public trust and cooperation, including an appropriate mix

of regulatory and non-regulatory measures incorporating incentives and sanctions.

7 *Sharing rivers for peace, development and security.* Trans-boundary rivers can be a focus for tension but also cooperation between and within countries, with the disruptive impact of dams requiring constructive cooperation to promote mutual self-interest and peaceful collaboration.

These criteria and guidelines were produced to help governments, developers and owners meet emerging societal expectations when faced with the complex issues associated with dam projects or alternatives. Adopting this framework will allow states to take informed and appropriate decisions, thereby raising the level of public acceptance and improving development outcomes. These priorities and principles come to life when applied within a practical project planning cycle, involving all stakeholders from planners to states, consultants and development agencies, developers and affected communities.

Taking forward the challenges

Dams and Development concludes with the statement 'We have told our story. What happens next is up to you'. The report, appropriately subtitled 'A new framework for decision-making', was not designed as a blueprint but instead to provide a starting point for discussions, debates, internal reviews and reassessments by governments, civil society organizations, the private sector, aid agencies, NGOs, academics and other stakeholders. It has since proved its value for exactly that purpose.

Collective learning and decision-making are necessary to enable these diverse stakeholders to work together to address issues at the earliest stages of planning, and to avoid becoming funnelled into the 'dam option' too early in the process. As Thayer Scudder, one of the twelve Commissioners on the WCD, put it in his 2005 book *The Future of Large Dams*,[4] the launch of the WCD report 'drew as much global interest in the landmark publication as in the unprecedented process by which it was born'. Often, common ground can be found without compromising individual values or losing a sense of purpose.

Response to Dams and Development

Responding to the WCD report in an open letter, ICOLD expressed concerns that it might be viewed as anti-developmental, emphasizing that a 'no development' policy will not alleviate poverty.[5] However, ICOLD saw synergies with its own commitment to sustainable development principles, demand-side management, improved watershed management, concern for natural and social aspects of the environment, and improved project planning. It also championed the WCD's 'emphasis on the fate of affected people and the needed protection of their rights'.

Nevertheless, ICOLD cast doubt that the WCD had fulfilled its mandate to review the development effectiveness of large dams, assess alternatives for water resources and energy development, and develop internationally acceptable criteria for aspects of dam design, operation and decommissioning. In short, the pro-dam ideology underpinning ICOLD found fault with the more cautionary tone of *Dams and Development*. Rather, it saw that 'The need for structural solutions, including more dams, is undeniable because there are no other practical solutions', favouring a pro-dam stance that gives a stronger voice to affected people and communities. Further, ICOLD 'seriously questions' the relevance of the eight dams selected for in-depth review, which it claims misrepresent more recent designs that reduce environmental and social impacts.

The ICOLD letter reminds the WCD that the 'objective of ICOLD is to minimize both social and environmental impacts of dams'. A noble aspiration, though focused on dams and not their alternatives, many of which can actually add value to dams and associated infrastructure by enhancing catchment yield and retention and decreasing the rate of sedimentation and export of potential pollutant and nutrient substances. The letter also highlights that 'ICOLD is concerned that such a cumbersome negotiation process, with mediation steps, review by expert panels, and requiring all detailed information about the potential impact on the ecosystem and the population, will, in fact, stall any new development projects'. This latter sentiment hardly squares with its support for minimization of social and environmental impacts and an 'emphasis on the fate of affected people'. Indeed, without comprehensive engagement, dialogue and supporting analysis, feeding back into options identification and appraisal and ultimately refinements to scheme design, it is hard or impossible to see how inclusive, equitable and sustainable considerations could significantly influence decisions relating to dams and/or their potentially more benign and net-beneficial alternatives.

The UNEP Dams and Development Programme (DDP)

Stakeholders generally agreed on the value of keeping the multi-stakeholder WCD dialogue going. This led UNEP to establish the Dams and DDP from November 2001, initially for a fixed two-year programme of work.[6] The purpose of the DDP was to promote dialogue on improving decision-making, planning and management of dams and their alternatives based on core values and strategic priorities established by the WCD. There was an explicit intention to achieve sustainable outcomes that benefit all, promoting multi-stakeholder dialogue at national, regional and global levels, producing non-prescriptive tools to help decision-makers.

The DDP was hosted by UNEP and guided by a multi-stakeholder Steering Committee representing UNEP's wider Dams and Development Forum, financed by contributions from donor countries. Phase 1 largely promoted dialogue at national, regional and global levels on the core values and strategic priorities of the WCD. It was extended from its original two-year lifetime until July 2004.

The focus of Phase 2, launched in February 2005 and completed in 2007, was upon the promotion of improved decision-making, planning and management of dams. In addition, the project was tasked with the production of non-prescriptive practical tools to help decision-makers comprising three main elements. The first of these was a database of summary information on existing policies, laws, criteria and guidelines concerning dam planning and management. The second element was a Compendium on Relevant Practices[7] on improved decision-making, planning and management of dams and their alternatives, providing worldwide examples of integration of key issues. The third element was an Experiences and Lessons Learnt Database collating information on good and relevant practices. The summary output of Phase 2 of the DDP programme was the 2007 report *Dams and Development: Relevant Practices for Improved Decision Making,*[8] which sought to take an approach that departs from that followed by most literature about dams by learning about positive ways forward from literature reviews and case studies, though also taking account of weaknesses. From this, it sought to produce non-prescriptive, practical tools based on the core values of the WCD.

Overall, the DDP took neither a pro- nor an anti-dam stance, noting that, where dams become a valid option on social, environmental and economic grounds, 'the question changes to how to build a good dam'. The intent was to apply better decision-making processes within the overall framework of sustainability to help realize the benefits of dams while avoiding many of the historic drawbacks. Stakeholder analysis and participation, inconsistently applied throughout the world, were recognized as crucial for engaging all affected people, with social repercussions remaining unresolved for many established dams. Dams, the DDP report notes, should continue to be an option considered alongside diverse alternatives for improving supplies of water and energy, but options identification and appraisal should cover both structural and non-structural approaches to water and energy, covering supply- and demand-side management and efficiency measures.

Dramatic strides forward were commended in measures to encourage, facilitate and compel dams to comply with laws, policies and other relevant norms over recent decades, and it was acknowledged that, while much remains to be done, 'there are a number of innovative and promising experiences'. The DDP concluded that, 'The core of the debate on dams is essentially about the role of dams in poverty reduction, social justice and the promotion of social and economic development,' though noting that successful compliance mechanisms often stand out as exceptions to general practice, with compliance being very uneven between countries.

There remains, however, a prevailing sense of malaise about the outcomes of the UNEP Dams and Development Programme. Although the DDP process achieved its initial aim of maintaining dialogue after 2000, it has not been seen as making much substantive progress in fulfilling its primary objectives of improved decision-making, planning and management of dams with development of practical tools to achieve the high and generally uncontested ideals established by the WCD.

The Beijing Declaration on Hydropower and Sustainable Development

Another high-profile event in the progression of international thinking about large dams was the United Nations Symposium on Hydropower and Sustainable Development, convened in Beijing in October 2004. The meeting engaged representatives of national and local governments, utilities and the private sector, United Nations agencies, multilateral financial institutions, other international organizations, non-government organizations, the scientific community and academia, and international industry associations in consideration of international commitments to achievement of the Millennium Development Goals and sustainable development.

The meeting concluded with the Beijing Declaration on Hydropower and Sustainable Development.[9] This reiterated that access to energy is essential to achieving sustainable development and is critical for meeting the Millennium Development Goals, noting that 2 billion people at that time lacked access to electricity. The Declaration was predicated on delivery of energy services in a 'reliable, affordable and economically viable, socially acceptable and environmentally sound manner'. This, the Beijing Declaration continued, would generate opportunities for economic growth, enhanced education, better healthcare, more training and employment, as well as higher productivity in business, thereby contributing to sustained poverty reduction.

Sustainable hydropower, steered from social, economic and environmental standpoints, together with energy efficiency and other renewable sources, was noted as offering potential for contributing to these goals. The Declaration also concluded that two-thirds of economically viable hydropower potential was yet to be tapped, with 90 per cent of this potential lying in developing countries. It also recognized the 'substantial adverse impacts on the environment', demanding that governments establish rigorous environmental impact assessment, mitigation and management measures that 'should give due weight to environmental and social factors, as well as economic and financial factors'.

The Beijing Declaration has, in reality, added little to the ongoing debate about dams. On the one hand, the Declaration reiterates a number of positive principles to improve dam performance. Yet, on the other hand, much of it appears to be founded on an inherently pro-dam set of development assumptions. Overall, it adds little clarification to the all-important issue of how to think through the needs, option development, appraisal and subsequent implementation and operation of water management on a fully inclusive and sustainable basis.

WCD+10: revisiting the large dam controversy

In 2010, a special edition of the journal *Water Alternatives* (vol. 3, no. 2),[10] comprising twenty papers, six viewpoints and four book reviews, was dedicated to assessing dam-related issues a decade after publication of the initial World Commission on Dams report. Collectively, this volume tested and largely confirmed the success of the WCD as an experiment in multi-stakeholder dialogue and global governance concerned with a subject fraught with conflict and controversy. It examined the influence and the impacts of the WCD on dam policies and practice, also taking account of other drivers that have become more influential in the intervening time, including climate change and new financiers of dams. The *Water Alternatives* special edition also contained a significant dissenting view noting that no dam-building country had accepted the central recommendations of the WCD, although the initiative had been constructive in leading to development of a coherent vision of why water infrastructure was central to growth and poverty reduction.[11]

Regrettably, it seems that the legacies of the world's 45,000 large dams continue to cause controversy, with few river systems remaining untouched by some type of dam. Displaced populations were estimated to have increased to between 40 and 80 million people by 2010, and the bulk of resettlement still occurs with minimal or no compensation, often in marginal lands, with the outcome that the poor and marginalized have, in the majority of cases, become or remained poorer. As many as 472 million river-dependent people have had their livelihoods negatively affected by dams.[12]

Meanwhile, large-scale alteration of natural hydrological regimes continues to exert substantial and generally negative impacts on fisheries, water-based livelihoods, aquatic ecosystems and a wider set of ecosystem services. Furthermore, it is the view of some scientists that many reservoirs emit large amounts of greenhouse gases, perhaps even as much as 4 per cent of all human-induced greenhouse gas emissions.[13]

Cumulatively, the special issue of *Water Alternatives* demonstrates the need for a renewed multi-stakeholder dialogue across a range of scales, building on some evidence in the intervening decade of true partnerships forming among stakeholders with the aim of creating transformative resource-sharing agreements.

6 | The state of play with dams

Dams and Development recommended that various dam projects 'in the pipeline' be appraised for conformance with its principles. Some of these appraisals have since been published online as part of a 'reality check',[1] and a large body of case studies was also compiled by the DDP to support decision-makers with positive case studies. There is also a broad scientific literature about methods for stakeholder engagement around identification of needs and the options that might best meet them.

This chapter draws upon this resource, as well as wider surveys and literature on water management schemes, to determine the current 'state of play' with dams as well as wider thinking about water management and appropriate solutions. This then goes some way towards addressing the critique of ICOLD that the conclusions of the WCD's 2000 report were founded on older dams to which contemporary design and operational considerations had not been applied. These various case studies are considered below more or less arranged by the flow of stages in development of a water management proposal and scheme.

Public engagement in the identification of water needs

Public engagement in environmental decision-making is now commonly accepted in democratic societies, and widely supported by international and national policy (the 1998 UNECE Aahrus Convention, Article 14 of the EU Water Framework Directive, the US approach to collaborative watershed planning, South Africa's National Water Act 1998, CSIRO guidance in Australia,[2] etc.). This requires a new relationship between expert and diverse lay understandings of issues that, in turn, promotes learning about different perspectives and optimal solutions appropriate to multiple local needs.

There is not yet a great tradition of public engagement in water needs identification leading to dam options. However, there are increasing instances of stakeholder engagement in the early stages of planning in South Africa, where multi-stakeholder approaches to water options identification through various stakeholder bodies are required by national legislation. However, in practice, competing demands and authorizations from different government departments and civil society organizations still contribute to widespread difficulties in achieving well-balanced representation and the active participation of all stakeholders.[3] Government leadership was found to undermine participation from community members, while pro-poor leadership by academics tended to undermine government and private sector involvement. By contrast, emergence of local fora, including, for example, the Kat River Valley Catchment Management Forum, provided a more inclusive basis for dialogue, placing greater emphasis on social mobilization, ensuring that local people, including women, were mobilized to take an interest in their environment. Engagement, then, even where compelled by statute and attempted on the ground, is no easy process.

Experience in the Mahaweli scheme in Sri Lanka, comprising a series of dams and water diversions implemented from 1977 throughout the 1980s under what was called the Accelerated Mahaweli Project (AMP) as a 'statement of political will', provides largely negative lessons.[4] The Sri Lankan government initially allocated 30 per cent of national capital development funds to the scheme, one of the largest integrated river basin development projects under construction in the world, to stimulate regional development with benefits radiating across the country, with the aim of self-sufficiency in electricity generation and rice production. However, the hierarchical Mahaweli Authority was unwilling to share responsibility for implementation with other agencies or to encourage settler participation, merely asserting that settlers would benefit though rice farming from project irrigation. Ultimately, none of the major goals was achieved. Major lessons from this classic failure of centralized planning included lack of involvement of intended beneficiaries, of understanding of their diverse water needs, and of monitoring and evaluation, with inadequate consideration of resettled people with a focus on housing but not on income generation.

The Skuifraam Dam within South Africa's Berg Water Project is part of the wider Western Cape System Analysis (WCSA). The Skuifraam Dam featured as a DDP case study, a WCD 'reality check' and in the scientific literature, as well as being the subject of a study commissioned by the South African government.[5] Recognizing the need to engage a broad range of stakeholders, though not yet compelled to by statute in 1989, DWAF set up a comprehensive public empowerment exercise engaging 1,100 people and organizations informing the WCSA *Evaluation of Options* study[6] and subsequently introducing the *Skuifraam Dam Feasibility Study* and Integrated Environmental Management[7] process. A Task Group elected by stakeholders selected options and commissioned additional studies, where needed, concluding with a set of options.[8] The Skuifraam Dam emerged as a favourite option, though consideration of other options seems to have been limited by a presumption already in favour of the dam in line with historic practices.

In a region where the fragility of the ecosystem presented a major obstacle to secure livelihoods, particularly for smallholders and landless people, farmer-participatory integrated watershed management in the Adarsha Watershed in Kothapally, India, found that 'The success of watershed management largely depends on the community's participation'.[9] Engagement of farmers in the watershed to collectively identify issues and technical interventions resulted in development of small check dams, field bunding (low embankments generally of soil) and gabions (baskets or cages filled with rocks) to promote groundwater recharge, protecting the utility of small wells. Also, critically, it looked beyond water supply to also consider soil, water and nutrient conservation through agricultural practices, improved tillage methods, tree planting and integrated pest management. Measured lasting successes from this programme included enhanced farm productivity and incomes and groundwater recharge, replacing the single-focus option of bigger dams to supply more water.

Very similar findings were observed for the engagement of poor rural communities in a coastal province of Vietnam, where a patient process of 'bottom-up participatory planning' proved particularly successful in helping people work together to escape from poverty.[10] This emphasized the value of investment in engagement, capacity-building and problem identification before reaching too quickly for solutions.

Options identification and appraisal

The Olifants River Water Resources Development project in South Africa featured in the DPP review as an example of positive stakeholder engagement, formerly excluded under apartheid, in the practice of identifying and assessing alternatives to meet long-term needs.[11] Many stakeholders emphasized that new resources should not be developed without first ensuring efficient use of water, shaping final recommendations covering infrastructural and non-infrastructural components. The exercise flushed out novel options for supply, including the raising of an existing large dam and the construction of a new one, combined with localized small-scale use of groundwater and measures to conserve water.

Multi-criteria decision analysis (MCDA) proved a successful tool for integrating different types of information during stakeholder engagement in the Sand River, Mpumulanga, South Africa,[12] allowing meaningful participation by stakeholders in the analysis of options. Hypothetical land use scenarios for the catchment were explored first by a project team and then with stakeholders, defining perceived problems in the catchment for which different combinations of land uses were used to build catchment scenarios. Options for optimal management were quantified, allowing preferred scenarios or 'directions of preference' to be identified for different zones in the catchment. This resulted in consensus about combinations of land management options that best and most equitably served the interests of all within the catchment. Measures included the wider catchment benefits of removal of some tree plantations for community conservation in the upper zone of the catchment, some expansion of irrigation and community conservation in the middle zone, and allowing for harvesting of natural products in some of the commercial conservation areas in the lower zone.

The Nepal Medium Hydropower Screening and Ranking project provided an example of good practice in the initial streamlining of multiple options into a smaller number to allow for more detailed appraisal. Nepal's 1992 National Hydropower Development Policy prioritized development of hydropower potential in many of its steep rivers as a key government objective. The screening process used a stakeholder-derived multi-criteria environmental assessment process that eliminated options that performed poorly against national legislation, were in designated conservation areas, protected parks and their buffer zones, which potentially disrupted infrastructure, where water could be abstracted from trans-boundary rivers, and where there was a high index of persons resettled and land take per megawatt. More detailed environmental impact assessment could then be undertaken on the seven remaining schemes.

South Africa's Department of Water Affairs and Forestry (DWAF) developed the Thukela Water Project (TWP) proposal, including two new dams (the Jana Dam and the Mielietuin Dam) in the upper Thukela catchment, ultimately to divert water into the Vaal river system to the north, to feed the economic heartland of the province of Gauteng.[13] (The Thukela study has already been referenced in Chapter 3, and will be discussed in greater detail in Chapter 7.) DWAF undertook a large number of studies in support of the Thukela proposal, including a feasibility report, an engineering report, evaluation of alternative water sources, a public involvement programme, an environmental feasibility report, and a social impact assessment. The swathe of DWAF studies conclude that the TWP was technically, environmentally (natural and social) and economically feasible, delivering a wide range of benefits, subject to some necessary design changes to limit repercussions for the river ecosystem. Public involvement incorporated approximately one thousand Interested and Affected Parties (I&APs), using a variety of fora and media, the location of the TWP Project Management Team in Ladysmith helping link with various regional development and economic forums within the uThukela District Municipality. However, for all this engagement, official studies seem to focus on the advantages to those receiving water to the north without detailed consideration of the inevitably significant changes to the Thukela river ecosystem. Many local benefits are ascribed to communities in uThukela municipality, yet the reality is that water is being taken from the environment that sustains them, and the seeming dismissal of the potential for significant issues stemming from the two proposed major dams and the abstraction of a huge volume of the river's net flow suggests a major blind spot in the capacity of decision-makers to conceive of the river as an integrated socio-ecological system. A further study has since been undertaken to quantify benefits and costs associated with likely changes across the Thukela catchment (addressed in more detail in Chapter 7).

A range of modelling tools proved effective in integrating different types of knowledge – expert, community and other – to improve stakeholder decision-making in three Australian case studies.[14] By modelling proposals arising from stakeholder dialogue through approaches such as integrated simulation modelling, participants are immediately able to perceive the broader consequences of their suggestions. These tools, if used wisely to serve community dialogue rather than dominate it, have proved effective in promoting deliberation, mutual understanding and improved stakeholder decisions.

Dam planning

As noted previously, South Africa's Skuifraam Dam represents a halfway house towards broader thinking, seeking to engage stakeholders despite an apparent presumption in favour of building the dam. Nevertheless, novel attempts at dialogue with a spectrum of potentially affected stakeholders built understanding and support for the project and also produced political momentum for demand management. As part of this process, 600 Interested and Affected Parties were identified and invited to participate in an Environmental Impact Assessment (EIA) voluntarily undertaken in 1995 (EIAs subsequently became a statutory requirement only from March 1998), covering a range of disciplines, including archaeology, botany, tourism, fluvial geomorphology, social aspects, economics, in-stream flow requirements and forestry. This process generated numerous mitigation measures and innovative approaches. However, official DWAF documentation still reiterates the perception that water reaching the sea is 'wasted', reflecting the dominance of a classic utilitarian world view, and the dam itself displaced some of the La Motte state forest, implying an underpinning assumption that the catchment ecosystem itself and its wider services is of subordinate value to the utility of water for public supply.

Dam operation

The third 'strategic priority' of the WCD was to address existing dams to better manage social and environmental issues, to consider evolving technology and to respond to changes elsewhere in the catchment.

The DDP reviewed the identification of options for dam operating regimes to address stakeholder interests under water use planning guidelines in British Columbia, Canada, covering both power and other water control facilities as part of the licensing procedure of the British Columbia Water Act. Water use plans were prepared through a collaborative effort involving the existing or prospective licensee, government agencies, First Nations (indigenous peoples), other key interested parties and the general public. Stakeholder engagement prior to submission for regulatory review and approval, with the objective of achieving consensus on operating rules for each facility satisfying their diverse interests, resulted in a better balance between competing water uses, with ensuing decisions founded on stakeholder consensus. Where no consensus was reached, active monitoring and adaptive management were initiated to test alternative flow regimes, opening the way for further stakeholder agreement on further improvements.

Significant collaboration with various stakeholders from the outset of relicensing of the Clark Fork project, comprising two hydropower dams on the lower Clark Fork river in the USA, was presented as an example by the DPP. An ongoing adaptive management process, known as the 'Living License', was established to promote ongoing problem-solving as well as generating detailed licence provisions, including funding mitigation measures and creating an external review body. These experiences led to the development of more cooperative approaches for (re) licensing of other dams in the United States. Stakeholder engagement was thereby found to add value even to established infrastructure, and can feed back into improved operating procedures.

The DDP also highlights a villager-led Thai Baan consultation to inform and consult on mitigation following construction of the hydro-electric Pak Mun Dam on the Mun river, a tributary of the Mekong. The initial focus was on the impacts of opening the dam gates, but this was subsequently broadened to cover wider issues. Researchers involved 200 villagers from 65 communities to collect data demonstrating the impact on the fishery downstream of the dam and the inadequacy of compensation. The Thai Baan case study illustrates the cost-effective contribution that poorly educated people could have made if included in earlier stages of impact assessment and development planning.

Another DDP example of practices to improve decision-making focused on the Eastmain 1A-Rupert diversion in James Bay, Canada. This scheme involved diverting some water from the Rupert river and constructing additional powerhouses at an already developed hydroelectric generating site. However, there were sensitivities owing to the significant cultural value of the river as it runs through the territories of six indigenous Cree communities. A series of informal meetings and public assemblies with senior Hydro-Québec managers and Cree leaders and communities led to the signing of a nation-to-nation agreement between the Cree and the government of Quebec, the Boumhounan Agreement, in 2002, which confirmed a partnership approach. The indigenous Cree were then involved at all phases of the project, from the concept onwards. The Cree provided ecological and traditional knowledge, and participated in a joint study group and field investigations to conduct environmental and social impact assessment data-gathering and analysis. The process was supported by locally employed Cree coordinators and fully equipped information and work offices in the communities, which provided a continuous forum for exchange, access to information and videos translated into the Cree language. The Cree were afforded time (more than three years) and financial resources to assess, consult and understand the nature and scope of the project, and were assisted by specialists and lawyers. Special funds were provided for a joint non-profit corporation for construction of remedial works and implementation of mitigation measures, and economic and community benefits such as training, employment, contracts and environmental guarantees. Under Canadian and Quebec legislation, a review panel comprising experts, including Cree representatives, held public hearings in the six Cree communities affected and in the cities of Chibougamau and Montreal. Hearings encouraged an exchange of views following public release of the impact statement, translated into relevant languages. In all, participation methods ranged from face-to-face meetings with key individuals, large public assemblies, joint data-gathering groups and field trips, collaborative discussions about project design and the development of economic benefits, and more formal public review procedures where the views of all parties could be shared. Civil society representatives noted that this case also illustrates how the principle of free, prior informed consent led to the success of the initiative. Many lessons emerge, including the value of early stakeholder participation and the necessity to back this up with adequate time, budget and capacitation to enable full engagement.

Environmental consequences

The Berg Water Project in South Africa, addressed already when considering the Skuifraam Dam, represented a good example of how legislation has enabled the active participation of stakeholders in the identification and assessment of options. The Berg Water Project addresses water supply in the heavily urbanized Western Cape region, relying on capture of winter flows in a large storage reservoir for release during the dry summer months. In addition to technical solutions, it was also recognized that water yield from the catchment has been reduced by invading alien species, which have also displaced unique endemic vegetation. As part of a national programme aimed at enhancing water security, improving ecological integrity, restoring land and promoting sustainable resource use, the project owner partnered with DWAF to provide employment for local residents by clearing the dam's catchment of alien trees and shrubs under the Working for Water programme (addressed in Part 2 of this book). The means by which the Berg Water Project engaged all relevant stakeholders has already been described above, but the ecosystem-centred remedy to improve catchment water yield is an instructive outcome.

The Grand Coulee Dam on the Columbia river in the United States was developed between 1933 and 1955 for hydropower generation and irrigation supply, a massive dam conceived in an era when impacts on the migration of fish, particularly salmon, and the consequences for the livelihoods of upstream native Americans and Canadian First Nations were inadequately considered. Production of salmon and other fish had been the centrepiece of the area's indigenous economy and culture. In 1951, the Colville Confederated Tribes filed a suit against the United States. Twenty-seven years after the claim had been filed, the Indian Claims Commission ruled in 1978 that the tribes were entitled to full compensation for all income losses associated with the dam, for which the US government provided in total US$66 million as historic compensation, including annual payments of US$15 million to offset ongoing reduced income opportunities. This time lag did little to enhance the acceptance of dams and wider hydropower and irrigation projects. We can learn from this that environmental impacts not only have substantial human impacts, but that even decades on they can incur substantial economic liabilities.

Social consequences

In early 2011 in southern Africa, Botswana's court of appeal squashed by the unanimous decision of five Appeal Court judges a previous 2010 ruling that had denied the Kalahari Bushmen access to water in a well in their ancestral lands.[15] The rights of the Bushmen to use their old borehole, as well as a right to sink new boreholes, was upheld on appeal under which the Appeal Court judges branded the government's conduct towards them as 'degrading treatment' after the Bushmen were forcibly evicted from their ancestral lands in the Central Kalahari Game Reserve by the Botswana government in 2002. The key lesson here is that top-down water management solutions that ignore stakeholder groups can result in infringement of human rights that may then require subsequent restitution.

The DDP identifies the Driekoppies Dam on the Mlumati river in South Africa as a useful example of scoping of communities affected by a proposed dam, covering loss of productive resources, impacts on economic activities, effects on settlements, housing, community facilities and services, community organizations and institutional relationships, historical and archaeological sites, population pressure and social dislocation. This evaluation enabled assessment of the significance of potential impacts, informing future project activities regarding the management of social change. It is significant that this appraisal did not result in changes to the foregone decision to implement the dam, though it did outline the scale of social disruption at the dam site.

Another DDP example of addressing the mitigation of negative impacts and the optimization of benefits from the early planning phase is the Upper Seti Storage Hydroelectric project on the Seti river in Nepal. Mitigation measures identified from the process included resettlement and land acquisition, a code of conduct for outside construction workers, the protection of archaeological sites and provision of additional social infrastructure and services. Suggestions for enhancement measures to increase positive impacts of the proposed project included improvement in agricultural practices, training, skills development, loan assistance programmes for small businesses, environmental awareness for conservation, and other community development initiatives. This is therefore another example of exploring social and environmental mitigation with stakeholders once 'top-down' decisions had been made.

The Ghazi Barotha hydropower project on the Indus river in Pakistan, built between 1995 and 2003, was regarded by the DDP as a useful example of practice on involuntary resettlement. Learning from prior experience, the World Bank had sought to strengthen management of resettlement issues by following best practices, including a set of monitoring arrangements overseen by a review panel including NGO representatives. The project required the relocation and rehabilitation of 179 families and affected the land of approximately twenty thousand households in fifty-four villages. The resettlement action plan included an integrated regional development plan to find locally acceptable solutions to grievances, as well as cash compensation for loss of production and acquisition of alternative land. However, implementation of the resettlement action plan would have benefited from a more continuous commitment from the developer and a more secure and independent source of funding.

Economic consequences

Brazil's Salto Caxias hydroelectric dam on the Iguaçu river, constructed between 1995 and 1999, formed another DPP case study of dispute resolution addressing indemnity rights and resettlement. This dialogic process led to the signing of agreements with representatives of affected people, with a proportion of compensation diverted into a municipality-led regional economic development plan that eventually led to the creation of a number of new small businesses. Engagement with all those potentially affected people led to improved and better-accepted agreements and compensation payments reflecting livelihood considerations.

Conversely, the costs of South Africa's Skuifraam Dam project were initially estimated at 620 million rand, shortly rising to R800 million and increasing with ensuing years and delays to R1.4 billion on dam filling from 2006. Some of this delay and inflation was due to retrospective inclusion of stakeholders in decision-making, and also accounting for previously overlooked environmental and social consequences.

The Shuikou hydroelectric dam, constructed on the Min Jiang river in China between 1987 and 1996, is another DPP example of economic resettlement planning undertaken in the early 1980s in the context of an emerging legal and regulatory framework in China. China had seen mounting pressure from people relocated by the construction of some seventy thousand dams, including 300 large-scale dams, over a forty-year period. This resulted in a 1991 Chinese regulation, revised in 1996, establishing post-resettlement and rehabilitation funds. This regulation recognizes that, even with well-planned resettlement, remedial measures still have to be taken beyond the end of the relocation period to address outstanding issues, including restoration of incomes of affected people. The Shuikou project caused the relocation of about 15,600 rural families and 20,000 urban-based people, with the dam builders preparing a resettlement plan following extensive consultations with affected leaders. The plan adapted over time to both the new Chinese resettlement regulations and, to a lesser extent, a 1990 version of the World Bank's involuntary resettlement guidelines. Villages were relocated, with displaced persons given serviced lots and the responsibility to build their own houses using compensation payments based on replacement costs. Significantly, the resettlement plan included an economic rehabilitation plan aimed at creating new production systems for affected people. A key lesson here is that livelihoods, not merely possessions, need to be addressed, and this is most effectively dealt with by inclusive stakeholder dialogue.

The DDP also reports that Norwegian legislation relating to taxes and licence fees contains mechanisms that ensure benefit-sharing from water management and hydropower projects with regional and local project-affected communities. However, the tax system in Norway limits powers for municipalities with more hydropower installations on their territory to raise tax revenues from power companies. Various strands of learning stem from this Norwegian case study, including the greater equity inherent in benefit-sharing agreements, but also the need for fiscal systems that do not prevent their practical delivery.

In the study of the coastal province of Vietnam cited previously, the participatory approach had a central objective, to 'improve the incomes and living standards of poor rural households and increase their participation in the development process'.[16] Significant efforts were put in place to ensure economic sustainability, including, for example, channelling innovative microfinance schemes through the Vietnam Women's Union and enabling the poor to benefit from greater access to markets.

Monitoring compliance and incorporating feedback in scheme improvement

Compliance, or rather the lack of it, was a major issue highlighted by the WCD,[17] with 'ensuring compliance' constituting the sixth of the WCD's seven 'strategic priorities'.

The Nam Theun 2 project in Laos was selected as part of the WCD 'reality check',[18] based on WCD guidelines. The assessment was completed by a former WCD Secretariat member who then served as a project manager of Nam Theun 2. The assessor concluded that 'the project has complied with so many of the WCD guidelines prior to their existence' and that it 'is an ideal testbed to check the workability of the WCD criteria and guidelines'. However, NGO scrutiny of the Nam Theun 2 scheme came to significantly different conclusions based on exactly the same guidelines, noting, for example, that other options for water and energy provision were not adequately assessed. In particular, the NGO consortium is reported as stating that 'The study focused on how the country could meet its commitments to provide electricity to Thailand, rather than on other options by which water and other resources could be utilized to provide revenue and alternative livelihoods'. Wider concerns relating to the Nam Theun 2 project include illegal logging and mining[19] as well as issues connected with forced displacement of people.[20] Different starting conceptions and interests can yield a fundamental divergence of conclusions, and one that would seem to be at the heart of any sustainability and equity test of big hydrological infrastructure.

Uganda's Bujagali Dam, spanning the River Nile near Bujagali Falls downstream from two other large dams, was another 'in the pipeline' test case reviewed as a WCD 'reality check'.[21] AES Nile Power claimed to have pursued 'principles of best practice in order to supply the energy needs of Uganda in a sustainable and environmentally prudent manner' that 'supports WCD's effort and are convinced that its project meets and exceeds the principles of the WCD's strategic priorities'. However, other viewpoints have been raised, significantly including those of the NGO International Rivers, which, based on the same set of guidelines, points out that no 'needs assessment' was carried out on the dam scheme, the dam will not bring power to the rural poor, no programme of demand management is in place, other options for renewable energy were available, and 'cumulative effects' with other neighbouring dams had not been considered.[22] The project also creates major risks for Uganda's taxpayers, contravening the WCD 'strategic priority' addressing risk. Other groups have expressed concerns about the dam's broader impact on the health of Lake Victoria. Again, we see scope for a marked divergence between 'official' and public opinions. No mitigation of impacts was put in place as a result of this appraisal.

A DWAF-sponsored review[23] concluded that South Africa's Skuifraam Dam proposal complied well with WCD guidelines in the planning stage. However, an influential consortium of trade union (South African Municipal Workers' Union, SAMWU) and environmental interests saw inadequate concern for environmental impacts. They also found that the dam provided for the rich while further marginalizing the poor through an inequitable tariff system applied by the water utility. The consortium also regarded the dam as having been imposed on people by blackmail, that it was only a short-term solution and that more sustainable options had not been seriously examined. SAMWU stated that, 'the era of supply-side tunnel vision is over'. When construction started on the dam, the Skuifraam Action Group shifted its focus from a strong media campaign to monitoring the project's impacts.

The DDP notes that the Brilliant Expansion project on the Kootenay river in Canada is a useful example of dam project monitoring. The operator hired a contractor as an independent socio-economic project monitor who reported on the impacts and benefits stemming from the expansion project within a 100-kilometre radius of the project site, reporting on employment and expenditure, including local hires across different social strata. We can learn from this that independent scrutiny of impacts across an appropriately wide area can help promote the acceptability of dam expansions, helping identify broad-spectrum problems that may improve further options for management or design.

Governance for sustainable water management

It is important in the modern era to review institutional arrangements better to reflect both inclusive stakeholder representation and the central importance of the 'carrying capacity' provided by ecosystems. There are no directly helpful instances in the WCD 'reality check' or the DDP, other than the 'root and branch' revision of laws in South Africa which in reality are still in transition to full implementation. However, the wider scientific literature contains relevant material. Other partial attempts, founded on grand ideals but generally thwarted by only partial implementation, include the establishment of Catchment Management Agencies in Australia and the visionary intent of the European Union's Water Framework Directive.

A study of Pani Panchayat (community-based bodies) in the Indian state of Orissa gives clear evidence that statutory provision alone is not sufficient to deliver efficient water management institutions. The Pani Panchayat, an attempt to decentralize and devolve management of water to community level to promote participation in decision-making, failed largely owing to poor community participation, especially among marginal groups and lower-caste people who perceived that elite members dominated the process.[24] Commitment to engagement must then entail capacitation of the less influential and articulate, with effective facilitation to avoid more powerful people merely entrenching their interests.

A river restoration study on the urban upper River Tame in Birmingham, UK, explored the largely ignored question of how a deliberative process can capitalize on local knowledge and lead to shared (academic, practitioner and public) learning and understanding.[25] This used a two-stage process, the first broadly framed at whole-city scale and the second focused on a restoration plan at the scale of a local playing field, and included a discussion workshop, information mailed to households around the restoration site, engagement with the local press, and attendance at district and ward committee meetings. Discussions generated consensus on both the 'physical' and 'emotional' characteristics of the ideal urban river, producing a linking concept of 'bringing a little of the rural into the urban' as a popular focus for shared learning before practical constraints were considered. Success in this case strongly rested on recruitment of representative interests, active facilitation, collaborative framing, optimizing interaction and managing expectations.

Social learning proved effective for resolution of conflicts over water management between farmers and nature conservation interests in the Netherlands.[26] Tensions arose from protests by farmers over a ban on the use of overhead sprinkler irrigation on grassland in summer, which had led to a rapid drawdown of groundwater, giving rise to wider public concern about the drying up of wetlands in nature conservation areas. A proposed national park designation also meant that all land use in the park area would have nature conservation as its sole purpose. The southern farmers and horticulturalists' union (ZLTO) determined that a shared perspective was lacking, advocating proactive multi-stakeholder collaboration based on shared learning and voluntary participation as the only way forward. ZLTO started working with local water boards to develop ways to help farmers use sprinkler irrigation more efficiently. An agreement was also formed to have the land classified as a 'national landscape', a legal status that allows for multi-purpose land use. As a result of dialogue, water boards began to recognize farmers as partners in the management of surface water and hydrological flows and, in return, farmers began to appreciate how their on-farm decisions had landscape-scale effects. This reduced confrontation between agricultural and nature conservation interests, leading to recognition of the value of shared learning and the roles of all players in management of soil water levels, with central government recognizing that 'top-down' imposition of regulations was not yielding intended results. This led the national water authority to experiment with 'open planning or interactive processes' on a regional scale to facilitate local stakeholders to negotiate new options for development within the boundaries of existing laws and regulations. Costs associated with this deliberative process were less than the costs of trying to enforce compliance though regulation. Thus facilitation of social learning became part of a new approach to cooperative governance, creating social capital and preparing the ground for addressing more complex processes beyond traditional technical approaches and mechanical application of regulation and market economics. The ZLTO example also demonstrates the lifetime economic efficiency of early engagement.

Meanwhile, the Okavango Delta Management Plan[27] (ODMP) to manage the biodiverse endorheic Okavango Delta in Botswana has demonstrated the value and importance of social learning. (An endorheic system is a closed drainage basin that has no outflow to other external bodies of water.) The Okavango formerly lacked a comprehensive water management plan, which, owing to increasing competition between large-scale agricultural users, subsistence farmers and tour operators, threatened the sustainability of the delta. The ODMP project worked with village-level *kgotlas* (community meetings) to consider the diversity of needs of everyday local as well as bigger-interest users, building appreciation across stakeholder groups and co-creating options to secure livelihoods while sustaining biodiversity. Communities felt a sense of ownership, helping to ensure long-term conservation of the delta. This approach was subsequently integrated into district and national planning in Botswana.

The learning from these selected examples is about learning itself: finding ways of engaging different interests to work together to find better outcomes addressing the concerns of all, and feeding them into adaptive management processes.

International drainage basins

A range of initiatives have taken place around the world to better coordinate the efforts and management of countries sharing drainage basins. As addressed in Chapter 10, strategic assessment of the 'southern African hydropolitical complex' highlights how, though potentially the subject of conflict, international rivers such as the Komati, Zambezi and Orange systems have in fact served as a basis for international agreement and peaceful cooperation. The DDP also highlights coordinated international efforts under the Zambezi Action Plan, or ZACPLAN, under which the governments of Botswana, Mozambique, the United Republic of Tanzania, Zambia and Zimbabwe signed an agreement 1987 on an action plan for the equitable, sustainable and consensual utilization of the shared water resources of the Zambezi basin. To this we can add the example of the Songwe River Transboundary Catchment Management project, sustainable water management of the Volta basin and establishment of the Lake Tanganyika Authority, all of which have linked a variety of sectors of society spanning Malawi and Tanzania in protection of Lake Nyasa (as described in Chapter 10). These demonstrate the value of integrated and collaborative thinking for maximizing the benefits to all people, regardless of political borders, who share a limited natural resource.

International organizations and donors were also noted by the DDP and the UN as making a valuable contribution to the Mekong basin in South-East Asia through the Mekong Committee, established in 1957, offering potential for economic development of the four riparian countries: Cambodia, Lao People's Democratic Republic, Thailand and Vietnam. This is another example of positive results from collaborative deliberation, promoted in this case by external funding agencies.

The DDP also highlights how resumption of Indo-Bangladeshi negotiations over the Ganges following disputes in the 1970s, as well as subsequent agreements about water sharing, provides a strong example of the collective benefits of international cooperation. Also relevant to this is the difficult history of negotiation between India and Pakistan over the waters of the Indus basin, ultimately deferring suboptimally to the different politics of the nations and the establishment of agreements for a quantitative division of waters between the two countries, leaving each free to carry out its own development independently. Lessons emerge here about both the value of dialogic processes and the practical difficulties of achieving consensus in contested cases.

Lessons learned

The case studies throughout this chapter demonstrate the 'state of the art' of dam planning, construction and operation. Controversy surrounds many schemes, but we can learn from them all. As recognized by the WCD, dams have delivered significant benefits around the world, particularly in arid countries, though proponents and NGOs seem often at odds about their relative merits. Certainly, they have often done so at significant and often avoidable costs. There is also consensus that the catchment is a logical unit for planning, with broad acceptance of WCD values, principles and guidelines, albeit with different interpretations and flexibility in implementation, but also disjointed implementation across the world. Nothing in this analysis obviates any aspect of the WCD guidelines.

There is something rather too sweeping, perhaps even disingenuous, about the claim of ICOLD that

> Today we are mitigating the environmental impacts of dams. In many countries, governments have mandatory requirements to take into account and plan to mitigate the possible impact which dams may have on nature and the environment when selecting where a dam should be built, as well as how it will be constructed and operated. By taking these predictions seriously, many possible consequences can be addressed in a positive way.[28]

Attempts to mitigate historic environmental harm arising from dams through post hoc management and improved design have not automatically resulted in contemporary fish passes, management regimes and mitigation schemes that adequately tackle environmental perturbations. It is easy to overstate the case for the sustainable management of dams, as in the case of the Bujagali hydropower project in Uganda and in DDP studies in Canada with claims to compliance with sustainable development principles. Best current practice perhaps, but can the outcome honestly be described as truly sustainable? It is not my intention to undermine progress made by ICOLD and its members, but rather to seek honesty and openness in the debate about the environmental impacts and the human, ecological and ultimately economic consequences of the building of a large dam. A large dam is, after all, a huge structure expressly designed to intercept substantial flows and volumes of water, big enough to trigger earthquakes, and diversions from them can replumb entire subcontinents; we are dealing with the biggest of all the 'big technologies' here, with consequences proportionate to their enormous scale.

The honest question, then, is not about environmental mitigation. The term mitigation, while addressing the minimization of harm, can often be construed as solving all ills and therefore presuming only minor disruption that can be relatively easily fixed rather than considered proactively as an integral element of decision-making and design. The greatest 'sin of omission' of our historic utilitarian view of water as a resource to be siphoned off to meet urban, irrigation and industrial needs is that it almost wholly overlooks, or at least assumes there are ready retrospective fixes for, implications for the landscapes and ecosystems from which it is withdrawn and the many people dependent upon them for their livelihoods. By focusing on growing water and energy demands solely on a 'predict and provide' basis, we tend to overlook opportunities for a whole range of alternative technologies, including, as just a few examples, water and energy efficiency measures, water reuse, and alternative forms of renewable energy, food production and security.

We have seen a transition in thinking about the ecological consequences of large dams, starting from a point of substantial ignorance or denial and moving towards the kinds of principles espoused by the WCD. We are learning more about the various costs of overlooking environmental, social and wider associated economic impacts, the potential to store up liabilities for the future, and the risk of increasing land claims and demands for redress of rights denied or stolen under former regimes.

Social discourse has, then, moved from overlooking people in the harnessing of water and its associated potential energy towards informing them of decisions already made, setting up compensation funds for disadvantages suffered, and ultimately making efforts to engage them in the decision-making process itself. This is a revolution in thinking, albeit as yet poorly populated by best-practice examples. Many schemes nevertheless demonstrate a degree of transition from the outmoded model of merely informing people of decisions made by 'experts' on behalf of 'the public interest'. Progress is being made towards some form of meaningful engagement in decisions of all potentially impacted constituencies sharing a destiny, including compensation where pre-existing rights and land claims can be verified. All of these people need to have both a say and a stake in the distribution of benefits and burdens from the earliest stage of needs and options identification and planning.

The reality of large dams is that they effectively remove one entire ecosystem and displace it with another set of biophysical conditions in which a new ecosystem will form. This occurs not only at the dam site but with major ramifications across substantial lengths of river and areas of drainage basins, all with direct and indirect consequences for the livelihoods and potential of people dependent upon them. To assess the wisdom and consequences of that, we need a more inclusive and far-sighted conceptual and decision-support paradigm that accounts for the dynamics of ecosystems and all who benefit from them.

7 | Dams and ecosystem services

Ecosystem services comprise the many societal benefits provided by ecosystems. The concept and application of ecosystem services have been evolving since the 1980s to support understanding of the natural environment and, in particular, how it supports human well-being. The evolving ecosystem services paradigm, including a variety of classification schemes, was included by the Convention on Biological Diversity (CBD) in 1995 in the 'ecosystem approach'. This approach is 'a strategy for the integrated management of land, water and living resources that promotes conservation and sustainable use in an equitable way', defined by twelve principles and five points of operational guidance.[1] The most powerful stimulus to integration of the many strands of ecosystem services science, and its application in international and national policy, was publication of the Millennium Ecosystem Assessment (MA)[2] instigated by the UN to assess the status of, and trends in, major global habitat types and their prognosis for continuing human well-being.[3]

To achieve this, the MA amalgamated diverse pre-existing classification schemes into a consistent framework comprising four major categories: 'provisioning services' (things that can be extracted from ecosystems such as fresh water, food and fibre); 'regulatory services' (processes that regulate the natural environment such as air quality, climate, water flows and pests); 'cultural services' (diverse aspects of aesthetic, spiritual, recreational and other value); and 'supporting services' (not directly exploited but including processes essential for the functioning, integrity and resilience of ecosystems). Though neither perfect nor complete, the MA typology nevertheless provides a broadly inter-comparable classification relevant across major habitat types and bioregions, and a useful framework for understanding the ways in which diverse sectors of society benefit from, or suffer by, interventions in the environment. It thereby exposes the complexity and multiplicity of interactions between social and natural systems, the knowledge gaps about how all ecosystem services are produced, and the need for methods to monitor them.

Ecosystem assessment

Ecosystem services enable assessment not merely of ecosystems but of their functions and capacity to deliver a wide range of human benefits. The MA Synthesis report[4] states that 'Everyone in the world depends completely on Earth's ecosystems and the services they provide' and that 'Over the past 50 years, humans have changed these ecosystems more rapidly and extensively than in any comparable period of time in human history'. Importantly, it continues, 'But not all regions and groups of people have benefited from this process – in fact, many have been harmed. Moreover, the full costs associated with these gains are only now becoming apparent.' Around 60 per cent of global ecosystem services are being degraded or used unsustainably, with circumstantial evidence of an increasing likelihood of non-linear changes in ecosystems. Degrading ecosystem services have disproportionate impacts upon the poor, contributing to growing societal inequities and disparities. Among the MA's conclusions are that 'These problems, unless addressed, will substantially diminish the benefits that future generations obtain from ecosystems'.

Freshwater ecosystems are one of the global habitat types most significantly adversely affected.[5] However, many ecosystem services have been overlooked and as often degraded through human activities, notwithstanding their irreplaceable importance, including, for example, fresh water supply, air quality and climate regulation, pollination, culturally valued landscapes and educational and recreational opportunities. Consequently, the ecosystem services paradigm is now substantially shaping international thinking, national policies and management practices, promoting deeper insights into practical application of sustainable development. This includes throwing light on some aspects of large dams and the balance of benefits and negative consequences for ecosystem services that such large-scale transformation of drainage basins implies across all ecosystem service categories.

Dams and ecosystem services

Dams significantly boost selected ecosystems services favoured by society, or at least by a cadre of decision-makers, particularly retention of fresh water and potential 'harvesting' of energy through hydroelectric generation. Additional provisioning services such as reservoir fisheries and cultural services such as navigation and/or amenity activities may also be planned, along with regulation of flooding by major alteration of the catchment hydrograph. The design of some also seeks to mitigate harm to services of concern – for example, mitigation of some of the flow impacts downstream through installation of multi-level spillways and dam management regimes. However, many services are overlooked, with all of the hazards that non-systemic management brings with it. Scale presents a real challenge, as large dams are nothing short of the substitution of one set of ecosystem functions for another, fundamentally changing not merely local conditions but also flows of energy, water, sediment, solutes and biota across broad landscapes with a raft of unforeseen or ill-considered consequences.

History is replete with examples of large dam schemes that have failed to live up to their grand visions owing to wider unintended consequences with significant associated costs. It is precisely this need for connected insight which the ecosystem approach is designed to serve, providing a framework to innovate and test options, addressing and structuring negotiation about their likely consequences for multiple stakeholder groups at a range of scales. Understanding these broad potential implications as an interlinked set of impacts of ecosystem services with associated 'winners and losers' within catchments may help us better appreciate the interdependence of people around water systems. It may then serve to support innovation and co-creation of multi-benefit solutions that may or may not include dams and/or other land and water management options, including better mitigation measures.

Hindsight across the past century highlights the naivety of a 'one size fits all' approach to dams that assumes all people will automatically benefit. An ecosystem-service-based appraisal therefore offers to fill a long-neglected gap, not merely addressing potential negative impacts but also, as exemplified by reforestation in the upper Yangtze basin (reviewed in Chapter 13), how an ecosystem-based approach can prolong the asset life and value of a major dam and associated infrastructure. The fundamental principle supported by an ecosystem approach remains achievement of the greatest and most enduring set of benefits for all in society and the protection of the ecosystem processes that support them.

Analysis of the ecosystem service impacts of large dams

The first step in undertaking such an assessment is to understand the types of marginal change across all ecosystem services likely to arise from construction and operation of a large dam, alternative water management scheme or other intervention. In this thought experiment, as indeed often in the case of appraisal of actual dam schemes, valuation of all these positive and negative impacts may not be possible.

However, a semi-quantitative 'likelihood of impact' scoring system published by the UK government[6] is helpful for screening, ideally through a process involving multiple stakeholders, the likely balance of impacts of any management intervention for each ecosystem services.

The table below collates the consensus views and rationale of various stakeholder workshops I have run in South Africa, the UK, Sweden and China to assess the generic likely marginal impacts and considerations of an illustrative 'large dam' proposal, relative to the 'baseline condition' of a semi-natural river valley. This uses a simplified version of the semi-quantitative UK government scoring system: + potentially positive; – potentially negative; o neutral; and ? not enough information to make a judgement.

TABLE 7.1 Ecosystem service, based on the Millennium Ecosystem Assessment classification: Likely consequences of generic dam construction relative to the baseline of a semi-natural river

Provisioning services
Fresh water
   + The primary purpose of most dams is to increase the amount of water available for human use.
   – Factors such as evaporative loss from dams and infrastructure may not be factored into overall assessments of benefits and, commonly, negative implications may arise from changes in flows of water elsewhere in the catchment.
   Note: Overall, the balance of benefits or costs can be judged only on a case-by-case basis taking account of all stakeholders throughout the catchment, together with the ways they access and use water, as potentially affected by the proposed dam.
Food (e.g. crops, fruit, fish, etc.)
   + Where commercial fisheries occur in reservoirs and also when land is irrigated by dam water, food production benefits may occur.
   – It is essential to understand impacts on water/silt flows on pre-existing river fisheries, and the production of subsistence, cash crop and commercial crops in wider river systems, which will generally be negatively affected.
   Note: We also have to consider the distribution of those benefits across society.
Fibre and fuel (e.g. timber, wool, etc.)
   + Irrigated crops such as cotton as well as irrigated forestry can enhance fibre production.
   – General disruption of floodplain-nourishing processes downstream in river systems can reduce natural fibre production in grazing land, floodplain forestry and reedbeds, and other river resources.
   Note: Again, we have to be aware of the potential to change the balance

of 'winners and losers', as well as crop types favoured.

Genetic resources (used for crop/stock breeding and biotechnology)
– Reservoirs are substantially less biodiverse than the endemic ecosystems that they displace, with knock-on consequences down river systems also tending to simplify ecosystems, potentially decreasing this service significantly.

Biochemicals, natural medicines, pharmaceuticals
– As for 'genetic resources' above.

Ornamental resources (e.g. shells, flowers, etc.)
– As for 'genetic resources' above.

Regulatory services
Air quality regulation
– Natural floodplain vegetation communities have a role in air quality regulation, including trapping of aerial particulates as well as geochemical transformations, which may be lost owing to habitat simplification.

Climate regulation (local temperature/precipitation, greenhouse gas sequestration, etc.)
– Natural floodplain vegetation communities have a role in cycling of atmospheric gases, while hydric soils tend to sequester carbon.
? Hydroelectric generation potentially cuts emissions relative to fossil fuel generation, but emerging knowledge about methanogenesis and nitrous oxide generation raises as yet unresolved questions about the overall contribution of large dams to climate change.

Water regulation (timing and scale of run-off, flooding, etc.)
+ Initially, reservoirs may absorb a pulse of floodwater, and the seasonal buffering of monsoon pulses is a design intent of some dams.
– However, there is no further buffering when dams overtop. Loss of river habitat in the inundated area, increase of impermeable development associated with the dam and degraded floodplain habitat downstream decrease the capacity of river systems to detain and infiltrate floodwater. Human settlement on downstream floodplains thought to be no longer at risk may exacerbate damage in the event of flooding.

Natural hazard regulation (i.e. storm protection)
– Loss of habitat complexity reduces the capacity of habitats to absorb storm and other energy.

Pest regulation
– Loss of ecosystem complexity reduces the stock of the natural predators of pest species.

Disease regulation
– Declining and smoothed water flows together with simplified habitats tend to promote diseases such as bilharzia, malaria, West Nile virus, Japanese encephalitis and others with aquatic vectors, while fast-water areas can promote the growth of the simuliid (blackfly) vectors of river blindness. Reduced river flows may also reduce dilution and the transmission of diarrhoeal diseases.

Erosion regulation
   – Sediment detention in reservoirs accelerates habitat erosion downstream in river systems owing to sediment starvation.

Water purification and waste treatment
   – Loss of habitat complexity, and standing water in which algae may bloom or aquatic vegetation may grow and decay, decreases many natural physico-chemical and biological water purification processes in river systems.

Pollination
   – Loss of ecosystem complexity reduces the stock of natural pollinators.

Cultural services
Cultural heritage
   + Lake habitat may be valued by some sectors of society.
   – However, there is a net loss of traditional landscapes and artefacts, inundated below reservoirs and affected by habitat change downstream.

Recreation and tourism
   ? Some people may benefit from tourism related to dam operation, fisheries and amenity, particularly in regions of the world with little open water, yet other facets of tourism in the dam site and affected river habitats downstream may be depressed. This includes perturbing the migration routes, spawning and nursery sites and other habitat important to wildlife with tourism or recreational value, and also depressing values for canoeing and other water sports as well as birdwatching and informal recreation.

Aesthetic value
   – A subjective measure as some find dams attractive, but the greatest impact will be loss of characteristic river landscapes and their associated ecosystems and cultural features.

Spiritual and religious value
   – Loss of traditional landscapes beneath reservoirs and in river reaches affected by habitat change downstream, including many examples across India and Egypt of sacred sites inundated by dam water, erodes this service.

Inspiration of art, folklore, architecture, etc.
   – Loss or degradation of natural landscapes and associated traditions is likely to be overwhelmingly negative.

Social relations (e.g. fishing, grazing or cropping communities)
   – Although new fishing, amenity, industrial and dam management communities may form, this impact is considered overwhelmingly negative as traditional crafts and livelihoods are lost together with their focal role in local community life.

Supporting services
Soil formation
   – Detention and accumulation of suspended matter in dams inhibits soil-forming and soil-fertilizing processes in river systems.

Primary production
   o The balance of overall productivity is hard to generalize, but excessive

production of some algal, aquatic plant and fish species in reservoirs has to be offset against displacement of the wider productivity by more complex ecosystems formerly existing at the dam site and in longer reaches of river affected by dam operation.

Nutrient cycling
 – Loss of ecosystem complexity and habitat structure along the river corridor, at the dam site and downstream is likely to suppress biogeochemical cycles including those affecting nutrient substances.

Water recycling
 – Reduction in habitat and ecosystem complexity throughout the entire river corridor is likely to reduce the cycling of water between wetland habitats, terrestrial and aquatic habitats, and the often complex interactions and localized cycles between air and water (i.e. recapture of evaporated moisture in complex riparian vegetation communities).

Photosynthesis (production of atmospheric oxygen)
 ? Most likely, a net negative impact but hard to generalize for all dams. Net photosynthesis in reservoirs is likely to be offset by reduced plant activity in the simpler ecosystems and degraded habitats at the dam site and along the whole affected river corridor.

Provision of habitat
 – New reservoir habitat may bring in new species, but is generally far simpler than the river habitat that it replaces. Dams also perturb downstream river habitat structure and functioning over substantial distances, as well as the connectivity of the river system.

This illustrative example highlights how all dams are different and need to be evaluated as such, ideally involving a representative set of potentially affected stakeholders. Discussions around intra-team disagreements in all of the workshops I have run, which inform this compilation, highlight how an ecosystem service assessment can provide a transparent basis for promoting dialogue about the balance of benefits and costs across interlinked ecosystem services, exploring connections across whole complex socio-ecological systems and innovations that might optimize them.

Virtually all of these broader services have been overlooked throughout our industrial history of intensive food growing, marine fisheries, forestry and urban sprawl, maximizing production of a selected few services with the unintended consequence of degrading overlooked services and ecosystem resilience. Exclusion of this breadth of benefits from the contemporary market externalizes them from established business, governance and development systems, reinforcing the 'tragedy of the commons'.

Our prior consideration of 'The state of play with dams' reveals the extent to which this applies to water management, with consequences for water systems and their many services to humanity. This has real and serious repercussions as water is inseparable from human needs. However, it is also true that, since ecosystem services relate to different streams of benefits to people, and the MA classification explicitly sought to encompass a breadth of value systems from the utilitarian to the aesthetic, spiritual and culturally relative, ecosystem services are amenable to valuation. Valuing services offers a means to bring them into societal calculations (a topic to which we will return in Part 2 of this book). One such pioneering economic assessment is the now well-known 1997 study by Robert Costanza and colleagues,[7] who estimated the absolute value of global ecosystem services at around $US33 trillion: more or less equal to global gross domestic product at the time. Another study published in 2002 assessed the cost of ecosystem loss worldwide as in the order of $US250 billion per annum, or in other words some 2–5 per cent of GDP.[8] The MA further confirms that the degradation of the world's major habitats threatens to halt or reverse progress with human development,[9] a conclusion endorsed by subsequent national studies such as the UK's National Ecosystem Assessment.[10] This has led the UN to question the extent to which the Millennium Development Goals[11] can raise people out of economic and water poverty in the face of this level of ongoing ecological degradation.[12]

These studies have contributed to a better understanding of the value of ecosystems, promoting application of the ecosystem approach to practical and often pressing problems.

Taking an ecosystem services view of dam proposals

To date, only two detailed ecosystem services assessments have been undertaken on schemes proposing dams and major water transfers. The first of these remains one of the most advanced studies of the broader consequences of different development scenarios across a major river system: the *Thukela Water Project: Reserve Determination Module*, Part 1: 'IFR scenarios in the Thukela River catchment: economic impacts on ecosystem services'.[13] As reviewed in Chapter 6, the Thukela Water Project (TWP) addressed different options for diverting the flows of South Africa's Thukela (Tugela) river, in the province of KwaZulu-Natal, northwards to serve the economic heartland of Gauteng. Already supported by a raft of traditional studies and engagement processes, the 'Economic impacts on ecosystem services' study took the more radical approach of exploring potential marginal economic impacts arising from changes to the supply of a range of ecosystem services in the upper sub-catchments of the Thukela system under different environmental flow regimes.

The economic value of the 'status quo' condition was deduced by interviews with representative households throughout rural and urban communities scattered across the major sub-catchments of the Thukela. Ecosystem services targeted by the study included fish (other than recreational fishing), reeds, sedges, waste assimilation, waste dilution, cultivated floodplain agricultural land, livestock grazing, whitewater rafting and kayaking, canoeing, recreational swimming, recreational fishing (trout) and recreational fishing (estuary). Ecological disservices were also addressed, including bilharzia (treatment costs), bilharzia (loss of productivity), pathogens (treatment costs of diarrhoea), pathogens (loss of productivity through diarrhoea), pathogens (treatment costs of cholera) and pathogens (loss of productivity through cholera). Total economic value was extrapolated by multiplying the household benefit or disbenefit by the number of households enjoying the ecosystem service within each sub-catchment.

'Out of river' implications (changes to the volumes of water available for abstraction and direct economic use) and 'in-river' services (the implications of changes to the level of services supplied by the volume of water remaining within the river) were then assessed as percentage variations on the basis of modelled changes to flow regimes under different water management scenarios, calculating economic variances from baseline conditions. This was determined for eight major tributaries, with four scenarios (three dam options and the status quo) using seventeen potential services (or disservices): some 544 individual economic assessments. To ease interpretation, numerical outcomes were presented on a colour-coded basis related to degree of likely change: pale blue (no problem); green (good); orange (caution); and red (bad).

For many dam/diversion scenarios, a different balance of benefits, as well as a different balance between beneficiary communities and those suffering disbenefits, was encountered in different sub-catchments across the river system. This emphasizes the hazards associated with broad generalization of impacts. Significant changes in ecosystem services were most often attributed to a number of factors. These included reduction of water volume and flow with associated habitat loss, possible saltwater intrusion in lower reaches of river, loss of reeds and sedges (or in some flow scenarios significant increases) with consequences for indigenous construction and crafts, impacts on the capacity of rivers to dilute and assimilate wastes, lowering of the water tables on floodplains, and compromised floodplain grazing, recreation and fishing opportunities. Increasing habitat available to vectors or direct transmission of debilitating waterborne diseases including bilharzia and cholera was also often highly significant. Under some 'development option' scenarios, there was a significant likelihood of significant increases in disease.

The 'Economic impact of ecosystem services' study did not explore all of the MA's ecosystem services. Instead, it focused on a subset representative of and appropriate to the sub-catchments of interest. It also omitted the likely implications of some broader ecosystem processes (sediment trapping, changing water use habits, increased evapotranspiration, etc.) which may have further influenced total marginal costs. However, the study provides a robust and graphic demonstration of the interdependence of multiple ecosystem services. It highlights the differentiated ways in which they can impact different sub-catchments and sectors of society under changed river management scenarios. The report helpfully summarized this complex analysis simply for decision-makers in both central and provincial government through the 'traffic light' colour coding. We would do well to learn from this innovative approach, a pioneer and exemplar of the kind of integrated and transparent assessment necessary to inform future strategic decisions, and to apply it more widely, not only throughout Africa but across the globe.

Another 2010 study used the MA ecosystem service framework to assess likely outcomes of the proposed Pancheshwar Dam on the India/Nepal border.[14] The Sangam, or meeting of rivers, at Pancheshwar in the Himalayas (Uttarakhand State, India) is the site of proposals to build the Pancheshwar Dam to control flow of the Kali river and its tributaries. The Kali (or Mahakali) river here forms the border with Nepal, with which the dam was conceived as a joint venture. At 315 metres high, the proposed Pancheshwar Dam would be the world's second-tallest dam, a rock-filled structure intended to harness hydroelectric power and water.

The ecosystem services study drew upon published sources, interviews on a site visit, polling experts both from India and the international community, and on online forums to explore marginal impacts across the substantial area of the Pancheshwar site. It addressed the significant ecological, cultural, spiritual and tourism importance of the site, as well as implications for disruptions to river ecosystems and to the many people dependent on them for substantial distances downstream. It was not possible to quantify or monetize these impacts, but 'likelihood of impact' weightings were determined on the basis of stated assumptions and supporting evidence. Planned beneficial outcomes included harnessing of water and energy; however, the broader 'filter' of ecosystem services revealed a far wider range of likely consequences for many other people potentially affected by the dam scheme, most of whom were omitted from planning considerations or consultation. This represents a serious democratic gap, as so often observed in major dam schemes, with an almost complete lack of engagement of local people and a paucity of published information. Furthermore, consideration of environmental and social consequences occurred only belatedly in the planning process, perhaps merely as a 'tick box' exercise, and almost certainly too late to have any influence on scheme design and decisions with their associated sunk costs and investment of political capital. Pointedly, no other options appear to have been contemplated or appraised, with no analysis of how people actually use water and energy and how else these might be more appropriately delivered without such major disruption to the catchment ecosystem.

The Pancheshwar Dam failed when the findings from the ecosystem services analysis were assessed against the seven WCD 'strategic priorities'. The proposed Pancheshwar Dam could therefore not be assumed to be sustainable, ethical or economically sound. The report's authors concluded that it would have substantial and long-lasting negative environmental consequences affecting people, livelihoods, cultural importance and high-priority nature conservation areas over a wide geographical scale. Negative effects would be most profoundly inflicted on rural communities largely omitted from planning considerations. The impacts of earthquakes on dam integrity also seem to have been overlooked, despite this being a highly active earthquake zone. The net value of the proposed Pancheshwar Dam to Nepal, India and beyond is then highly questionable; some potential positive outcomes appearing overstated with negative consequences substantially ignored. It is not clear who will pick up these costs. This has ramifications for the perceptions of India and Nepal on the world stage in terms of overlooking the interests of the majority of their people, also infringing risk assessment criteria required by many potential funders.

At the time of writing, Marxist influences in Nepal have put the future of the Pancheshwar Dam proposals in doubt. Also, during an advisory visit I made to China, access to the various websites on which the then recently published Pancheshwar Dam report was posted were suddenly blocked from within China; it appears that the findings were not palatable to all governments with pro-dam proclivities!

Ecosystem services, dams and water sharing

The value of taking an ecosystem approach is clearly demonstrated by this rudimentary application to the topic of dams; large dams do not so much modify catchment ecosystems as replace them with wholly new systems with a different set of characteristics and associated ecosystem services. This has major implications for all people sharing catchments, all of whom need to inform management decisions if sustainability and equity are to be achieved.

Through extension of the kinds of assessment tools represented by ecosystem service studies of the proposed Thukela and Pancheshwar schemes, society can begin progressively to reimagine the role of the water cycle in society, providing the necessary stimulus for appropriate and innovative management of fundamental resources, including fresh water. A great deal more needs to be done to bring the ecosystem approach into the mainstream of decision-making, something that the UN and the wider international community are keen to promote. Ecosystems are far from expensive externalities, as framed under neo-classical economics, but are instead important sources of fundamental resources upon which all depend. We are witnessing the early phase of a long-overdue recognition that society and its many activities exist not in some abstract sphere but in intimate interdependence with the ecosystems of which it is an indivisible part.[15]

8 | A new agenda for dams

Ecosystem services are significant not merely in terms of broadening our perspective of the natural world and its supportive processes, but also of the diversity of humanity dependent upon it, the diverse value systems held by these people, and their unavoidable if commonly overlooked interdependencies. This integrated framework, then, provides us with a new way to bring into political and business calculations the often historically overlooked value of the natural world and its functions, and what 'best value' may actually mean for optimizing outcomes for all in society over the longer-term future. Equity, sustainability and long-term economic efficiency are thus brought into a new paradigm of natural resource management, stewardship and sharing.

Stewardship and allocation of resources are of course the essence of governance, never more so than for critical and limited natural resources such as water. Reflection on the history and balance of outcomes of dam schemes sheds light on wider issues concerning the relationship of people with water and the hydropolitics that drives it, and the importance of a new hydropolitics.

The shifting politics of large dams

Dams, large dams in particular, may be emblematic of a psyche of mankind 'triumphing over nature'. This, let's recall, was summed up succinctly by Jawaharlal Nehru's 'temples of modern India', as well as the conflation of 'big engineering' with nation-building in Egypt, China, the USA, Turkey and beyond. That Nehru regretted his statement within his own lifetime is well documented; he later frequently referred instead to 'the disease of gigantism' to describe the proclivity of large dams and related large infrastructure schemes to accelerate depletion of forests, displace native people and appropriate huge sums of public money through corruption, all in the name of a blinkered, technocentric model of progress. Set in opposition to this were Gandhi's ideals of locally appropriate technologies and lifestyles founded upon sufficiency rather than competitive Western development.

Yet it would be unfair to blame dam visionaries such as Jawaharlal Nehru, Gamal Abdel Nasser and Herbert Hoover for a failure to foresee the far-reaching impacts of large dams on the environment and, often, the very people they were intended to help. These twentieth-century pioneers took decisions in a simpler age, envisaging simple lines of cause and effect from their positions in the upper echelons of power and assuming a uniform pervasion of the immediate benefits of the projects that they helped bring into being. It is as certain that future generations will be as struck by our own naivety about the web of interdependencies, consideration of which is essential to underpin sustainable progress.

War and peace

Where there is competition for a limiting, critical resource of any kind, there is the potential for conflict. Water scarcity, for example, was regarded by Anthony Turton as likely 'to limit South Africa's economic development, potentially elevating the issue from WRM [water resource management] to the level of national security concern'.[1] Indeed, Turton highlights how the 'securitization' of WRM can become a driver of future conflict if left unmanaged, and that 'desecuritization' is not just a technical management task but a political priority necessitating engagement of all affected stakeholders. The cross-border nature of rivers can exacerbate tensions around the sharing of water, increasing friction between Turkey, Syria and Iraq, between India and Pakistan, across southern Africa, and in the Nile Basin. In a detailed analysis in November 2011,[2] *The Economist* magazine questions whether the 'unquenchable thirst' of India, Pakistan and China over the waters and power generation potential of the region's great rivers could create rivalries threatening South Asia's peace, resonating with the now often-repeated prediction by World Bank vice-president Ismail Serageldin that 'Many of the wars of the 20th century were about oil, but wars of the 21st century will be over water unless we change the way we manage water'.[3]

Yet wars over water are already long established. The Six Days War of 1967 had competition for the waters of the Jordan river at its heart. The Arab League, angered by Israel's construction of its National Water Carrier, which had appropriated much of the water of the Jordan river for Israel's uses, began to dig canals to divert two of the major tributaries of the Jordan: the Hasbanin and Wazzani Springs. Israel's response was to shell and destroy both projects. Retaliatory attacks by Syria, Egypt and Jordan were swift to follow. In the ensuing war, Israel seized Gaza and the Sinai peninsula from Egypt, the Golan Heights from Syria and the West Bank from Jordan, all but the Sinai peninsula important as sources supporting Israel's water security. Diversion of water from the Mesopotamian wetlands also became a potent weapon of war waged by Saddam Hussein's forces against Iraq's Marsh Arabs.

However, other contrasting research reveals much more historical evidence of water playing the role of a catalyst for cooperation. The 2006 UN report *Ten Stories the World Should Hear More About* was subtitled 'From water wars to bridges of cooperation – exploring the peace-building potential of a shared resource'.[4] This was published at the launch of the UNESCO project *From Potential Conflict to Cooperation Potential*,[5] promoting water security in the twenty-first century by focusing on the development of tools for the anticipation, prevention and resolution of water conflicts. This project noted that there were more than 3,800 unilateral, bilateral or multilateral declarations or conventions on water across the world; 286 of them treaties with 61 referring to over 200 international river basins. It further recorded that the preceding half-century had witnessed more than five hundred conflict-related events over water, seven of which had involved violence. According to UNESCO, 145 nations have territory within a trans-boundary drainage basin, 21 lie entirely within one, and 12 countries have more than 95 per cent of their territories within one or more trans-boundary basins. Approximately one third of the existing 263 trans-boundary basins are shared by more than two countries.

The UN report was informed by a number of case studies demonstrating the effectiveness of the cooperation approach. These included Bolivia and Peru working together on the management of water basin resources around Lake Titicaca through the creation of the Autonomous Water Authority. Progress was also acknowledged with restoration of the northern Aral Sea through cooperation between countries sharing its drainage basin (Kazakhstan, Uzbekistan, the Kyrgyz Republic, Tajikistan and Turkmenistan), including projects such as completion of the Kok-Aral Dam and rehabilitation of waterworks along the Syr Darya river to help farmers irrigate their lands. In fact, waters have returned to wide swathes of the Aral Sea, and local fishing fleets are at work again, leading World Bank president Robert Zoellick to state in 2009 that 'the return of the North Aral Sea shows that man-made disasters can be at least partly reversed'.[6]

This international appraisal is backed up by a critical assessment of the 'southern African hydropolitical complex', providing heartening evidence that international agreements on water sharing were a catalyst for dialogue, enduring agreements (even throughout periods of armed conflict) and also a mechanism for negotiating peace between countries at war.[7] Dams on cross-border rivers are inherently likely to be rather better considered in some respects than those over which nation-states have sole control. A Global Development Study[8] commissioned by the Ministry for Foreign Affairs in Sweden took evidence from three case studies (the Jordan river, the Kagera river, which is an upper tributary of the White Nile, and the Mekong river, which spans South-East Asia) and other studies of trans-boundary river systems and groundwater, demonstrating the unique considerations in each case and also how vested interests had often already appropriated more than a fair share of resources, whether through colonial-era agreements (in the case of Egypt) or by military intervention (Israel). The Global Development Study found that a more open dialogue between co-riparian nations based on benefit sharing could promote positive-sum outcomes, including overall water volume, hydropower and trade in food.

The Mekong Region Water Dialogues[9] is an ambitious IUCN programme designed to improve water governance in the Mekong Region by facilitating transparent and inclusive decision-making and to improve stakeholder involvement in environmental decision-making, accountability, transparency and protection of rights such as access to information among business, government and civil society between the four riparian countries (Cambodia, Lao People's Democratic Republic, Thailand and Vietnam). However, the effective absence of both China and Myanmar (Burma) from the 1995 MRC Agreement governing the Mekong river constitutes an ongoing threat to successful development within this basin, particularly in the light of plans for further major dams upstream in China.

The concept of 'soft power' describes the use of attraction and cooperation, rather than coercion whether by force or by payments, as a constructive means of persuasion.[10] This approach and term is now widely used in international affairs, including for example by China and the USA, as a means for the resolution of international and other conflicts. US general Wesley Clark noted for the resolution of wars that soft power 'gave us an influence far beyond the hard edge of traditional balance-of-power politics'.[11] The approach has also been related to interstate and sub-national tensions over trans-boundary waters,[12] in which cooperation and conflict were observed not as polar opposites but as often coexisting. Neither was regarded as uniformly beneficial or harmful, with cooperation sometimes perpetuating conflicts through uncritical acceptance of traditional forms of arrangements such as river flow allocations. Recognizing and seeking to critically appraise areas of both existing cooperation and conflict in political negotiations is seen as a means for innovation and eventual mutually beneficial collaboration.

Water sharing cannot therefore be dissociated from the securitization agenda, respecting the sovereignty, rights (particularly of the poor and frequently marginalized) and aspirations of bordering countries. The oft-cited inevitability of 'water wars' is therefore far too simplistic, and in fact widely contradicted by water-sharing arrangements around the world. Political arrangements are fundamental to this process of engagement and sharing, and must address the behaviour of whole catchments rather than allowing local or solely national demands to fragment the broader-scale processes upon which the benefits of all depend. The key investment here is in dialogue to recognize and address complex and potentially conflicting needs, yet to be open to win-win innovations and departures from traditional technical, political, economic, land use and other solutions. The building of these forms of capacity represents more insightful and useful targets for funding by development aid agencies and other international financing.

The politics of technology

Technology choice is in reality political choice. In the most overt cases, we see this in the naming of large dams or reservoirs, from the Hoover Dam to Lake Nasser, after their political champions or indeed their depiction as monuments to a particular model of progress such as Libya's Great Manmade River. But, regardless of the name on the structure, a decision to invest in massive technology to hold back large reserves of water for piped supply and hydropower production, or for inter-basin transfers, is no light undertaking, with commensurate impacts on the character of catchments and the diverse livelihoods dependent on them. Intensive centralization in the management of water mirrors that of electric power generation, directly so where large-scale hydroelectric schemes are part of dam design, and the difficulty of integrating into a centralized infrastructure the kinds of local embedded renewable energy solutions that work best in supporting dispersed local needs. British people of a certain age will recall with a wry smile the promise of energy 'too cheap to meter' from the new era of nuclear generation plants of the 1950s, an expression of trust in the perception of the 'white heat of technology' to transform the lives of all citizens for the better. More than sixty years down the line, we are now horribly aware of how these most honourable of hopes and intentions have been fatally undermined by a raft of unintended and unforeseen environmental and social costs. Some of them will be expressed over geological timescales, entailing huge financial costs, public disquiet and, in the post-9/11 era, anxiety about terrorism and broader security issues arising from the international proliferation of nuclear technology. So too the industrialization of farming and food processing that sweep aside locally adapted strains and practices, the imposition of strict curricula in education excluding minority values and traditions, and the process of industrialization itself which values uniformity rather than diversity.

However, while centralization of this kind brings with it substantial 'economies of scale' when viewed in narrowly economic terms, we are now learning about the effectiveness and inclusivity of localized solutions. These include embedded renewable energy generation, protection of locally adapted crop strains and farming practices, disease transmission issues arising from long-distance haulage to centralized stock slaughterhouses and processing units, distributed computing and the internet, and locally modified educational curricula. This is undoubtedly also true for water management systems adapted to local environmental conditions and to local needs, traditions and wisdom. From centralized banks 'too big to fail' down to microfinance that empowers women and local minorities in profitable ventures tailored to local need, lessons are to be learned about the full economy of our dependence on nature. Lessons about resilience being dependent, as in ecosystems, on diversity and apparent redundancy contrast with realization of the costs consequent from industrial-scale over-exploitation of ecosystems.

Dams are, of course, a classic example of a big centralized solution to issues of water supply and/or energy generation, augmented locally by utility for navigation, hydrological and other designed benefits. As such, they have suffered the same kinds of myopia as society's other addictions to 'big technology' solutions with their raft of associated unintended consequences. Many people have benefited, certainly in the short term. However, in the absence of inclusive and equitable thinking, aquatic ecosystems and the many people dependent upon them most certainly have not thrived in the overwhelming volume of cases.

Dams and other 'big engineering' schemes may be sexy, but they are not the only type of technology. Our historic 'sins of omission' include overlooking many of the potential unintended consequences of dams, and addressing exactly who it is that they really serve. In considering water, energy, food and other interconnected needs on a more sustainable and equitable basis, we have clearly often overlooked serious consideration of alternative, locally adapted options for managing the water and wider catchment systems they share.

Yet neither the politics of centralization nor localism and local accountability are automatically individually superior. For example, local people may elect to over-exploit a water resource, thereby compromising the well-being of others living downstream. A balance of the ideologies of centralization and localism has to be struck, and particularly in the context of maintaining a sustainable relationship with the finite 'carrying capacity' of water and catchment ecosystems. And, in a heavily overpopulated world, technology undoubtedly has a vital role to play in helping us achieve sustainability, particularly as we approach a global population of 9 or 10 billion by 2050. Indeed, throughout human history, technological innovation has been one of the main driving forces enabling humanity incrementally to overcome constraints of food and water availability, transport, predation and disease. What matters is the technology choice and the means by which it is chosen, respecting the needs of the diverse people it affects as well as the functioning and resilience of ecosystems vital to their long-term future.

Nehru's changing stance towards dams and grand technology in general reflects a broader societal awakening to environmental problems with their associated consequences and the need for a more integrated approach to development. By not seeking to hear and account for the voices of the silent majority in technology and management decisions, we exclude them from the sharing of benefits but certainly not from the apportionment of costs. We also blind ourselves to a win-win mix of technologies optimally beneficial to all. For this, we need better understanding of the natural dynamics of the water cycle, its many meanings and values to all the people who interact with it, and practical tools to provide us with a comprehensive view of all of the potential consequences of water management options.

Large dams have delivered significant benefits to society and may well have an important continuing role but, as neatly summed up by the consortium opposing the Skuifraam Dam, 'the era of supply-side tunnel vision is over'. We are now better informed and placed to avoid the social and ecological blind spots that have blighted our historic technology choices. As the Skuifraam Dam case study also demonstrated, we may just be running out of ecosystems and livelihoods to plunder to serve the needs of ever more thirsty players in the 'First World economy'. We will certainly have to innovate along more ecosystem-based lines if we are not to continue undermining resources critical to the longer-term well-being of all.

TWO | **Water in the postmodern world**

9 | Water in the postmodern world

Pre-industrialized humans were preoccupied substantially with access to primary ecosystem-derived resources to meet their needs. It is perhaps ironic that, after a cycle of industrialization that has seen us massively alter the Earth's ecosystems to yield a limited set of benefits for the most affluent, our focus is again brought back to how we can continue to secure access to ecosystem resources on a sustainable and equitable basis for our burgeoning population. As Sir John Beddington, the UK government's Chief Scientific Adviser, neatly described in March 2009, the world will face a 'perfect storm' of food, water and energy shortages by 2030 without radical interventions.[1] Beddington warned of public unrest, cross-border conflicts and mass migration in the worst-affected parts of a world constrained by primary resources to meet a growing population under the impacts of a changing climate. The way we conceive of and manage water is a vital constituent of resolutions of these potential conflicts.

Learning our way to sustainability

Daunting and pressing though these threats to continued human well-being are, we can take heart from the fact that we are a learning species. Our inherent ingenuity has historically enabled us to find new ways to appropriate natural and human resources for our own benefit, apply our wits to tackle problems and progressively build upon our sum total of knowledge and technical capability. This uniquely human quality has seen us rise not merely in population but in the construction of successive civilizations, proliferating across every continent from the poles to the equator, wetlands to deserts, and high mountains to coasts and islands. Over a mere 8,000 years, we left behind hunter-gathering for settled farming then propelled ourselves onwards through agricultural revolutions, industrialization and the information technology age. Progression from Spinning Jenny to Space Shuttle took us just two centuries; transition from programmable computer to PC just four decades. Our capacity for rapid and paradigm-changing innovation is impressive. It is never more needed than today.

It is only since the 1960s that humanity has, in any broad sense, begun progressively to realize the scale of negative, unintended consequences arising from our historic pathway of industrial and agricultural innovation. The convergence of environmental, social and economic considerations into the holistic concept of sustainable development has therefore been relatively rapid, and we have since spawned a plethora of tools to help us make better decisions. It is undeniable that the pace of change in our thinking, decisions and proportionate actions must massively accelerate. However, shifting mindsets, at least in some parts of the world with respect to large dams and water management in general, demonstrate aspects of the required transition.

Systems thinking has made a critical contribution, fostering recognition and shaping responses related to the reality that all things are intimately interconnected. Sustainable development, ecosystem services and the ecosystem approach, and integrated management frameworks for water and other key resources are all examples of systems-based conceptual and management tools, albeit that the practical integration of systems perspectives into governance remains as yet partial and slow. The prevalent global market predominantly continues substantially to externalize many, perhaps most, adverse and long-term impacts on people and the environment from short-term decision-making. If we are to achieve sustainability, as indeed we must if we are to attain a just and secure future, systemic perspectives cannot be solely the province of academics but must become swiftly integrated into governance and markets.

Ultimately, we will be judged by future generations inheriting from us either a world that is already impoverished in natural beauty, productivity, diversity and resilience or which is restored to a condition enabling all people to live fulfilled lives. The power to minimize or reverse this damage, or watch passively as degradation accelerates, lies uniquely in our hands today. And water, as a common, fundamentally important and frequently limiting resource, is a potent medium through which to enact these bold intentions.

A new agenda for water management

This changing world-view has in turn affected the ways in which society has come to think about water resources. Historically, we might have focused almost entirely upon local interventions for local benefit, such as damming a stream for local supply, locating and diverting water from deep aquifers, or constructing flood walls to 'defend' a town or agricultural land. But parochial assumptions based solely on local cause and effect and founded on assumed rights have often blinded us to the broader ecological and societal ramifications of our decisions, the consequences of which will inevitably return to haunt us.

Rather, every person on Earth is a beneficiary of the many functions of catchments, each simultaneously sustained by and influencing the movement of water through land and water bodies. Water is fundamental to people. It has often been the basis for many place names (fords, bridges, mouths, hams, ports and wells) and defined the character of localities and even whole civilizations. Proximity to fresh water in particular has defined the nature and trajectory of human settlements across the world and throughout the millennia, generally limited by the 'carrying capacity' of local resources and their relatively minor modification to amplify selected human benefits. People, then, are an important, often dominant influence upon the water cycle, so the social context of catchments is of prime importance in understanding and better managing humanity's relationship with the water environment.

This pattern of human development close to water remained the case through to the era of 'megawater', when the power of technology began to make possible the spread of cities and economic hubs in arid regions and beyond the local 'carrying capacity' of other localities. We have already cited Johannesburg and Pretoria, Beijing and northern China, but we can add many more, including California and the Middle East. Today, humanity has stopped moving to sources of water; now water is being moved to cities. The technological means by which this is achieved are diverse and often massive, including, for example, water transfers and tankering, the shipping of vast water containers, imports of water-intensive foods, timber, cotton and other materials, and the 'mining' of fossil groundwater. However, the very power of this technology is breaking the link between people and water resources, with oil resources and their use in pumping, diversion and transport schemes generally becoming the new limiting factor with all the insecurities that this implies in a climate-changing, resource-depleting world. The disconnection of people from their place in the landscapes and the aquatic and other ecosystems with which we have co-evolved as a species is seen by authors such as Edward O. Wilson,[2] Ted Roszak[3] and David Suzuki[4] as a major contributor to human malaise and the capacity of modern societies for environmentally and socially irrational behaviours, including the devaluation, over-exploitation and inequitable sharing of basic natural resources.

But, faced with Beddington's 'perfect storm' and the learning from the Millennium Ecosystem Assessment and other authoritative studies, we have to recognize that human demands are manifestly outstripping ecosystems at all scales right up to the global. The agenda changes from one of continued entrainment of remote resources, at no assumed cost to ecosystems and people, to a model of development conscientiously safeguarding the ecosystems that constitute the primary resource upon which future human well-being depends. The way that we must regard and manage water in the postmodern world is founded on a radically different world-view to that of our industrial past, which has largely been responsible for the pressing problems we are facing today. Tomorrow, we must learn about and manage consistently the way that water and other natural cycles operate, safeguarding through sensitive use and management the habitats that capture, retain and purify water and stabilize seasonal flows while also recharging groundwater, regenerating soils and supporting wildlife. And we have to learn to do this quickly before the well runs dry.

Draining the communal well

Today, water reserves are being used up or polluted faster than they can be replenished. Problems with over-exploitation of surface waters are far better understood and publicly acknowledged than that of groundwater, out of sight and often out of mind, and which many regard as a panacea for water shortages. While in some countries groundwater resources are well managed with respect to risk management of potential contamination and accounting for withdrawal versus recharge rates, groundwater is frequently 'mined' and depleted on a demonstrably unsustainable basis throughout much of the world.

Around 1.5 billion people worldwide were reliant upon groundwater for drinking in 2000, 10 per cent of whom were known to depend on depleting groundwater.[5] By 2012, an estimated 1.7 billion people were living in areas where groundwater was being used more quickly than it can be replenished.[6] As pumps have become more powerful, deeper and deeper aquifers have been tapped, often accessing what can only realistically be viewed as fossil water deposits, the regeneration rate of which is minuscule in comparison to rates of exploitation. As a consequence, over-pumping of aquifers is now commonplace on every continent with water tables receding as pumping exceeds natural recharge. For example, under the North China Plain, which accounts for 25 per cent of China's grain harvest, the water table is falling by roughly 1.5 metres per year, and probably much faster in some places. Drainage of north Chinese aquifers has effectively dried up the lower Yellow River for much of the year, including its associated lakes and springs, turning formerly productive grasslands into dust bowls. The poorest farmers with the shallowest wells and weakest pumps are left without water. The same thing is happening under much of India, particularly the Punjab: the country's 'breadbasket'. In India, where bullock power has been the traditional power source to abstract water from wells of around nine metres (thirty feet) deep across the state of Gujarat, today tube wells sunk to depths of up to 396 metres (1,300 feet) are running dry owing to petrochemically powered pumps intended to advance the well-being of society. Meanwhile, whole villages in parts of Gujarat have had to be abandoned as shallow wells have run dry owing to powered groundwater abstraction, while in other places across the country water tables have retreated to as much as a mile deep yet are still pumped as intensively twenty-four hours a day as state aid to stimulate agricultural production includes free electricity. Each year, Indian farmers are reckoned to pump from beneath their fields more than twice as much water as the monsoons replace, resulting in plummeting water tables right across the subcontinent. Industrial-scale groundwater abstraction in Rajasthan has seen whole villages abandoned as crops fail and livelihoods become non-viable. In the United States, water tables are falling under the grain-growing states of the southern Great Plains, shrinking the irrigated area. Of the world's 6.1 billion people in 2000, 480 million were being fed with grain produced by over-pumping aquifers.[7] Other estimates suggest that up to one billion people around the world are eating food grown using underground water that is not being replaced. Drop by drop, the long-term implications for the sustainability of aquifers, together with potential for food production, are ominous. These issues are compounded by the collateral pollution of scarce groundwater as it is over-harvested, or the intrusion of deeper groundwater enriched in potentially problematic substances. UNESCO estimates that there is a US$5 billion market in the remediation of contaminated groundwater and land throughout Europe,[8] reflecting greater hidden costs from these 'out of sight and out of mind' issues, with the World Bank estimating in 1990 that the long-term loss to Nigeria from environmental degradation also stood at about US$5 billion annually or the equivalent of the nation's annual budget.[9]

A surprising number of countries now not only exploit but depend upon non-renewable 'fossil' water resources, which may be up to tens of thousands of years old. Unwisely, yet inexorably, the water table is depressed as pumping bills spiral. The Nubian sandstone aquifer beneath the Sahara desert is one of the largest bodies of fresh water on the planet, the remnants of pre-Ice Age swamp up to six thousand years ago but now retreated to about 490 metres (1,600 feet) down below ground. This resource is being tapped by Libya to offset saline intrusion and over-pumping of groundwater in the coastal strip. Fossil water is increasingly seen not as a backstop but as a fully exploitable resource, from Australia to Libya, South America, China, Jordan, South Africa, Taiwan and also Saudi Arabia, which derives 90 per cent of its water from such aquifers. Sixty per cent of India's irrigation water is pumped from below ground, with no confident estimate of how much of this is non-renewable or causing problems elsewhere in drainage basins. Long-term water strategies founded on non-renewable resources clearly guarantee profound future problems.

Pollution from agriculture, industrial and municipal sewage, and salinization from irrigation have also reduced the availability of clean fresh surface waters, increasing dependency upon vulnerable and often declining groundwater reserves. For example, some 40 per cent of Kuwait's formerly huge groundwater reserves are not only polluted but permanently unfit for drinking as a result of Iraqi forces setting fire to oil wells at the surface during the Gulf War of 1991.

Therefore, though often implicitly assumed a boundless resource, groundwater is in fact a vulnerable, limited and often non-renewable resource, over-exploitation of which can only deepen societal vulnerability. The World Commission on Dams concludes that

> Not only surface water is under pressure. The growing rate of extraction of freshwater from rivers and lakes is matched by increasing extraction of ground water, with many aquifers now seriously depleted. The volume of ground water withdrawal, primarily for irrigation but also for municipal and industrial use, exceeds long-term recharge rates. In many parts of India, Pakistan and China, the water table is sinking at the rate of one to two metres a year.[10]

Without adequate recharge and a management regime sensitive to the balance of recharge and withdrawal, the exploitation of groundwater is at best a 'sticking plaster' and at worst an investment in future crisis. For these and other reasons, we need to become not only more efficient in the ways we use water across its whole cycle but also more measured in the rate at which that we extract it and how we explore and protect alternative sources.

The United Nations characterizes countries with limited availability of water as water-stressed or water-scarce, depending on the amount of renewable water available. Water-stressed countries have fewer than 1,700 cubic metres of water available per person per year, such that water is often temporarily unavailable at particular locations. This necessitates difficult choices about allocation of available water between personal consumption, agriculture and industry while also maintaining water-dependent ecosystems. Water-scarce countries have fewer than 1,000 cubic metres per year, often insufficient to provide adequate food and economic development and to avoid environmental difficulties. According to statistics from ICOLD (the International Commission on Large Dams), 2.3 billion people currently live in river basins that are at least water-stressed, 1.7 billion live in basins where scarcity conditions prevail, and by 2025 these numbers are projected to be 3.5 billion and 2.4 billion respectively. A UNEP estimate in 2006 suggested that about 1.1 billion people across the planet lack access to clean drinking water. Lack of sanitation is a major public health problem for about 40 per cent of the world's population, resulting in thousands of avoidable deaths each day and the debilitation of many more people. As world population continues to grow at an annual rate of 1.3 per cent or 77.3 million per year, this can only get worse under current water demand projections. By 2025, 2 billion people will be living in parts of the world chronically short of water on current trends; climate change can only compound the situation. This is why access to clean water and sanitation is such a significant component of the UN's Millennium Development Goals.[11]

Working with the flow

Ecosystem services are significant in highlighting the many dimensions of the natural world beyond mere utilitarian value for the generation of quick profit. They thereby challenge the legacy worldview, formed during a bygone industrial age, that 'nature' is a largely boundless resource to be tapped in the name of 'progress'. Ecosystem services systematize the many types of benefits that people derive from ecosystems, and the diversity of stakeholders and value systems affected by the way ecosystems are managed.

By bringing these different aspects of societal dependency, including the needs of future generations, into a common framework of understanding and decision support, ecosystem services go beyond a mere pedagogic or management tool. They usher in a new politics reflecting, and potentially respecting, the rights of all in society in the sharing and management of common ecosystem resources, and supporting insight about 'feedback from the future' of the wider consequences of decisions and actions.

Notwithstanding a dense legacy of vested interests, anachronistic legislation and ingrained habits and expectations, this broader world-view, and hopefully in time the new politics that it illuminates, may just be a fulcrum around which equity and sustainability enter the mainstream of societal concerns.

Shifting hydropolitics

The post-apartheid democratic government of South Africa was quick to recognize that the way water and other natural assets are shared in an arid nation was the means by which societal transition, respecting the rights of all, would be achieved. This world-view frames water not just as a physical good, but as the lifeblood of ecosystems supporting wildlife, fertile soils and a wealth of local traditions and livelihoods. A decade before, Uganda had become the first nation on Earth to embed sustainable development as a driving principle of governance, and to institute as a key element of this a National Wetland Programme recognizing the many societal benefits flowing from its productive yet dwindling water-dependent ecosystems. The USA too, from the late 1980s and into the early 1990s, began to recognize the important functions of wetland systems and the need to delineate and conserve them for the benefit of ecosystem services and their role in the quality, hydrology and ecology of the wider water environment.[12] Australia too began in an institutional sense to factor the importance of wetland systems as central to protection of water resources across the continent into its thinking from the late 1990s.[13] Europe placed the 'good ecological status' of all of its water resources centrally into policy and regulation following publication in 2000 of the EU Water Framework Directive, which integrated and superseded a fragmented set of legislation covering aspects of the quality, utility and wildlife of the water environment.[14]

Respect for water, not as a dammed, piped and tapped commodity but as a natural cycle sustaining living landscapes, is fundamental to the long-term viability of governance for all in society. As Uganda had concluded in the late 1980s, it is indeed a central plank in the politics of sustainability. It will be ever more so in a climate-changed, more densely populated and resource-constrained world. The new politics must necessarily work with the flow of water through landscapes and ecosystems, and also the flow of societal needs, reflecting the ways that all people use or access water.

The era of the dam as uncontested icon of progress in the modern age is therefore long gone in many parts of the world. A myopic perspective of nature purely as a boundlessly exploitable economic resource needs to be challenged for the continued well-being of ecosystems and human livelihoods. Dam design and operation have undoubtedly moved with the times, with progress towards offsetting some environmental and social impacts as well as a transition towards engaging broader constituencies of stakeholders in their management. However, dam-related decisions worldwide do not yet fully reflect the fact that large dams do not so much modify ecosystems as represent a wholesale replacement of one set of ecological services with another. Meanwhile, other industrializing countries are, rather depressingly, seeing the same rush for status and the yoking of natural resources that has been the cause of so much unintended harm to ecosystems, their services and the diverse communities dependent upon them.

It is for this reason that this section of the book shifts attention to alternative means that can help rethink the management of water in the landscape to help support diverse human livelihoods on a more equitable, sustainable and efficient basis. Some of these techniques are novel. Many more are traditional and/or rediscoveries of ancient techniques adapted to sustainable yield and use in often harsh environments. Many more technical innovations are yet to be innovated or rediscovered. Some are of highly localized value. None is a universal panacea. However, all can constitute jigsaw pieces that may be helpful in uplifting and sustaining livelihoods adapted to their niche in our ever more populated landscape. All rest upon a less intrusive, and sometimes a restorative, approach to ecosystems as the basis for supporting human livelihoods. None wholly obviates the need for dams and heavy engineering where they support cities, but all can deliver real human benefits and even serve to prolong the life and enhance the value of engineered infrastructure.

A wide diversity of authors – including, for example, Peter Gleick,[15] Ian Calder,[16] Fred Pearce,[17] Constance Hunt,[18] Mark Everard[19] and many others – have written about the importance of shifting towards ecosystem-centred thinking in the management of water and other crucial ecosystem resources. As we have seen, the 'ecosystem approach' emerged in the late twentieth century as a policy response emphasizing the importance of placing ecosystems and their services at the centre of decision-making. Championed initially by the Convention on Biological Diversity[20] and the UN, increasing numbers of national governments round the world are recognizing it as a powerful means to develop more sustainable practices that help halt the precipitous decline in supportive ecosystems. We will touch upon instances of how this ecosystem-centred thinking has already influenced policy shifts in our relationship with fresh water.

Peter Gleick, a prominent critic of the assumptions of the developed world about dependence on 'big engineering' solutions to water supply, emphasizes instead the efficacy of small and local schemes, which may offer more appropriate and sustainable solutions to addressing local needs. Gleick sums this up eloquently as a 'soft path' towards water management solutions worldwide, highlighting many instances of how big engineering schemes often create more environmental, economic and social problems than they solve.[21] Gleick, along with many commentators, points out that the challenge is not that we are running out of water but that the ways we manage it are often inappropriate. Echoing this sentiment, Fred Pearce, another vocal and cogent champion of more sustainable approaches to water management, says that, 'Water is the ultimate renewable resource. We never destroy water. It always comes back in the rains. Our problem is not that we are running out of water. It is one of mismanagement – made worse by our interfering with the predictability of the water cycle through our influence on climate.'[22] Mark Everard adds that

> ... water and the other vital resources ... are inescapably our common foundation and legacy. Rather than concern ourselves merely with shared grazing, our preoccupation today needs to be with sharing of the 'common' of the vitality and productivity of the Earth's entire biosphere. This is both the sole common habitat for all of humanity and the wellspring of our collective future. Our busy, populous human lives have already reached out to the ends of the Earth and are threatening tangibly to consume the vital resources that underwrite both its and our prospects for the future.[23]

Underpinning established presumptions in favour of heavy engineering approaches to water management is the conception, seen already in case studies reviewed in this book, that value is ascribed only to water that is withdrawn from the environment. However, many people around the world use or depend on water not as a piped and treated product but as it moves through the ecosystem. Natural flows of water support their harvesting, cropping, stock management, domestic and other uses. Thus, livelihoods are matched to the supportive capacities of ecosystems without recourse to Westernized, water-thirsty lifestyles that depend upon industrial water supply infrastructure with its associated economic drivers. Sustainability, for many of us who share this world, may revolve not so much around an agenda defined by mega-engineering, and frequently fostered by development aid funding in which consultancies offer engineering 'solutions', but one instead with people and ecosystems at its heart.

Neither is this a purely rural or developing world concern. Even for those instances where heavy hydrological engineering may be essential to serve urban and other geographically concentrated demands, the ecosystem- and people-centred approach can add longevity and value to necessary infrastructure only by better controlling sediment, nutrient and other pollutant inputs, as well as contributing to more dependable flows and reducing flood risks through hydrological buffering. In all situations, we must avoid blinding ourselves to preconceived or ideologically driven water resource solutions. All types of solution may have a role in a technology mix in which the resilience of supportive ecosystems and people constitutes the longer-term focus.

Flowing down a new channel

The following chapters explore alternative approaches to water management serving different aspects of human interaction with the water cycle. These include ecosystem-based approaches to landscape-scale management, catchment production and storage, and water consumption and use, presenting wider options and broader ways of thinking considered subsequently in terms of the flow of water through society and the role of markets before we then turn to nature's water infrastructure.

Of course, the water cycle constitutes a contiguous whole that we fragment at our peril through management and other interactions, so it is necessary also to consider different conceptual frameworks and decision-support tools to shape a more sustainable form of hydro-politics: we will turn to this in the third part of this book.

10 | Managing water at landscape scale

One of the fundamental requirements for socio-economic development throughout the world is access to adequate clean water and energy. Part of the purpose of dams is to contribute towards fulfilling both, including their role in food production, accommodating variations in the water cycle to regulate river levels and diverting water to match demand. However, this does presume that everyone in the world requires piped and wired solutions, or that the world has enough material resources from which to make those pipes and wires. For many, perhaps the overwhelming majority in global society, 'heavy engineering' solutions may be far less appropriate. What matters is the way water moves through landscapes to enable growth of crops, support fisheries and other resources, and becomes available for a variety of direct human uses close to settlements.

Thinking of the benefits of water fluxes through the landscape, rather than constrained in reservoirs and conveyed in pipes, is a rather different way of thinking about the management of water to meet the diverse needs of people. From this perspective, it becomes apparent that water 'used' by ecosystems is not 'lost' to humanity, but rather supports natural processes beneficial to people, including soil formation, nutrient cycling, support for wildlife including fisheries, and indeed water purification and storage. Even when water is 'lost' to the atmosphere, it will return as rainfall, and when 'lost' to sea it will have supported important estuarine nursery areas for fish, birds and other wildlife as well as conveying nutrients and other important constituents to coastal seas. The need for integration in management of inherently integrated systems leads various authors to argue that water management needs to be reconceptualized as 'land and water management',[1] with increasing integration of atmospheric management[2] and the indivisibility of water management from ethics.[3] The various models of water management developed to address these needs and the potential conflicts between land and water users form the substance of this chapter.

Catchment management

Competing uses of water resources, including abstraction, diversion, navigation, appropriation for power, food production, waste dilution, recreational uses and a host of other water uses in an age of rising population, give rise to increasingly complex conflicts. As the body of management interventions evolved in response to localized acute problems – pollution abatement, flood defence, abstraction management and so forth – it is unsurprising that they were initially poorly integrated. However, from the latter quarter of the twentieth century, the concept of catchment management arose to address increasing contention over different facets of the water environment. Within the context of fresh waters, the drainage basins of rivers force an integrated approach since they touch upon all aspects of human activities, cross geopolitical boundaries and interact with both terrestrial and marine ecosystems. Consequently, integrated management initiatives have come more frequently from the aquatic than from the terrestrial perspective.

The underlying principle of catchment management is to take a whole-catchment approach that explores and better accounts for the complex interaction of variables and interests across drainage basins, which are acknowledged as fully interdependent. This is a logical and intuitively appealing concept, acknowledging that the many different uses of finite water resources are interdependent not merely with each other but also with the character, functioning and integrity of the catchments of which they are part and the societies that they support and with which they otherwise interact.

However, realization of grand ideals in the messiness of the 'real world' has been, at best, mixed. True integrated science and practice involves processes of participative decision-making, not merely the assembly of collections of data joined only by the staples that hold the catchment plan together. Appropriate methods are essential for the integration of topics and collaboration of different sector interests.[4]

Integrated Water Resource Management

Integrated Water Resource Management (IWRM) builds upon the principles of catchment management but takes them to another level, building in principles of equity, sustainability and, implicitly, efficiency and the co-creation of sustainable solutions. IWRM is thus implicitly synonymous with the sustainable development of catchment systems, taking account of the interdependencies of ecosystems, people and their activities. Over the past several decades, IWRM has become the dominant water management paradigm globally.[5] International consensus on modern approaches to IWRM was substantially achieved under the four principles of the *Dublin statement on water and sustainable develop-*

Box 10.1 The four guiding 'Dublin Principles' for IWRM[6]

Principle No. 1: Fresh water is a finite and vulnerable resource, essential to sustain life, development and the environment

Since water sustains life, effective management of water resources demands a holistic approach, linking social and economic development with protection of natural ecosystems. Effective management links land and water uses across the whole of a catchment area or groundwater aquifer.

Principle No. 2: Water development and management should be based on a participatory approach, involving users, planners and policy-makers at all levels

The participatory approach involves raising awareness of the importance of water among policy-makers and the general public. It means that decisions are taken at the lowest appropriate level, with full public consultation and involvement of users in the planning and implementation of water projects.

Principle No. 3: Women play a central part in the provision, management and safeguarding of water

Women play a pivotal role as providers and users of water and guardians of the living environment, requiring positive policies to address women's specific needs and to equip and empower them to participate at all levels in water resources programmes.

Principle No. 4: Water has an economic value in all its competing uses and should be recognized as an economic good

Within this principle, it is vital to recognize first the basic right of all human beings to have access to clean water and sanitation at an affordable price. Past failure to recognize the economic value of water has led to wasteful and environmentally damaging uses of the resource. Managing water as an economic good is an important way of achieving efficient and equitable use, and of encouraging conservation and protection of water resources.

ment, developed in the run-up to the Rio de Janiero 'Earth Summit' (reproduced in Box 10.1). These were agreed at the International Conference on Water and the Environment,[7] with a broad international consensus about the importance of adopting an IWRM approach to water policy and practice achieved at the Global Water Partnership forum.[8] The *Dublin statement* recognizes that water resources and quality are mediated through catchments that function as integrated ecosystems, including interdependencies between land and surface and groundwater resources. It also acknowledges that environmental, social and economic processes are intimately interrelated, and that the engagement of multiple stakeholders in water management is required to develop better understanding, build ownership and ensure effective implementation.

IWRM rests upon understanding the character and functioning of catchments and the capacity for landscape units to intercept, store and purify water across the drainage basin. This necessarily constitutes the basis for monitoring and adapting water usage to bring exploitation into balance with the needs of the environment and those with whom it is shared. Co-creation of management strategies in catchments, involving all in society who have legitimate needs, is therefore central to IWRM, replacing top-down 'command and control' systems of environmental management imposed by the politically and often economically powerful, supported by a technical elite. This also reflects the fact that human pressures, modifications and aspirations for rivers and connected landscapes mean that the catchment is as much a social construct as a biophysical one.[9] Co-created agreements between diverse stakeholders are essential to enduring management that is accepted as reflective of the needs and realistic aspirations of all, balancing society's legitimate demands while maintaining essential ecological services and their associated benefits. IWRM is thus more than an integration of different considerations about the catchment, but instead a framework for participation in governance to promote equity and well-being for all in the context of the water resources that support them.

IWRM principles are becoming more widely appreciated and implemented around the world, including their embedding within legislation such as the European Water Framework Directive, the Australian State of Victoria's Catchment and Land Protection Act 1994 (the CaLP Act), South Africa's National Water Act 1998, and across the Americas.[10] Catchment management was also implemented as a new concept in Papua New Guinea in 2007, centred on the Lake Kutubu catchment, developing catchment management capacity in which stakeholder participation was seen as fundamental to the objective of protecting biological diversity and ecosystem processes while also promoting sustainable management and resource utilization. The co-creation by stakeholders of the Lake Kutubu catchment management plan was central to widespread support and subsequent uptake, leading to wider implementation of IWRM principles across the country.

We are rather better furnished with examples of what happens when we fail to make these connections. For example, a 'dead zone' now of some 17,350 square kilometres (6,700 square miles, larger than the state of Connecticut) has progressively formed in the Gulf of Mexico as a consequence of excess nutrients pouring down the Mississippi river system as a result of agriculture, maximizing one set of benefits in one locality yet hostile to wildlife and imperilling the US$ multibillion fisheries in a massive area of the distant ocean.[11]

IWRM certainly has many critics.[12] Common issues raised include, for example, that IWRM is a nebulous, catch-all concept lacking a clear 'roadmap' to implementation, and that it overplays win-win situations while downplaying trade-offs. Also, that it has a high dependence on strong and functioning institutions, and that there are no metrics to evaluate success. All of these criticisms are fair, as IWRM is indeed more a statement of aspiration and broad principles than a prescriptive solution. It does not, and certainly should not be imposed to, replace local and collaborative solutions. However, as illustrated by positive examples above, it has served as a helpful conceptual framework to address issues of concern for a number of participants.

Adaptive water resources management

Since many catchment attributes, services and interdependencies remain poorly understood, and human responses and climate change impacts are uncertain,[13] management actions can often give rise to unintended consequences. In the face of these and other uncertainties, inflexible implementation has often thwarted the best intentions of catchment management and IWRM implementation. This has led to recognition of the need for *adaptive* water resources management (AWRM). The essence of adaptive water resource management is that human involvement and ownership are required at every stage of IWRM to identify optimal outcomes and to modify management regimes towards their delivery on the basis of experience and outcomes.

Mostert[14] defines public participation as 'direct involvement of the public in decision-making', resolving three principles central to social learning: reflection on goals; reciprocity; and respect for diversity. This goes far deeper than traditional information campaigns or consultation on a few expert-derived options. Holling[15] frames adaptive management as a principle to improve environmental management through learning, adopting an action learning approach (learning by action and reflection on outcomes) in dialogue with key stakeholders sharing a common interest in their home catchment. As yet, society is grappling with the full implementation of adaptive water resource management, with all the transitions in water and land management institutions, perceived threats to vested interests, and the engagement and deliberative processes that this must entail. However, trends in attitude to environmental management already reviewed suggest that catchment management will continue to move towards increasing internalization of integrated environmental, social and economic principles.

Today, the implementation of IWRM/AWRM principles across the world remains patchy, with wide regional variation in the emphasis on the integrity of catchments, equity for the diverse communities within them, focus on water efficiency and the degree of participation of stakeholders. Ultimately, all of these elements are necessary for the identification and achievement of sustainable water resource use which respects natural limits defined by catchment functioning. Overlooking, for example, the fundamental importance of catchment functioning, upon which the delivery of diverse human benefits flows, risks undermining the 'carrying capacity' of catchments. Continuing inequities across social groups within catchments are likely to undermine social stability, resulting in unsustainable behaviours, including appropriation of a disproportionately large share of water by dominant groups of people as well as future water and land rights claims. These retrospective claims for historic abuses are materializing today in Australia, South Africa, Zimbabwe, the USA and various other parts of the world, including fuelling the ascent of Welsh nationalism, where the rights of indigenous people were formerly overridden by a politically and/or economically powerful elite. The ultimate aim is participation of all stakeholders sharing catchment resources, engaged in the co-creation of strategic solutions serving the best interests of all.

Adaptive management can not only be instituted in new management schemes, but has an important role to play in readdressing some of the unintended consequences of historic management choices. An example of this in action is seen in the Glen Canyon Dam Adaptive Management Program[16] established in 1997, which sought to mitigate at least some of the harm to the ecosystem and public enjoyment of the Colorado river in the USA, including the reach running through the Grand Canyon (a World Heritage Site). By any standards, the Glen Canyon Dam is a major structure, a concrete arch dam 220 metres (710 feet) high and 480 metres (1,560 feet) long sited across the river in northern Arizona and holding back the country's second-largest reservoir (Lake Powell), which has a volume of 3,747,000 cubic metres (4,901,000 cubic yards) and extending upstream into the state of Utah. The Glen Canyon Dam controls water resources and hydroelectric power affecting seven US states and Mexican provinces. Unintended consequences of primary concern include severe threats to rare and diminishing species such as humpback chub (*Gila cypha*) and the loss of sandbanks and other important recreational and ecological habitats as part of a wider erosion of geomorphological processes. The Adaptive Management Program was developed to establish an organization, representing the interests of all US states affected by the dam and its impacts on the Colorado river system, to change the operating regime of the dam with the objective of improving the values for which the Glen Canyon National Recreation Area and Grand Canyon National Park were formed. The primary modification has been to the way that water is released from the dam, emulating to some extent a more natural regime of flood pulses that re-creates some of the lost habitat of ecological and recreational importance. Adaptation is built into the process, with the outcomes of monitoring and additional research influencing future dam operation.

Akin to IWRM, AWRM also has its critics. However, as a process of social dialogue feeding back into improved management to achieve agreed outcomes it serves as a valuable conceptual framework, as exemplified by the Glen Canyon example.

International solutions

Where drainage basins span political boundaries, be they national or regional, there is clearly a potential for competition or conflict. However, as reviewed in Chapter 8, agreements over the sharing of water resources can not only provide a focus for peaceful negotiation but have often served as a basis for healing of conflicts, maintaining peace and securing resources between nations.

A number of examples of collaboration to achieve better outcomes than competitive exploitation are found across all continents, including Africa. In central Africa, the Songwe River Transboundary Catchment Management project is a component of a broader ecosystem approach towards the conservation and sustainable utilization of the resources of Lake Nyasa (also known as Lake Malawi or Niassa), which supports the needs of some 1.6 million lakeshore inhabitants in the riparian states of Malawi, Mozambique and Tanzania. Since 1998, the WWF Southern Africa Regional Programme Office (SARPO) has supported national and regional consultative workshops with various stakeholders in the three countries to try to establish a common approach of sustainable management of the Lake Nyasa basin, responding to threats including nutrient and sediment loadings into the lake that have increased by 50 per cent within a century. The Songwe river catchment was identified as accounting for the greatest inputs of these sediments, leading to instigation of the Songwe River Transboundary Management Project as a collaborative IWRM programme involving forestry, water, agriculture, fisheries, tourism, local government, local communities, the private sector and relevant NGOs from Malawi and Tanzania to protect the lake basin's natural resources and those dependent upon them. In West Africa, a partnership of national and international organizations has been initiated to promote international cooperation between Burkina Faso and Ghana around sustainable water management of the Volta basin.[17] In the Lake Tanganyika basin, collaborative working between research institutes and riparian states (Burundi, Congo and Tanzania) has established common goals, developed specific actions and established the Lake Tanganyika Authority for the sustainable management of the lake's water resources.[18]

Opportunities and needs

India's rivers are of huge importance to the beliefs and livelihoods of its billion and more people, yet suffer substantial problems related to over-exploitation by competing uses. A chronic lack of integrated catchment management exacerbates these problems, particularly given the disproportionate political power of states compared to the federal government, fuelling competition and not infrequent conflicts over sharing of water where major rivers cross state boundaries. As India rapidly industrializes, with the emergence of a new, affluent middle class and changes to traditional ways of life across society, pressures mount daily on river systems such as the great rivers of the Deccan Peninsula (the Krishna, the Godavari and the Cauvery) and to the north in the Ganges, Narmada, Mahanadi and Brahmaputra systems. Outmoded, utilitarian views of water are far from dead in India, with many new proposals for dam and water transfer schemes threatening the vitality of its water systems. Equally, levels of urban and industrial pollution are rising sharply with economic prosperity, together with spiralling demand for energy and water. This occurs at a time of intensifying pressure for development within areas containing habitat critical for water capture, storage and purification, significantly in the narrow coastal mountain range of the Western Ghats adjacent to the Arabian Sea coast which is critical for intercepting virtually all of the monsoon rains feeding all the Deccan river systems. Piecemeal exploitation undertaken with regard only for local advantage and not the integrity of the whole system, exacerbated by changing climate and rising population, threatens the integrity of entire river systems and the millions of livelihoods dependent on them.

The weight of political and economic power in state governments in India, reinforced by its polarization across social classes and religious castes, today erects significant obstacles to true catchment-scale vision, public participation and co-creation of catchment management strategies targeted at sustainable and equitable outcomes. The need for integrated water resource management across India is starkly apparent as all of society, regardless of politics, state identity, income and caste, is codependent upon the supportive capacities of river catchments, and people will ultimately prosper or wither together with the fate of the core resources upon which they depend.

India is far from alone in failing to fully embrace the principles and practice of IWRM. For example, a failure to reverse flawed historic water management decisions in the Aral Sea region, with its associated devastating social, economic and environmental consequences, suggests that strategic and integrated planning is not a regional priority. Equally, the massive diversion of water from China's southern monsoon rivers to the over-exploited 'breadbasket' and industrial heartland to the north of the country suggests a regime predicated upon promoting only certain aspects of the national economy to the detriment of entire drainage basins and their influence on regional character, climate, habitat maintenance and livelihoods.

As a resolution stemming from the World Conservation Congress at its 4th Session in Barcelona, Spain, in October 2008, the United Nations urged governments that have not already done so to keep their promise to adopt IWRM. This commitment under the Johannesburg Declarations signed at the 2002 UN World Summit on Sustainable Development includes adopting a strategy for the implementation of IWRM. Within this are required measures to protect and conserve ecosystems that produce water, to create institutional frameworks that improve water governance, and to incorporate IWRM's implicit concept of sustainability into water regulations.[19] This, the UN resolution continues, requires the design and implementation of economic instruments to promote the conservation of ecosystems that produce and protect water, and to inform civil society about the new water culture through environmental education programmes.

A water vision for South Africa

The emergence of South Africa from an oppressive regime into democratic government in 1994 provided for it a 'clean slate' from which to reassess much of its legislation with the long-term intention of achieving a fair and sustainable society. In this semi-arid and water-limited nation, equitable, adequate and sustainable access to fresh water is a pressing issue. Indeed, the sharing of scarce water is, in many ways, the vehicle of transfer of power and access to resources from the white minority under apartheid rule into the hands of all people. This is a particular challenge in a nation comprising 49 million people, where 59 per cent of the water used nationally is for irrigation. Most of this irrigation is undertaken by the historic owners of land and abstraction rights. The complexity of the situation is compounded by many international agreements regarding river flows to and from the neighbouring countries of Swaziland, Lesotho, Mozambique, Zimbabwe and Namibia.

The old apartheid laws were iniquitous with respect to water, land and in many other respects. From the 1600s, waves of European colonizers incrementally appropriated South Africa's scarce water resources to create fertile farmlands and industrial enterprises in an otherwise arid landscape. Exclusive access to water was progressively cemented in legislation, such as the Irrigation Act of 1912, which stated that water constituted the sole property of the owner of the land on which it rose and that 'He can do whatsoever he pleases with it and neither the owners of lower-lying land nor even the public can claim to be entitled to make any use at all of that water'. Differential access to water was a key factor deepening social divisions during the apartheid era, under which white-only elections, jobs, land and, effectively, access to water were progressively legalized. By the time apartheid was dismantled in 1994, clean, potable water was being piped into the homes and farms of virtually all five million white South Africans, while approximately half of the nation's black population of some thirty-five million lacked access to safe water.

In the immediate post-apartheid era, the incoming democratic government of South Africa instituted a period of dialogue with the South African public, initiated by the Department for Water Affairs and Forestry (DWAF), on the selection of fundamental principles to underpin new legislation. The outcome of this first phase was the emergence of twenty-eight principles that collectively served as informal 'terms of reference' for the drafting panel of the National Water Act 1998 (Act 36 of 1998, or the NWA).[20]

The primary three principles driving the NWA are those of equity, sustainability and efficiency. These broader principles cover diverse issues from empowerment of historically marginalized, mainly black communities, to catchment-scale thinking, proceeding by consensus, and devolution of decision-making. Principle 23 is particularly helpful in this latter regard, stating that 'the responsibility for the development, apportionment and management of available water resources shall, where possible and appropriate, be delegated to a catchment or regional level in such a manner as to enable interested parties to participate'. This principle of subsidiarity is largely behind the division of South Africa into Water Management Areas (WMAs), each comprising agglomerations of catchments in major drainage basins. While some duties remain with central government, such as the setting up of strategic reserves to support basic human needs, the vitality of river ecosystems, water to service international agreements, and for 'strategic needs', stakeholders are central to the way that the remaining water is shared in their catchment. New Catchment Management Agencies (CMAs) are scheduled to be formed to oversee the implementation of multi-catchment IWRM in the WMAs, the NWA specifically requiring delegation of management and regulatory powers and duties from the minister down to emerging CMAs. To achieve this significant transformation, DWAF's 2007 *Catchment Management Strategy Guidelines*[21] emphasize the need for a strategic adaptive management approach supported by learning principles underpinning the flexible and adaptive implementation of IWRM.

The NWA's bold intent supplants historic rights and assumptions about water, introducing a new set of principles to be achieved by co-creation and agreement upon novel management devolved from central government. Nowhere else in the world has such a brave departure been undertaken in such a sweeping manner, no doubt impelled by the 'clean slate' of radical democratic reform. Constraints upon the necessary financial and expert resources to achieve catchment-scale vision and true public participation present serious challenges to the effective implementation and discharge of the responsibilities of the CMAs, but support from the international community is forthcoming to promote this global 'live experiment' in the implementation of IWRM/AWRM in the modern world.

Watering our future

There is, then, evolving awareness about the need to manage humanity's relationship with water systems, competing water users and resilience for the future. This includes the inseparability of the management of water, landscapes, food production and people. Management of landscapes explicitly to increase recharge, retention and reuse of water is essential for food security as an integral element of 'green growth'.[22]

Nevertheless, there remains a great deal of resistance to change, much driven by vested interests and the lack of political courage to take proportionate action to safeguard the future, and this despite emerging understanding of the systemic interactions between different facets and beneficiaries of aquatic and catchment ecosystems. Food production systems are a classic example, post-Second World War perspectives of which led to maximization of provisioning benefits (food, fibre and timber) while inadvertently degrading water resources, biodiversity, nutrient cycling and the many other benefits provided by the functions of ecosystems. A growing body of work is exploring ways in which food production and other water management priorities can be brought into greater harmony.[23] This depends on better understanding of ecological landscape processes and of appropriate valuation of their many benefits to society beyond food production. Recognition and valuation of wetland processes in particular, addressed in a human-centred way acknowledging the many supportive services they provide, may herald a new paradigm of water and resource management.[24]

We are therefore in transition, starkly evident in the South African context but no less profound elsewhere in the world, as we seek governance systems and ways of thinking about water that are appropriate to development needs in the third millennium AD. Without it, we may not escape this millennium without major catastrophe.

Integrated constructed wetlands: reanimating the Anne Valley

Inspiring examples of working with natural processes are to be found in the landscape of southern Ireland. In the Anne Valley in County Waterford, Ireland, trout dimple the main channel and the fringing pools, sticklebacks shoal in quiet backwaters and waterways, and abundant marginal wetlands are profuse with water plants, eels, a variety of birdlife, and a returning population of otters. Sea trout and salmon too have now returned after decades of absence, running the seven or so miles of main river and its many tributaries to complete their life cycles. Above the sea wall, mullet drift upriver through the defunct tidal flap into muddy creeks and the roots of phragmites beds, venturing upstream sometimes as far as the crag upon which sit the remains of Dunhill Castle. A walkable and driveable track along much of the valley floor provides access for working farmers and enjoyment for walkers.

However, a quarter-century before, the Anne Valley had been wicked dry by arterial drainage, like so much of the southern Irish landscape, and otherwise converted by intensification of agriculture, commercial forestry and peat harvesting that so profoundly altered the character of extensive Irish wetland landscapes.[25] Arterial drainage had been undertaken with the best of agricultural development intentions, but also in part owing to poor understanding of the true value of wetlands and, indeed, the perception of them as 'waste places' representing threats such as breeding grounds of diseases,[26] sources of flooding[27] or perennially fertile areas resilient to perpetual agricultural production.[28] It has been suggested that the disconnects which exist between scientists, policy-makers and a broader society may also result from epistemological failures and a broader structural incongruence between markets and the environment.[29]

The main Anne Valley river channels, if that was by then an accurate descriptor, had been straightened to rush water seawards, encroached by silt and vegetation to become little more than straight ditches of stagnant water that could, in places, be easily stepped across with dry feet. Little valued by people nor inhabited by wetland life, the worth of the farmed landscape had become questionable with the worst excesses of intensification fouling run-off in wet weather and putting already struggling farm businesses at constant risk of crippling prosecution. The landscape that the older farmers grew up in had been lost to progress, seemingly for ever, along with the fish and fishing, wildlife and beauty of the landscape. The restoration of the Anne Valley started in 1988, with the development of the concept and practice of what is now termed integrated constructed wetlands (ICWs).

The use of constructed wetlands is of course not new. We meet them in the pages of this book and elsewhere in the context of SuDS (sustainable drainage systems, also variously known as WSUD and 'source control').[30] We see wetlands also included as elements of 'green infrastructure',[31] polishing reedbeds tacked on to the end of conventional waste water treatment plant,[32] as a means to buffer water-vectored nutrients,[33] and other man-made systems intended to boost biodiversity. Wetlands have also been used as managed washlands and other techniques for working with natural processes for flood risk management,[34] as contributors to food production systems within developed and developing countries,[35] and increasingly as essential components in climate change adaptation and mitigation strategies.[36]

However, the ICW concept takes this to a whole new level, the 'I' (for 'integrated') of 'ICW' including 'landscape fit' to harmonize the systems within natural, aesthetic and working landscapes. ICWs are in essence cascades of shallow wetland cells, each heavily vegetated with emergent plants and no more than 200 millimetres deep and generally far closer to 100 millimetres when wetted. These aerobic wetland systems almost totally eliminate loadings of organic matter, ammonium and faecal microbes. However, it is in practice difficult to monitor the final output all year round as, for much of the time, the evapotranspiration and interception of plants in the wetland cells mean that there are no emissions from the final ICW cells into streams winding down to the Anne Valley. ICWs also constitute aesthetically pleasing amenity, angling and birdwatching resources (cultural ecosystem services) as well as intercepting and attenuating silt and nutrients from point sources (farmyards, septic tank pollution, etc.) and run-off from fields and tributaries that coincidentally sequester carbon, create microclimates, hold water in the system and regulate flooding downstream (regulatory services). ICW wetland cells also create dynamic habitat for wildlife and places where nutrient cycling and soil formation occur (supporting services), as well as maintaining genetic stock of local species and supporting farm profitability through better management of pollution and other net costs (provisioning services).

I undertook a research visit in late 2011 to see the sixteen farm or village waste water treatment ICWs in the Anne Valley. These comprise mainly whole-farm-scale systems. One ICW treats effluent from the community-owned Dunhill Ecopark, comprising a community centre, a number of small business units, including a food processing company, and collectively employing just over one hundred people, and the drainage from two large Gaelic football fields, the business centre's extensive roof area and its curtilage, including car park, and a greenhouse unit. Perhaps surprisingly, the Dunhill Ecopark ICW is biodiversity-rich, with not only a profuse and ever-changing assemblage of vegetation but also warblers in the summer, waders in the winter, among a variety of other birds, dragonflies and other organisms. Furthermore, this is not a system fenced off as a hazard; it is indeed completely unfenced and the bunds separating the cells are all accessible and walkable, the whole system constituting a well-used and appreciated community asset enjoyed not merely by workers on their breaks but also by families taking picnics and by dog-walkers and birdwatchers, meeting further the wishes and needs of the local community that owns it. Another ICW system in the Anne Valley intercepts the output from a septic tank taking the sewage from 250 or so people in the nearby village of Dunhill. Many other ICWs treat farmyard-soiled water, including milking parlour wash water, animal-soiled yards and roofs.

On this trip, I encountered a kaleidoscope of attitudes to ICWs and their many simultaneous benefits when surveying a number of local farmers, regulators and residents in the Anne Valley, as well as Jimmy Deenihan, TD (the Minister for Arts, Heritage and the Gaeltacht), Éamon de Buitléar (renowned wildlife film-maker who has championed the ICW concept since its inception), a number of directors of the Irish EPA (Environment Protection Agency), and various regulatory and planning staff within Waterford County Council. Some of the things said to me about the ICWs were that, 'There are direct farming benefits', 'people don't want to visit treatment works but they do want to go to ICWs', 'driven by economics: finding a solution that was cost effective, environmental and practical'. Also that they can 'mitigate clear felling impacts of forestry', 'It has added amenity value to those villages' and that 'They treat water very effectively and very economically and they've wider environmental benefits providing aquatic ecosystems'. The comments continued with 'They are very educational; we have school visits', 'There is no energy required [for treatment]', 'They are absorbing CO_2'. And some of the farmers were happy to tell me that 'It sorts itself out; there's no maintenance beyond the extensions we've made to the system', 'It is labour-saving', 'I like the ducks!' and 'I can sleep at night [without fear of prosecution]'.[37] This wide support, ranging from self-interest to community advantages as well as wider global environmental concerns, highlights how considered design of ICWs in landscape context delivers not merely physical and biological reconnections but also real value to the diversity of local people and livelihoods which are integral to these living landscapes.

These successes are far from merely anecdotal, but have been tested through in excess of thirty peer-reviewed scientific studies spanning delivery of multiple ecosystem services,[38] their efficacy in the treatment of contaminated water in agricultural landscapes with low environmental impact and ecological gains,[39] cost-effectiveness in treatment of this waste water,[40] treatment of domestic sewage[41] and livestock waste water[42] and enhancing wetland biodiversity.[43] Lysimeters (experimental dip wells) tap into groundwater beneath these ICW cells, confirming no significant percolation of contaminants through the cell beds which, as is generally the case in wetland systems, become self-sealing. The shallow depth and extensive vegetation are important because these are predominantly aerobic systems, not only processing ammonia and organic wastes far faster than anaerobic processes found in wetlands with deeper water but also lessening associated methane and odour generation problems.

A larger number of much smaller ICWs intercept potentially sediment- and pollutant-burdened streams and surface run-off where farmed hill slopes meet the valley bottom, creating trout-rich habitats that also 'polish' and slow down and retain water before it enters the main stream. Indeed, the final 'polishing' cells of many of the larger farm-scale 'treatment' systems serve as trout ponds, some providing an additional revenue stream for the farmers and around which I found plenty of evidence of otter activity. Plantings of alder, ash and other stands of wetland-tolerant trees provide additional landscape, microclimate and habitat functions around the smaller valley-bottom ICWs, providing wildlife corridors to reconnect remnant parcels of ancient woodland and newer plantations of larch, pine and other drier-ground species up the hill slope. The net impact on restoring landscape aesthetics is striking and much appreciated by local people.

All of this has been achieved through application of principles of restoration ecology, integrating control of point and diffuse sources in the agriculturally dominated catchment landscape with other requirements to achieve multiple beneficial services.[44]

The integration of large treatment-oriented ICWs with the smaller interception systems in the valley bottom is also important for optimizing benefits for ecology, hydrology, quality, aesthetics and amenity. This has bolstered community support, connecting people with the management of water and land by addressing social, economic and environmental concerns, including enhancement of the efficacy of this predominantly farmed, economic landscape. 'Reanimation' is a term now often used to describe the extensive and dramatic regeneration of much of the Anne Valley, retaining rather than rapidly shedding water and reintegrating the multiple, beneficial functions of the formerly widespread wetlands that had been eliminated from the landscape at huge and largely uncounted ecological, social and economic costs.

While an exemplar, the Anne Valley Project does not stand alone. Another major ICW system treats leachate from a partially unsealed former landfill site in Dungarvan, also in County Waterford, in which, remarkably, I found dense stands of opposite-leaved pondweed (*Groenlandia densa*), a scarce *Red Data Book* species that is explicitly protected under Ireland's Flora Protection Order, 1999. Perhaps twenty other ICW systems operate across County Waterford, with further examples in Dublin city and in Counties Monaghan, Limerick, Wexford and Kerry.

A major trade-off for ICWs perceived by some regulators is that they have a greater physical land-take than many narrow-disciplinary engineered solutions. For a small farm of marginal productivity, where every scrap of land is essential to maintain profitability, this may indeed be an obstacle too far, as it may also be where geotechnical solutions to cater for unsuitable soil types are prohibitively expensive. But often, land best suited to gravity-fed cascades of ICW cells lies close to the source of yard run-off along drainage lines in the landscape that might naturally have been wetted systems, and these are often already spoiled by farmyard waste. It may also be too steep to be really productive, or perhaps waterlogged and rushed-up, and so therefore of limited value precisely because of its natural wetland character prior to drainage. Once again, 'landscape fit' helps turn marginally useful land within mosaic landscapes into functional and beneficial systems that add value rather than merely consuming land, addressing 'real world' farming problems in an economically efficient way quite aside from the many wider benefits they generate for wildlife and communities. Just two of the quotes that I heard from farmers during the 2011 research were: 'Before we installed the system, the washings were just lying there on the field and the cows wouldn't eat that grass', and 'The ICW took some land out of production, but this was marginal land so there was in fact no real loss'.[45]

ICWs were enshrined in the Irish government's design guidance within the Water Services Investment Programme 2010–2012.[46] In the press release supporting this, John Gormley, TD (the Minister for the Environment, Heritage and Local Government) stated that, 'ICWs have the potential to begin a modest reversal of these losses and to provide many of the ecosystem services of the lost natural wetlands', and that 'These are the type of solutions we must aspire to – they are natural, very good for the environment, they can assist in flood relief and the by products are also beneficial'.

It is important to acknowledge that ICWs are no panacea for all ills. However, there are seemingly limitless opportunities to deploy ICWs more widely, realizing simultaneous low-energy treatment, biodiversity, fishery, social and a stack of other integrated benefits. Yet, perhaps predictably, there remains some resistance in Ireland and elsewhere to their wider uptake despite their community acceptance, the large number of peer-reviewed scientific papers demonstrating efficacy, and explicit Irish government design guidance.

The regulatory community is hampered by discipline-by-discipline and frequently reductive traditions and legacy regulations and economic instruments. So bringing regulators along with this big and connected vision is inevitably challenging, for such is the nature of innovations that break with established norms and vested interests. It is indeed interesting that, when the benefits are large, there is greater resistance to change, perhaps because they span so many narrow fields of interest. Yet ICWs would appear to have a useful role, for example, in making progress towards the enticing yet elusive concept of 'sustainable intensification'[47] by using the potential functions of landscapes in an integrated way, in addition to additional ecosystem service, social and economic ecosystem services benefits.[48]

This type of thinking, including but also extending beyond ICWs as an intermediate technological approach, can make a major contribution to aspirations to take an ecosystem approach in policy-making and implementation. ICWs, then, offer a potent, self-beneficial jigsaw piece that may contribute to a wider transition in policy and practice, addressing water and other resource management in a truly integrated way. ICWs, along with more progressive examples of green infrastructure, SuDS/WSUD and river restoration (all addressed in greater detail later in this book), constitute exemplars of what are beginning to be termed 'systemic solutions', which exploit, restore or emulate natural processes to provide low-input, multiple ecosystem service outcome solutions.[49] It is timely that these more systemic approaches progressively supplant our patchwork of inherited, narrowly framed technical and legal 'fixes', better to address emerging understanding of the complexity and inherent interconnectivity of ecosystems and people.

Connections

Thinking of water in a truly integrated way, in terms of its interactions with landscapes, people and economic uses, as has been the case with ICWs in Ireland's Anne Valley, provides a radical 'real world' example of what is possible. Integration is the key, as water is not treated separately from all it touches – land, atmosphere, nature, people and economic activities – but as an integral element of the socio-ecological system. Technology is at an appropriate scale, tailored to fit the natural and social landscape to achieve multiple, simultaneous benefits, including the rebuilding of overall landscape resilience and wetland functioning, which is known to serve as a buffer against the effects of climate change.[50]

Neither nature nor people are set aside in favour of single-solution engineering, but are part of the processing 'machinery'. This is true integrated management of water at a landscape scale.

11 | Catchment production and storage

The production, purification and storage of water in catchments is a natural phenomenon, part of the great and renewable cycle of water on this planet, and core to many crucial ecosystem services upon which all of humanity depends. Uplands are particularly important zones within catchments for the interception of water from the atmosphere, returning it to ground level from circulation in the atmosphere after evaporation from the surface of open water, wetlands, plants and soil, and subsequent distribution and condensation in the atmosphere. The 'sponge effect' of these upland zones, together with other wetland habitats and areas in which surface waters exchange with ground-water distributed throughout catchment systems, serves the function of water storage that buffers river flows between dry and wet periods. The interaction of co-evolved living and non-living components of these ecosystems is also essential for the physico-chemical processes that purify water.

Ecosystems also slow the passage of water through landscapes, recapturing water that re-evaporates within local water cycles that, even in parched landscapes, can result in vegetated or forested gorges where streams carve down otherwise arid hillsides. Evolution has finely tuned these gully ecosystems to increase water retention and residence time within the catchment. Forest systems too, with as much as 90 per cent of the rainfall of the extensive rainforest of the Congo basin generated by the forest itself. All of these various processes within catchment systems are vital for the provision of their diverse ecosystem services, maintaining the viability of whole catchments and climatic systems and sustaining dependent human livelihoods.

Water in the landscape

Changing attitudes to water in the landscape are exemplified not merely in the way that water is harvested but also how floods are managed. The changing paradigm of flood management illuminates some broader principles pertinent to water production and storage across catchments.

Traditional flood management of rivers around the world has been based on such industrial principles and language as 'flood defence'. This stems back to a Victorian paradigm when humanity saw itself as apart from nature, charged with the task of 'taming' the dark forces of the natural world and of 'uncivilized' people in other nations. So our empire-building forebears went out to civilize the world, coincidentally annexing resources to fuel domestic industry. In so doing, they exported with them development, theological and environmental management perspectives in which nature was largely perceived as a villain and not a provider. And so, for centuries, as human populations and industrial enterprises boomed and spread out on to floodplains and other flat habitat naturally formed by the episodic overspill of water, we perceived ourselves as engaged in a perennial battle against dark forces seeking to swamp, quite literally, a technocentric model of progress. Society threw up militaristic flood banks, like fortifications to hold back warlike tribes, against periodic inundation of 'reclaimed' land by swollen rivers and coastal waters. We also often dredged the heart out of channels to turn them into little more than arteries to shoot water seawards. Of course, all of this water and its associated energy have to go somewhere. The consequence of upstream flood defence solutions was all too frequently intensified flood peaks, concentrated and filled with eroded matter, hitting downstream reaches and settlements with greater volume and intensity, exacerbating the likelihood of damage. And, of course, the drainage of floodplains for agriculture and other 'progressive' purposes has, and continues to have, the same downstream consequences. So the old model of 'fighting nature' merely concentrated natural forces elsewhere in river catchments, with the need for higher defences, deeper dredging and all manner of other practices to combat natural forces in a battle that was ultimately unwinnable.

In Europe and the USA at least, a new paradigm of 'flood risk management' is beginning to take root out of recognition of the inherent value of the hydrological functions we have strangled out of many river catchments. Investment in flood resilience through catchment-scale planning has been recognized as a critical and beneficial contribution to adaptation to climate change through such authoritative analysis as the UK's 2007 *Pitt Review: Lessons Learned from the 2007 Floods*.[1] Progressive flood risk management practices focus less on 'defence' and more on risk management, exploring how best to emulate natural processes by dispersing and retaining water within areas of catchments that are not so heavily built up. This 'new dawn' approach acknowledges catchments as functional entities, recognizing and seeking to optimize or even regenerate their natural sponge-like properties.

The transition is not an easy one, despite the evident benefits when viewed at the whole-catchment scale. After all, after centuries of environmental over-management, vested interests and expectations about protection of assumed land and riparian rights, it is hard for a farmer or other landowner to accept that low-lying riparian meadow should be 'surrendered' to flood during winter spates. After all, recent decades of agricultural subsidy have reinforced farming practices that maximize profit while wholly overlooking the natural functioning of the land and the broad range of benefits to society that accrue from protecting it. Nor do we yet have an economic system that is sympathetic to owners of land which may be critical to hydrological functioning at catchment scale, providing them with an incentive to hold back from maximizing profit through food production, as if that were the only value of the land, despite the costs incurred by the many who share the benefits of the catchment. We are certainly beginning to understand rather better that soil properties may be a crucial factor in flood prevention,[2] and that decentralized management of landscapes makes a substantial cumulative contribution to overall flood management.[3] We are thus at last taking furtive steps towards reversing historic trends, recognizing the value of flood control achieved by floodplains rather than levees.

Some areas, of course, need to have their defences maintained. For example, a city with a long history and important heritage and economic contributions probably does need to be protected from flooding, if not for good ecological reasons then for overriding cultural, safety and economic ones. So the habitat taken by the city's 'footprint' needs to be mitigated not merely for the benefit of wildlife but to restore floodwater detention, fish recruitment and a wide range of other functions that the urban infrastructure takes from nature. Thus, mitigation in this instance balances net impacts of development, seeking to replace those functions 'consumed'. Restoration or protection of critical flood storage habitat can detain floodwater that might exacerbate flood risk in the protected area. The key principles here are that, applied strategically, such mitigation can rebuild natural functioning lost through development, and that the most damaging types of development should not be permitted at all in areas important for various natural processes.

Managing the source of water

This overview of modern approaches to flood risk management illustrates that there are alternative, ecosystem-centred approaches to the sustainable management of catchment hydrology to enhance human benefits that do not depend upon cocooning human activities behind ever-higher flood walls. The way that people use not only fresh water but also the landscapes that produce it has a profound influence on the characteristics and viability of water resources. Throughout the evolution of human societies and of the land use, urban, industrial and other technologies that have underpinned it, broader consequences for water resources have generally not been a defining feature. However, in the modern era of greater environmental awareness, particularly about the role of water as a critical factor limiting development of a burgeoning human population across the globe, the need for improved stewardship of water and catchment processes across the landscape has never been greater.

Across the arid world, a wide variety of in-field rainwater harvesting methods have been developed, emulating natural water infiltration processes at field, and sometimes wider, scale. These relatively simple, 'intermediate technology' innovations replicate the principles of natural systems, some of them 'upscalable'. Tractor-driven 'mechanized basin ploughs' that create rows of basins that collect water from short rainfall events, allowing it more effectively to percolate into the soil, are a good example.[4] Further examples include contour ploughing and vegetation barriers, mulch-filled ditches, and many more land use techniques besides. A fascinating innovation to enable farming in the Sahel is seen in the *ziä* system in Burkina Faso, entailing digging basins in a staggered row in 'unused' land early in the dry season, with mounds of spoil piled downslope of the pits to help divert water into the basins.[5] As the dry season continues, wind-blown soil and organic matter are intercepted by these *ziä* basins, which are then filled with additional organic matter, including manure, plant debris and compost. This attracts termites which dig tunnels into the bottom. When the rains return in April, the streaming water collects in these basins, infiltrating down through the termite burrows. The resulting deep pockets of moisture are safe from evaporation, and families can then plant crops in the basin bed.

Modelling studies of the role of riparian and catchment land use in water quality across several European countries found positive relationships between riparian grassland and river water quality.[6] Water 'farming' through the use of grasslands to store episodic floodwater can reduce downstream flood risk and build resilience which, from an economic perspective, is preferable to the potential loss of arable or horticultural crops, with the additional benefit of less entrainment of sediment from bare soils.[7] The influence of habitat units in the landscape upon aquatic ecosystems is complex, including issues of scale, soil type, topography, climate, land use and interactions with other landscape units, all of which influence significantly the ecosystem services that they provide,[8] though local benefits may or may not automatically create benefits at large catchment scale.[9]

As population pressures have increased demands upon water resources, with modification of landscapes decreasing natural supply, compounded by the impacts of a changing climate, the value of the ecosystem services produced by critical habitat across the broader landscape has gradually become more evident. Today, the role of landscape management for ecosystem services, particularly the reliable supply and moderation of flows of water, is more than theory or aspiration and far from localized in application. This awareness of the value of land critical to water yield is in fact not entirely novel. In parts of the USA, Australia (including large areas of land around the Australian city of Sydney) and the UK, historic foresight has set aside land explicitly for its capacity to intercept, store and purify precipitation. For some of these protected zones, subsequent land use has compromised the yield of clean water, necessitating an adaptive revision in policy and practice by landowners and managers. Increasingly, land management plans, often backed up by public subsidies, have been applied across the wider, non-protected landscape to protect the quality, quantity and other aspects of water resources.

Five inspiring large-scale case studies are outlined in the following paragraphs, one in each of the world's major continents, demonstrating the benefits for water production that arise from large-scale management of landscapes.

A prominent and substantially cost-efficient American example is the New York City water supply. The Department of Environmental Protection of the City of New York delivers over 1.2 billion US gallons (4.5 billion litres) of water daily to 9 million people. While early residents drew water from local sources, urban growth necessitated accessing remote sources. In 1905, New York City identified the Catskill mountains as a prime source, constructing various reservoirs and dams throughout the Catskills through to 1928, turning in 1927 to additional sources in Delaware County. The Catskills–Delaware system, known as the Cat/Del system, was implemented in stages between 1937 and 1964, today providing New York City with the largest unfiltered surface water supply in the world. However, by the 1980s, industrial-scale agriculture and forestry, tourism, residential and industrial development were posing increasing risks to raw water quality, while increasingly stringent public health standards were coming into force. The vast cost of installing expensive filtration plant – $US4–6 billion (£2.1–3.2 billion at then-current exchange rates) in capital costs plus annual running costs of more than $US200 million (£160 million) at 1990 prices – drove city planners to think in broader terms. Cost-benefit analysis suggested that a comprehensive 'watershed protection programme' would cost substantially less than filtration. However, making this work was going to be a tough challenge. Top-down, punitive regulations had generally ended in failure elsewhere. Consequently, city planners opted to explore an urban–rural watershed protection partnership offering simultaneous benefits to city residents and communities in the Catskills and Delaware catchments managing the water-yielding landscape. This instigated a process of dialogue, mutual understanding and consensus-building between farmers and city representatives. By the end of 1991, an urban–rural watershed protection partnership had been developed, including targeted, economically efficient integrated agricultural pollution controls at individual farm business scale backed up by grants, inclusion of forestry interests, land acquisition programmes and ecologically based land management. By January 1997, the constituent parties had formalized a comprehensive Memorandum of Agreement, to which the city committed funds of approximately $US350 million (£190 million), in addition to the costs of various other initiatives in the watershed. The total cost of the watershed protection programme is approximately $US1.3 billion (£700 million), a fraction of the capital and operating costs, let alone the wider environmental impacts, of traditional filtration solutions. This truly partnership-based approach, linking rural and urban stakeholders in a mutually beneficial arrangement based on the ecosystem services provided by the land, is key to maintaining the city's pristine water quality as well as the viability of farming for the foreseeable future.

SCaMP, the Sustainable Catchment Management Programme, represents a pioneering European example. SCaMP was instigated by the British multi-utility company United Utilities, the water service provider for the north-west of England. United Utilities is a major landowner, holding 57,000 hectares (140,850 acres) of upland principally to protect the quality of water entering reservoirs and rivers but also supporting nationally significant habitats for animals and plants. SCaMP was developed in partnership with wildlife NGO the Royal Society for the Protection of Birds (RSPB). The first phase, formally funded by water service income between 2005 and 2010, entailed working with tenant farmers to alter land management practices and agreements and also undertaking additional capital works to restore upland habitat in ways that are simultaneously beneficial for water production, scarce ecosystems and agricultural production methods stabilizing farm incomes. Reinvestment of water service charges into upland restoration therefore can represent a cost-effective approach to averting the costs of increasing water treatment and potential water shortages lower in the catchment. SCaMP therefore presents a 'win-win-win' scenario for biodiversity, society and economic performance.[10] SCaMP has since become something of an exemplar for putting ecologically based concepts at the heart of investment and a more sustainable form of British water resource development. It has influenced other catchment-based water resource protection schemes in the UK (such as 'Upstream Thinking', addressed in Chapter 13) and elsewhere in the world.

An African example, the Working for Water (WfW) programme, has also demonstrated the benefits of landscape-scale, community-based integrated management. The quality and quantity of water running off South Africa's arid and semi-arid landscape has been compromised not merely by land use but also significantly by invasive alien plant species. Many alien plants, particularly trees, have far greater evaporative loss compared to native, drought-adapted species,[11] with rooting depth a key factor in depleting water recharge.[12] Numerous studies across the world assess the scale of loss of water through alien vegetation. In Australia, 'the evaporative loss of one hectare of willows is enough for about 17 households each year' and 'potentially, more than 5.5Ml/year of water could be saved per hectare if willow canopy were removed where trees stood in-stream with permanent access to water'.[13] In South Africa, the most widely accepted estimate is that invasive alien species could use 17 per cent of mean annual run-off (MAR) if left to invade, though one (albeit contested) paper claims a staggering 91 per cent reduction in MAR in the arid Namaqualand coast of the Western Cape. Clearance of invasive species from river catchments was undertaken as part of the National Water Conservation Campaign, established early in South Africa's democratic era as evidence suggested that removal of water-hungry vegetation could prove more cost effective than the construction of infrastructure such as dams or filtration plant. One of the initiatives spinning off from this Campaign was the WfW programme, an innovative scheme providing jobs for the least advantaged in society to control problematic invasive plants. WfW was established in 1995 with a budget of 25 million rand to control invading alien plants for the enhancement of water security, ecological integrity, the productive potential of land, the quality of life of marginalized sectors of society through job creation and poverty alleviation, and the economic benefits of wood, land, water and trained people. Today, WfW is one of the biggest conservation programmes in the world, with an annual budget approaching R600 million (including the KwaZulu-Natal Invasive Alien Species Programme, or KZN IASP[14]). However socially oriented WfW may be, its outcomes include conservation of a significant amount of water otherwise 'lost' to MAR. Studies to improve the targeting of removal of problem species in the most impacted places provide preliminary assessments of the costs, benefits and progress of WfW, demonstrating a considerable set of benefits associated with improved water yields[15] and additional benefits for further ecosystem services.[16]

As an Asian example, the restoration of traditional johads and associated land management practices in Rajasthan, India, demonstrates the benefits of community-based management that addresses the ways that water flows through landscapes. Excessive pumping for industry and industrial-scale farming are radically depleting groundwater in India's northern desert state of Rajasthan, exacerbated by the impacts of deforestation.[17] Running against government momentum towards industrialization, which appears to lie at the root of water resource mismanagement, Rajendhra Singh, sometimes known as 'the Rivermaker' or 'the Rainman of Rajasthan', has for many years been pursuing community-scale development work through the NGO Tarun Bharat Sangh[18] (Save the Rivers Mission). Singh's work has centred on the revival of a range of traditional water management skills, significantly including the restoration of tank systems known in Rajasthan as johads, which help local communities to help themselves attain better and more secure access to water resources. Johads, as well as other traditional landscape modifications including 'anicuts' which comprise simple mud and rubble check dams constructed across the contours of slopes to catch and conserve rainwater, provide not only a direct reserve but also significantly increasing percolation and recharge of groundwater. The revival of johads is backed up by advice on farming methods requiring little water, leaving as much as possible to recharge groundwater. Success did not come quickly or easily, with trust-building among local people presenting a key initial challenge, though a community-based approach that involves local people in their own water conservation schemes is central to success. This community-based approach has also run Singh into both legal and physical conflict with government officials driven by engineering-focused laws relating to prohibitions on stopping the flow of water, including the perceived interception of water from manifestly failing 'big technology' solutions such as large dams and irrigation projects.

However, by 2010 some ten thousand johads had been constructed by communities across the state, with benefits for wildlife and farmland productivity, as well as helping address issues such as flash flooding, soil erosion, and the soil salinity and alkalinity issues often associated with dam-based irrigation in arid regions. The cumulative impact of these localized schemes has included overall hydrological improvement in some areas, reviving springs and streams as well as larger rivers, including the Ruparel and the Arvari rivers, which had dried up, leading to mass emigration from the area. By restoring water flows through the landscape, Singh's work has regenerated a region that had formerly witnessed severe aridity and depopulation. It is ultimately community ownership and participation which enables a technology to become sustainable; for his participatory work, Singh was awarded the Asia-wide Ramon Magsaysay Award[19] for community leadership in 2001. Some industries are, however, engaging with aquifer recharge to buck the trend and the negative press. For example, SABMiller has helped fund four water recharge dams located on natural fissures in Rajasthan, retaining monsoon rains long enough to replenish the aquifer.[20] This move has reportedly seen the groundwater rise by 9 metres, which equates to the needs of SABMiller's brewery in the area. There appears to be further potential for a hybrid of modern methods and traditional and locally adapted water management techniques.

Catchment-based management of the Murray-Darling river provides an Australasian example. Australia is the most arid continent on Earth. The Murray-Darling river is a significant water resource, draining around one seventh of the Australian land mass – a catchment of 1,061,469 square kilometres (409,835 square miles) – including one of the most significant agricultural areas in Australia. Most of the basin is flat, low lying and far inland, receiving little direct rainfall. Given that it is the primary water resource for the city of Adelaide and many other communities and enterprises throughout its 3,375-kilometre (2,097-mile) course, conservation of the Murray-Darling river is of critical importance for many of the benefits it provides. Given the erosive nature of many of Australia's soils and the relatively low population density, catchment management is critical for protection of the river and its benefits. For this reason, issues such as farmland and forestry management, invasive vegetation control, riparian erosion, pesticide and other agrochemical controls, practices to control diffuse pollution from urban areas and a wide range of other catchment control measures have been central to the integrated catchment management plan for the Murray-Darling basin.[21]

Success breeds success

Successes in some areas of improved water management create successes elsewhere. For example, the success of South Africa's Working for Water programme means not only that the scheme has continued since 1995 and been honoured by numerous national and international awards, but that it has spawned related initiatives across South Africa. There are three such closely allied integrated employment and catchment protection measures, targeting appropriate restoration initiatives for an identified set of environmental benefits that in turn yield societal benefits: Working for Woodlands restores forestry functions benefiting catchment hydrology, biodiversity, characteristic landscapes and supply of sustainable fuel wood; Working on Fire addresses the control of wildfires through invasive vegetation management; and Working for Wetlands restores wetland habitats with their many critical ecosystem services simultaneously with job creation.

In South Africa, the Rietvei is a dam and surrounding wetland of great significance for the supply of water to the adjacent city of Pretoria. Here, as in fifty other wetlands around Pretoria, the water service provider, Rand Water, is investing significantly in management of the wetland area in partnership with the Working for Wetlands programme to protect the capacity of these important habitats to intercept, store and purify water for public benefit. The dam and wetland site also serves as a popular recreation area for fishing, boating, birdwatching and more general enjoyment of wildlife, barbecues and picnics and general leisure activities.

Some commentators suggest that the Working for Water model was also influential in the decision by former US president Clinton to initiate the Comprehensive Everglades Restoration Program,[22] one of the largest natural capital restoration projects in the world. By restoring degraded swampland, the Comprehensive Everglades Restoration Program has many major benefits: it helps overcome water quality problems resulting in greater availability of higher-quality water due to natural purification; it boosts biodiversity, including protection of a number of vulnerable species; it adds value to the tourism industry; it restores natural floodwater controls; and it serves a range of other associated benefits stemming from ecosystem services.

Globally, attitudes to land use subsidies are showing signs of change, with a broadening recognition that food production is merely one among many important service outputs of land and landscapes.[23] The Australian Landcare scheme,[24] for example, seeks to work with land managers who benefit from reduced erosion and improved practices while also decreasing silt and nutrient loads entering rivers. The UK's network of voluntary Rivers Trusts is a highly successful northern hemisphere example, undertaking farm advice work to bring efficiencies and innovations to farm businesses while simultaneously promoting the ecological health of river systems for biodiversity and angling gain, which then stimulates associated ecotourism.[25] Ireland's ICWs, reviewed in the previous chapter, also embrace this approach. The US Conservation Reserve Program (reviewed in Chapter 13) also reflects a major transition from simple land retirement towards maximizing production of desirable ecosystem services, including water resource protection. Major changes to the European Union's Common Agricultural Policy (CAP) were seen in 2002 and further changes are scheduled for 2013, shifting land use subsidies from production of commodities towards a greater emphasis on agri-environment support, reflecting wider societal benefits arising from appropriate use and management of farmed land. These include heritage, biodiversity and a variety of other facets of ecosystem functioning, including supplying clean fresh water. All of these initiatives further demonstrate the effectiveness of placing the functioning of catchment ecosystems at the centre of planning to improve hydrology, water quality and other ecosystem functions beneficial to catchment communities; people benefit when ecosystems function better, and they do so more sustainably than when over-relying on end-of-pipe or end-of-catchment solutions.

Local-scale water harvesting

The principle of water harvesting need not be considered just at larger scales. Rain falls, watering vegetation and percolating into groundwater, running off into rivers and streams and accumulating in wetlands and bodies of standing water. Some returns to the atmosphere as evaporation, and a proportion of this may be trapped as mist or condensation among complex vegetation structures in close and efficient localized water cycles. At different points in its greater planetary cycle, humanity appropriates water for beneficial uses. A diversity of innovations throughout human history and cultures have intervened to harvest water more locally to meet local livelihood needs.

Across the arid world, a wide variety of in-field rainwater harvesting methods have been developed, emulating natural water infiltration processes at field, and sometimes wider, scale. These relatively simple, 'intermediate technology' innovations replicate the principles of natural systems. Some of them, such as 'mechanized basin ploughs' and also Burkina Faso's innovative *ziä* system to promote crop production in the Sahel, as noted already, are 'upscalable'. Many more locally adapted systems are to be found around the world.

Fred Pearce's excellent book *Keepers of the Spring: Reclaiming Our Water in an Age of Globalization*[26] provides an eloquent and persuasive overview of the wide range of traditional small-scale water harvesting techniques found throughout the world. One example that prefaces the book is the rediscovery of a system of 'spring-flow tunnels' in the vicinity of Jerusalem, which, though of uncertain origin, date from between 2,000 and 2,700 years ago. This innovative system comprises a system of shallow-gradient tunnels honeycombing the underground strata of the hills surrounding the ancient city, tapping groundwater to produce a steady flow of water fed into terraces of vegetables and oranges in an otherwise arid landscape. Some Palestinian farmers still make use of these ages-old systems, also filling pitchers for use in the home. Yet, elsewhere in the region, the tendency today is to plough fields flat to aid industrial-scale farming methods fed by mechanically pumped boreholes or transfers of water from the distant Sea of Galilee, modern Israeli engineers trusting more to mechanization than the apparent vagaries of springs.

Pearce observes parallel technologies harvesting groundwater through gravity in balance with recharge rates throughout the world. This includes *laoumia* tunnels that intercept meltwater from the mountains of Cyprus, diverting it from 'mother wells' into tunnels running slightly downhill to feed water into villages. While the technological system is ingenious, it is backed up by equally crucial social systems for sharing water, in which landlords paying for the digging work have first call on the water with the remainder shared through the agreement of a committee of local farmers distributing rights to ensure that the whole community has a share, and equally ensuring that the whole community shares the costs of repairs. As with the 'spring-flow tunnels' around Jerusalem, both the technical performance and the social infrastructure supporting this system are compromised today by the mechanical pumping of water from deep boreholes which depresses groundwater levels.

This model of man-made underground rivers tapping groundwater is emulated across the world, including, for example, in the *karez*, which comprise a network of mounds and underground canals and boreholes used successfully since the Western Hang Dynasty, around two thousand years ago, surrounding Turfan in China's Gobi desert, where rainfall is reportedly unknown.[27] Pearce identifies broadly similar *foggara* in North Africa, *karez* in Afghanistan (where the *mughani* are a separate caste of well diggers passing skills secretly from father to son) in addition to those found in China, *aflaj* in the Arabian peninsula, *surangam* in parts of India, and *qanats* in Iran, which may be 3,000–4,000 years old and are still shared by often thousands of co-owners. These widely distributed systems differ in size and precise design and operation, often reflecting local hydrology and geology. However, their inherently similar core principles may reflect the spread of the basic technology as dominant nations conquered neighbouring countries throughout the Middle East, across to Spain and the Canary Islands and to Libya, Morocco and Algeria on the African shores of the Mediterranean and through into Pakistan and China. Where these technologies spread, the social order of many villages was often found to be constructed around the cooperative sharing and maintenance of this water supply infrastructure, reflecting the fundamental importance of securing water in arid regions.

India's tank system is another instance of a locally appropriate water harvesting mechanism that has persisted for at least three thousand years, harvesting water from landscapes at a sustainable pace. Tanks, comprising pits dug into the landscape to intercept monsoon run-off, groundwater and sometimes incorporating springs, are pervasive across southern India, where they still contribute to nearly a third of the total irrigated area. These and many similar systems are common throughout South-East Asia, many serving multiple benefits, including production of seasonal crops such as fish and lotus.

Tanks are particularly important in predominantly rain-fed areas. There are thought to be about 120,000 tanks across southern India, though the recent renaissance of johads in Rajasthan will doubtless have boosted this number significantly. By intercepting natural groundwater flows, as well as channelling run-off during periods of rainfall, including monsoons, for storage in tanks, as well as regenerating groundwater reserves, the tank system enables water to be harvested from the landscape for human uses at a largely sustainable rate, and certainly as compared to deep-well-pumping alternatives with all of their associated problems. Like any such system, they require agreements about water allocation, including whether pumping is allowed and if so by whom and when, periods during which the tank is left alone to fill naturally, and that no one will exceed their share through a transition to water-hungry crops such as sugar cane. Many tanks, particularly larger ones, also serve multiple functions, including aquaculture, recreational angling, drinking, bathing and washing, which may include sacred and ritual purposes. In fact, the building of water storage tanks often combines practical and sacred needs. Tanks can also serve as important resources for wildlife, for example attracting many bird species. Tanks, then, like spring-flow tunnels, may serve as cornerstones in social systems in those regions dependent upon them. For tanks that are predominantly designed to intercept water running off landscapes, dug into low-lying areas into which monsoon rain naturally flows, slow percolation of water also gives these pools an important role in recharging wells. A recent progressive decline in the efficiency of tanks, due to factors as diverse as inadequate maintenance, reduced storage capacity, seepage in the delivery systems and poor water management techniques, poses a serious threat to the agricultural economy of rain-fed areas dependent on tank irrigation, with poorer farmers particularly affected. However, the revival of johads in Rajasthan is a rediscovery of a long-lived but recently abandoned form of the tank system. It has been dramatically successful in regenerating water systems, involving community-based collaboration and locally appropriate food production, to the significant advantage of local communities and the ecosystems that support them. Rajasthan's now widespread restoration of johads has been hard won, but has offered significant benefits at scales from farms and families to communities and whole regions once again working in sympathy with natural flows of water through the landscapes that support them.

One of the interventions in local water harvesting that is more equivocal in terms of benefits is the small-scale dam. Small-scale dams, many less than a hectare in size, are common across Australia, New Zealand, parts of Europe and the USA, South Africa and elsewhere as a means to intercept and store run-off for domestic, agricultural and other uses. All will impact flows of water (that is what they are intended for) as well as sediment and solutes. However, as observed previously, the scale of dam impacts is more or less related to its size, though it is not possible to set a *de minimis* on the scale of dam likely to be inconsequential to overall catchment functioning. Furthermore, there are growing concerns, particularly in the USA, that all dams have to be assessed periodically for safety purposes. Each has to be assessed on its own merits – taking account of size, proximity to watercourse, impacts on groundwater flows, impacts on water yield accessible by other users, etc. – and it is strongly suggested that this is done on the basis of impacts on the full range and sharing of ecosystem services within catchments.

Rainwater harvesting

We have explored above how innovations such as tanks, bunds and terraces can harvest rainwater as it runs off the land. However, the gathering and storage of rainwater directly from man-made impervious surfaces is another important innovation in some regions of the world, with the potential for far greater uptake. Traditionally, rainwater harvesting has been practised most often in areas of water shortage, including arid and semi-arid landscapes, providing supplies for domestic use as well as for watering livestock, small irrigation plots and the replenishment of local groundwater.

This is a technology that is already relatively mature and well known, so we will not devote much text to it other than to note that it is applicable not merely to roof water but also to the interception of water running down hillsides, from car parks and other impermeable urban surfaces. Some systems may treat this water while others may not, depending upon the use of water and the likelihood of contamination. For water collected from paved urban surfaces, low-input treatment options such as SuDS (sustainable drainage systems, also known around the world as WSUD and 'source control', as explained later in this book), which comprise a suite of technologies including infiltration basins, detention ponds, reedbed and grass swale filters, etc., may provide adequate cleansing for further use. India's tank systems are in effect a rural method to intercept and harvest rainfall. In some arid parts of the world, including for example Gansu province in China and in semi-arid north-east Brazil and Bermuda, large rooftop rainwater harvesting projects have official support and make a major contribution to water availability and security. Indeed, in Bermuda, the law now requires new construction to include rainwater harvesting adequate for the needs of its residents.

Opportunities exist in other water-stressed parts of the world where cheap methods for rainwater harvesting would make a substantial difference. One such example is in Zulu tribal lands in KwaZulu-Natal in South Africa, where water harvested from the roofs of traditional homes could go some way towards meeting domestic and small-scale irrigation needs. However, an obstacle that I have identified here and also discussed with representatives of the South African plastics industry is that most drainage guttering is extruded straight, whereas curved lengths would be required to fit around the roofs of traditionally round Zulu buildings. The simple innovation of suitably shaped guttering might help address some local water scarcities, matching livelihood needs with appropriate technologies rather than automatically assuming that damming a river will best support the needs of people in these dry tribal lands.

Various technologies are available across the world, some addressed in the preceding section, to harvest rainwater from fields at various scales. Practical examples are presented in the form of guidance to rural farmers in arid regions of South Africa, where a guide, *On-Farm Application of In-Field Rainwater Harvesting Techniques on Small Plots in the Central Region of South Africa*,[28] defines water harvesting as 'the process of concentrating rainfall as runoff from a larger area for its productive use on a smaller area'. This guidance takes a ten-stage approach to building local communities sharing best practice and the practical conversion of fields using techniques such as bunds and troughs filled with stone and straw mulch. Experimental plots running over a number of years demonstrate the potential to reduce total run-off to zero and evaporation from the soil surface considerably, enhancing maize and sunflower yields by up to 50 per cent compared to conventional techniques and potentially also recharging groundwater. Outreach methods ranging from songs and plays to farm and demonstration site visits, videos and websites, broadcasts by television and radio stations, newsletters, conferences and a range of other methods have accelerated uptake of these beneficial management measures, enhancing livelihoods and local food security. Further examples are contained in volumes such as Vanclay et al.'s book *Realizing Community Futures: A Practical Guide to Harnessing Natural Resources*.[29]

Moisture from thin air

Efficient gully and valley ecosystems found throughout the arid areas of the Earth, beautifully adapted by evolution to retain and efficiently recirculate moisture, have been addressed earlier in this chapter, as has the substantial recapture of moisture released from the Congo's extensive rainforest. The importance of rainforest habitat on India's Western Ghats for the whole Deccan peninsula is also described elsewhere in this book, the forests significantly enhancing the interception of moisture from humid air blowing in from the Arabian Sea. Nature has evolved beetles, herbs and trees efficient in the capture of moisture from thin air, such as the Norfolk Island pine, which evolved by capturing moist air on Norfolk Island off eastern Australia but is now a common standard tree planted around the world. Demonstration of the benefits of forest ecosystems for water capture and storage is also provided by the many negative examples around the world of major hydrological disruptions resulting from deforestation.

The planting of shade trees, commonplace as a method to control soil temperatures, erosion and moisture levels in Kenya but also providing shade and a cooler, water-efficient microclimate in tea and coffee plantations in India, is one technological application of this natural process. There is also a wide range of more high-tech innovations. One such is a fog-trapping scheme in Chile, where arrays of nets installed along the ridge of the 790-metre (2,600-foot) El Tofo mountain in 1992 harvest moisture from clouds blowing in from the Pacific Ocean. As moist air is blown in through these huge sheets of plastic mesh, it accumulates in droplets that are gathered in tubes feeding down the hillside to serve the people of the fishing village of Chungungo. Local and modest in scale, this and similar projects could provide local solutions to the needs of many such scattered, water-scarce communities. The method is cheap, low in maintenance, requires no specialist skills for the necessary renovation work, and is potentially durable. It is even conceivable that fog-harvesting may help provide water to allow reforestation of formerly wooded areas, the restored forests then continuing the water harvesting function as well as yielding a wide range of other benefits to society. Pine trees, with their needle-like leaves, are known to be particularly efficient at the capture of water from moist air. In Peru today, fog catchers dot the deserts around Lima, the world's second-largest desert city after Cairo with a population of 9 million, providing a significant water source to augment an extremely low rainfall, typically of less than 4 centimetres annually, and the erratic flow of meltwater from dwindling Andean glaciers.[30] Sandwiched between the cool, moist Pacific winds and the Andes, humidity in these deserts can reach 98 per cent, including frequent thick, white sea fogs from which water is being harvested by networks of mesh hung from bamboo frames. This technology is accessible, not to mention hugely cost efficient, for other coastal communities in Peru and beyond.

Human exploitation of this biological phenomenon is not new. For example, nomadic tribes in Saudia Arabia traditionally obtained their clean water by placing cisterns beneath certain types of trees known to trap water from moist air during periods of intense fog. In both its tree-based and technology-enhanced forms, this is certainly a naturally founded approach to water harvesting that may just have an important future serving humanity in some arid coastal areas, as well as upland zones where natural water-capturing habitats have become degraded.

Thinking at catchment scale

Clearly, we have a pressing need to promote catchment production and storage of water in the light of the widespread examples of land drainage and other big, engineering-centred water supply technologies that degrade the very water-producing ecosystems they tap into. However, it is also important to sound a note of caution: many ecosystem-based technologies – fog-harvesting, spring-flow tunnels, tanks and the like – do not actually create more water. Targeted reforestation and also the protection of critical upland moor and peat habitats may increase the water yield and storage of catchments, but we have also to be aware of the potential for perverse knock-on impacts on the hydrology of the whole drainage basin and indeed climatic systems, and others dependent upon them.

But, above all, we need to overcome the 'big technology' assumption that only abstracted water has a value. We often hear the term 'wasted' water applied to that which flows out to sea, percolates into the ground or is in other ways 'unused'. If we have learned anything from this chapter, it is surely that water within ecosystems yields enduring and multiple benefits that are lost if we merely try to suck the landscape dry for immediate human utility. In reality, this 'wasted water' has real if often poorly appreciated value for the sustainability of catchment systems and their dependent communities. Water percolating into the ground is not 'lost' but is serving useful purposes for ecosystems and for the many ways people rely upon them, including production of food and extraction of water elsewhere in the system.

Conservation or restoration of whole environments, not just novel methods to extract water, needs to be our major preoccupation.

12 | Water flows through society

Once it is harvested from the environment, the ways water is distributed and used have major impacts upon water efficiency. Consumption and reuse are therefore hugely significant to the sustainability of the environments that produce water and to the equity with which extracted water is shared to meet the needs of all people. Water-efficient household appliances can make significant differences in urban areas where residential customers account for the greater part of water demand.[1] However, this is also a well-trodden topic that is more than adequately covered elsewhere. It will not therefore be addressed here; instead we will devote attention to several facets of the wider 'water metabolism' of modern society.

Sustaining livelihoods

A 'big technology' world view, focusing on such mechanisms as large energy generation plants with distribution to scattered communities and users, automatically conceives of water infrastructure in terms of centralized storage and treatment with subsequent broad-scale reticulation. Aside from the impact of dams, we have also seen that industrial-scale groundwater abstraction and distribution pipes and canals can be environmentally, socially and economically inefficient. Widespread losses occur through leakage and evaporation with a high level of energy consumption, risk of contamination, drying up of wells supporting the needs of many people, salinization of land and contributions to aridity through depressed groundwater and dried-up wells. Heavy centralized infrastructure can also deny needy people access as the water speeds on its way to big commercial applications and rich centres of population.

Many of the ways that people use water to meet their livelihood needs may be better served by local water harvesting than by complex piped systems. In Asia, for example, the most rice by far is produced within walking distance of where it is eaten.[2] Production systems here are most often designed to intercept natural flows of water through landscapes. Though 'low tech' in Western industrial terms, the kinds of terraced agriculture common throughout Asia are remarkably efficient in terms of the conservation not only of water but of soil and nutrients. In areas such as the hill slopes of the Western Ghats of India, where the upland forest habitat serves a crucial role in the capture and storage of water upon which the river systems and hundreds of millions of people across the otherwise arid Deccan peninsula depend, water is used so efficiently at local scale that it barely has any impact on catchment hydrology. This sophisticated and well-adapted form of terraced farming is found from Thailand to Java, Bali, India, Cambodia, Sri Lanka, the Philippines and even as far afield as Peru; cultures may come and go, but the system persists.[3] This form of localized communal approach to the tapping of environmental flows of water, both through soils and in the form of capture of rainfall to meet local needs, has underpinned great civilizations upon which empires have been built, even if the vital technologies supporting the livelihoods of most of their people have been almost entirely overlooked.

In his book *Keepers of the Spring*,[4] Fred Pearce elaborates on various examples of the interception of subsoil flows of moisture for the benefit of crop production, for example the use by Papago Indians of rocks and brush arranged over broad landscapes to divert rainfall and soil moisture towards the best soils. Remarkably similar systems are found in other arid areas such as Israel and Yemen. Other tribes of American Indians from Mexico and across South America use low stone wall terraces for similar purposes. These schemes are characterized by many similarities, ranging from their huge scale across seemingly dry landscapes to their dependence upon deep and long-standing knowledge.

Efficiency in use

Sustainable and equitable use of water depends not just on how the water is used, but also what it is used for. Many of our developed-world habits were innovated in countries with less water stress and on the assumption that more water could be abstracted from remote resources with no thought of consequences for its former or other potential users. Water efficiency has not historically been a defining feature of industrialized society.

Nevertheless, as the importance of water conservation becomes more pressing across the world, we are seeing progressive innovation of water-efficient and water-free technologies across all spheres of domestic and industrial water use, from water-free urinals to efficient and recirculating industrial processes. There is huge scope for further progress even in as developed an economy as the UK, where organizations such as Envirowise (a government-sponsored environmental advisory service) state that 'Many companies could save up to 50% of their costs by implementing simple, inexpensive water minimisation measures'.[5] However, we will devote little more space here to the rather better-documented innovations and opportunities of domestic and industrial water-efficient applications in the developed world, taking continuing progress here as a given, albeit an overdue one.

Virtual water

As developed-world society begins to embrace less thirsty lifestyles, owing as much to shortages in increasingly water-stressed conurbations as to environmental concerns, we are seeing a gradual spread of low-flush toilets and highly efficient showers, washing machines and other domestic appliances. However, it is often what we overlook which is the most shocking.

About one thousand cubic metres of water a year are required to raise our individual food needs, compared to about one cubic metre per year for drinking and 3.5 cubic metres for domestic use.[6] Accounting for the water 'footprint' in growing, production, processing, packaging and transport, it takes a shocking 140 litres of water to make a cup of coffee, a hamburger may take 2,400 litres of water, while a pair of blue jeans could account for as much as 11,000 litres.[7] While a 50-gramme bag of a basic salad in the UK costs about £1, its production wastes almost fifty litres of water; worse still, production of a similar-sized bag of mixed salad takes 300 litres of water.[8] When you eat a steak that was raised in Texas, you're effectively drinking 15,000 litres of water entailed in growing the cow.[9] The term 'virtual water' describes that consumed in the production process of an agricultural or industrial product,[10] unseen in the final products but representing a very real facet of global water consumption. The economic advantage enjoyed by richer and generally moister countries tends to enable them to exploit the water resources of other nations via global supply chains. Many water-intense commodities may derive from poorer and often drier nations seeking to enhance foreign revenue as a priority, but not necessarily mindful of consequences for domestic livelihoods and therefore of the inefficiencies of the invisible 'export' of all this water. This may be particularly the case in markets for such water-intensive crops as forestry products, cotton, sugar, tobacco and rice,[11] as well as water-hungry processes such as mining. Developed countries may unwittingly be importing huge amounts of 'virtual water' through trade, used in often poorer countries to grow the crops and commodities that we eat, wear or base 'value add' manufacturing upon. Today, globalization underpins modern developed world lifestyles, but we may be blind to the geopolitical inequities through factors such as 'virtual water' that underwrite our richer-world lifestyles.

According to one UN assessment,[12] Britain imports nearly fifty cubic kilometres of virtual water a year; about eight hundred tonnes for every member of the population. The age of empire may be long gone in terms of occupation of foreign soil, yet the superior bargaining power it has ceded us means that much of the already developed world still appears to exert an entrenched form of 'hydro-colonialism' as well as other forms of asymmetric exploitation of the resources of poorer nations. Furthermore, by 'exporting' a model of development that is conflated with industrialization, we are creating dependency on and vulnerability to fossil fuels while devaluing local self-sufficiency and manual labour in emerging nations, globalizing agriculture in ways that transfer control to transnational corporations in an export-first, rather than food-first, culture, the costs of which include local food and livelihood security.[13] This raises not only significant questions about equity and prudent economics, but also about our own supply chain security as, when water resources dry up, so too will the sources of cheap goods to which we have become accustomed. There is also growing interest in accounting for the 'groundwater footprint' of goods and lifestyles, reflecting the vulnerability of this depleting yet often neglected global resource.[14]

Some argue that water-stressed countries should, instead of concentrating on production for export to generate foreign revenue, invest in importing foreign food, particularly water-intensive grain such as wheat, as an economically efficient way to release water for other more productive and basic needs.[15] Yet for struggling economies, short-term profit is hard to forgo in the face of long-term sustainability and security, and the habits are hard to break. The distribution of profits and ultimate costs also entrenches short-termism. For the far-sighted nation intent on sustainable and equitable water use, low-water crops are a must. By shunning the immediate pressures of the water-addicted global marketplace, clever national planners may pre-empt tomorrow's requirements as the whole world becomes more water-limited, constricting the supply of water-intensive commodities in global markets.

'Water grabbing'

With globalization comes a more direct acquisition of the water resources of other nations, often referred to as 'water grabbing'. The term itself derives from large-scale and increasing land acquisitions for agricultural production, including biofuels, which are commonly referred to as 'land grabbing'.[16] However, it is often intimately connected water systems which are the prime targets and drivers, though, by virtue of the complexity of hydrological systems, implications for unequal power relations, statutory and basic human rights and ownership, this is often poorly understood and also commonly excluded from negotiations.[17] Many examples are to be found across the world. In sub-Saharan Africa, it is often water resources which underpin the projected productivity and crop suitability of land acquired through foreign investment, competing with other domestic water uses.[18] In West Africa, land acquisition for biofuel growth almost wholly ignores local needs for both land and water for crop growth.[19] In India[20] and Mali,[21] reallocation of land rights to serve export markets is generally at the implicit expense of the needs of local people. Further examples are seen in the privatization of hydropower development in Turkey[22] and the Mekong basin,[23] mining operations in Peru,[24] and in the playing out of power relationships between Palestine and Israel.[25]

Often, it is the lack of an integrated approach to land and water management which creates opportunities for foreign investors to exploit the water resources of local people.[26] This is yet another example of the kind of 'hydro-imperialism' noted for the invisible trade in virtual water, which can only serve to disempower local people and keep them in a spiral of hydrological and intimately connected food and economic poverty.[27] It can also stem from a conflation of the 'development' and the Western, oil-dependent model of industrialization which tends to centralize power in transnational corporations rather than favouring the needs of local people.[28] The net result is a new form of colonialism, dispossessing small farmers and indigenous people of land and water for the sake of investors.[29]

The 'blue revolution'

The famous 'green revolution' of the post-Second World War era saw massive gains in food productivity as the power of science was unleashed on agriculture. Innovations in breeding, engineering, chemistry and husbandry saw huge advances in terms of the production of food per unit of land. As populations grow and no new land magically appears, the pressure on productive soils for foods, biofuels, fibre, chemical feedstock, dyes and other biologically derived matter will continue to rise. However, a by-product of the 'green revolution' was greater inputs throughout the production process, including energy, chemicals and water. The analysis in this book suggests that this increase of inputs, particularly of water, cannot continue unabated. Looking ahead, the scarcity of water is likely to overtake the scarcity of land.

Water was not the limiting factor of the first green revolution. However, it may well be in the future with a shift in thinking about productivity from efficiency per unit of land area towards benefits per unit of water. The benefits of the green revolution are fast fading away in countries such as India, Pakistan, northern China and Mexico. Massive irrigation from new sources may simply become untenable, with efficiencies in rain-fed farming becoming hugely more important for food security than irrigation schemes. Efficient use of water is the basis of a necessary 'blue revolution'.

As Max Finlayson, president of Wetland International, says of the need for a blue revolution, 'Our immediate challenge is feeding an additional 70 million people each year and reversing ecosystem degradation.'[30] Many factors may contribute to a blue revolution. Gender issues come to the fore, acknowledging the significant role of women in water conservation around the world, yet their voices commonly remain overlooked in higher-scale decision-making.[31] We have already addressed the need for crop selection based on suitability for growth under different conditions, a traditional practice from which we have much to learn and would do well to do so rather than persisting with our more recent industrial-agricultural methods and crop choices reliant upon excessive inputs that threaten other aspects of ecosystem integrity and human equity. Selective breeding has a further role here to maximize water efficiency, in much the same way as it changed land efficiency throughout the 'green revolution'. A shift to high-energy Western-style diets also needs to be reassessed, not only to better reflect the 'carrying capacity' of local conditions but also for public health and economic benefits. And, of course, innovative technologies and more sensitive economic signals have a big role to play.

Modern plastics – durable, light, flexible, modifiable in property through blends of additives and many of them, at end-of-life, recyclable – may have a major role to play in various aspects of water management. These range from water capture technologies as diverse as fog nets to impermeable roofing, gutters and pipes, storage tanks and irrigation equipment. Appropriate plastic applications may promote a cheap transition on all scales of farming towards highly efficient drip irrigation, delivering it to the root zone for maximum uptake rather than relying on the all-too-common practice of daytime spray irrigation, which sees a huge proportion of water merely re-evaporated back into dry air. Modern laser levelling equipment, in common use for various groundwork applications, can also help significantly to improve land topography during tillage for the benefit of water, soil and nutrient conservation. We need not just look forward for innovations of value, as many long-standing and traditional land use systems were founded on principles of the efficient use of water. In the UK, for example, the post-medieval water meadow system endured, and in some localities persists still, for upwards of four centuries as a means to harness water and its load of warmth, nutrients, oxygen and vegetation control properties to promote agricultural intensity in a pre-industrial age with no additional inputs.[32] We have also already seen how traditional Asian paddy and terracing systems have endured for millennia as an efficient and often low-impact means to exploit local water resources. The range of technologies amenable to promoting water efficiency in production is long, and possibly without bounds, if we can just shift the framing question from maximizing 'crop per land area' towards 'crop per drop'.

Treating water as an economic good in all its competing uses was not only the fourth of the four Dublin Principles of IWRM, but was endorsed at the UN's 1992 Rio de Janiero 'World Summit' and features among the twelve principles of the 'ecosystem approach' promoted by the Convention on Biological Diversity. We have already described farming subsidies in India that include free electricity for round-the-clock pumping of deep and ever-retreating aquifers, which seem only to promote wasteful use while degrading wider landscapes and the prospects of those dependent upon them. We have explored how dam schemes in Nigeria and other places have been designed for targeted benefits, yet end up draining larger wetland areas upon which the unaccounted livelihoods of many people formerly depended. There are many other examples of how pricing for access to water without taking account of abstracted volumes merely promotes wastage, a likely transition to water-hungry cash crops and possibly salinization of land as part of a 'tragedy of the commons' in which the interests of poorer people and communities have no entry in the ledger of costs and benefits. There is a need for practical realization of the kinds of wise economic policies that create incentives for equitable sharing and efficient use of water which are implied by the Dublin Principles and wider aspirations to the sustainable use of water. The economics of water are addressed in more detail in Chapter 13.

Farming for water

The 2002 'Curry Report' to the UK government[33] emphasized that land performs many beneficial functions, ranging from carbon sequestration and water production to support for wildlife and amenity, in addition to food production. The diversion of large tracts of US and European land almost exclusively to food production since the Second World War has had profound implications for these wider benefits,[34] which we now understand better through the lens of ecosystem services. The UN's Millennium Ecosystem Assessment identified agriculture as the major cause of wetland degradation and loss, boosting provisioning services while depressing regulatory and supporting services, notwithstanding the importance of wetland systems for catchment functioning.[35]

Whereas post-war US and European agricultural subsidies have largely rewarded maximization of food production with only a token diversion of support through agri-environment schemes for additional but generally poorly targeted benefits, Curry's report is one of a range of initiatives across the globe recognizing that land can be 'farmed' for a wider range of ecosystem service benefits. This is substantiated by lessons learned in Chapter 11, taking examples from all five continents of how co-management of land and landscapes for food, water and other beneficial services promotes sustainable development, including economic efficiency and the support of diverse livelihoods. Many other significant water-related initiatives connected with farming around the world include the 2008 FAO report, 'Scoping agriculture–wetland interactions',[36] and the Ramsar Convention's Guidelines on Agriculture, Wetlands and Water Resource Interactions Project (GAWI).[37]

Much remains to be done to change the current paradigm of farming, which through reward systems tends to liquidate most ecosystem services to maximize the yield of just a few, such as production of food and fibre with some diversification into chemical feedstock and biofuel. Redressing established practices and assumptions is essential for the restoration of crucial climate, air and water regulating services, as well as cultural and supporting services necessary to secure our collective future, and to retain the viability of both ecosystems and farming. Restoring the water capture, purification and storage services of farmed land is of great importance, and is already constituting a significant step towards farming for a sustainable future.

Multi-use systems for water provision

One of the common consequences of 'big engineering' is 'top-down' planning, implicitly assuming that water use in all communities is similar to that in the more economically and politically empowered sectors of society where decisions are most commonly made. Yet the reality is that people use water in a wide variety of different ways to support multiple livelihood needs, covering irrigation, bathing, washing, drinking, cooking, laundry, cleaning, livestock, gardening, field irrigation, tree growing, aquaculture and fisheries, small-scale businesses like brewing and many more uses besides. Delivery of piped and treated water according to the developed-world model may be neither appropriate nor affordable for many of these diverse and often widely geographically dispersed activities.

It is from this recognition that the multiple use water services (MUS) approach was developed as a policy mechanism. Initially, this started as a donor-funded, multi-country action research project from which local operational learning was scaled up into a policy learning process.[38] Today, MUS is a more widespread approach, though with potential for far wider uptake to address the disparate needs of diverse rural populations across the world. The essence of the MUS approach is to overcome compartmentalized, single-use planning within the water sector, basing planning for service provision instead at grassroots level through a community-driven water services approach addressing the different ways that water is required to support domestic, productive and other purposes.

MUS rests upon cooperative governance, engaging the broad range of water users critically in assessing their plurality of water needs and including the different perspectives of the poor and including both women and men. Where communities design their own water systems, they usually do so with multiple uses in mind. The challenge is therefore for water 'professionals' to think in such integrated ways, including engagement of those they are tasked with supporting, including water services that are effective in supporting livelihoods and tackling poverty. The focus needs to start at household level working upwards, rather than with a presumption in favour of a 'big engineering' solution, such as a dam, working downwards to the different constituencies which need to be connected. As we have seen repeatedly in this book, there are very many instances of dams providing for the needs of some but inadvertently eroding the ecosystem services supporting the needs of many more people. When people need to adapt their livelihoods to inappropriately designed schemes that do not meet multiple needs, this may be inconsistent with allocation schedules or may otherwise perturb the hydraulics of piped networks. At the very least, efficiency and sustainability are compromised, and there are ethical arguments to be addressed where control of these 'illegal activities' – generally ineffective owing to enforcement difficulties – serves to deny the genuine multiple water needs of the people that engineered, single-use schemes purport to assist. The fault here lies not with the good intentions of the engineers nor the demands of rural populations, but in the mismatch between technological provision and real-world needs.

It is only by prioritizing the actual water needs of a population that optimal means can be determined to satisfy them, including household-level technologies, small and localized collective technologies, or medium-scale schemes. These may entail more distributed technologies yielding water closer to the point of need, including rainwater harvesting from roofs and the landscape, water collection from springs routed locally to crops, standpipes and other local methods of providing water for homes and livestock, piped infrastructure designed flexibly to permit for multiple off-takes, and water-efficient delivery systems such as plastic drip irrigation to enable farmers to benefit more from small local water sources. Solutions must also address means, both technical mechanisms and social agreements, for sharing excess water from one use with others. This approach takes better account of all available water sources, however small, and the delivery of water services, including conveyance and storage, more local to the multiple uses of water in households, homesteads and small settlements.

Often, there is a cultural clash to be overcome, on the one hand between organizations with centralized, single-use tendencies (such as bodies licensing or retailing water, domestic water service planners, the irrigation sector, livestock and fisheries departments, and so forth) and 'bottom-up' sectors of society (for example, local NGOs, smaller municipalities and farmers' collectives) more deeply rooted in the multiple uses of water. These sectoral and organizational boundaries need to be overcome if the real needs of the population are to be met efficiently and ethically in water planning systems.

Various knowledge-sharing networks have been established around the world to both upscale and outscale learning about MUS approaches, including in South Africa, Nepal, Thailand and beyond. The driving principles are collection and efficient use of local water resources to their full capacity, maximizing their societal value by taking account of quality, quantity and seasonality, and also taking better account of local water sources and the range of technologies and agreements that can best safeguard and assure efficient use. A case study on the upscaling of MUS in Bushbuckridge (Bosbuckrand) Municipality in Mpumalanga, South Africa, identified the importance of building capacity among officials and community members. It enabled them to better understand the connections between water and the livelihoods of the many stakeholders in a catchment, the need to engage representatives of those multiple stakeholders in participatory assessments at local scale, and to establish and facilitate a multi-stakeholder platform for collective analysis and planning.

Waste water recycling

The Industrial Revolution model that has framed a great deal of thinking about resource use was, as we have discussed, founded on a range of now anachronistic assumptions, including a poor grasp or complete oversight of the natural limits of resources. The model established at that time, and which still underpins market systems, is that natural resource and human ingenuity should be used to create products with utility and economic value and that a growing market will result in a booming economy and a greater throughput of materials in the economy. Undervaluation and depletion of resources are unfortunate consequences in the absence of agreements or regulation; another is the accumulation of waste from all this material throughput. We see both consequences contributing significantly to the raft of problems facing us today, contributing to inequitable shares of limited resources. And, of course, the linear 'use once and throw away' model also affects historic and inherited attitudes to water.

Water is, naturally, an infinitely renewable resource that is distributed and purified by cycles throughout the biosphere. It is also possible to recycle it closer to the point at which it was used by society and, as environmental pressures bite, we can expect to see a growing trend towards the efficient and cyclic use of water. Accordingly, we are seeing the emergence of a range of water-efficient systems in the home and industry, as well as 'greywater' recycling of slightly contaminated water. At a grander scale, sewage treatment infrastructure seeks to purify more grossly contaminated waste water before discharge to the environment, where natural purification processes complete the job of polishing the water into an adequately clean and exploitable condition. These developed-world technologies need not preoccupy us too much as they are well documented elsewhere, though it is noteworthy that the slow uptake of water-efficient technologies is hampering sustainable water use and costing its potential users substantially in terms of wasted water.

The application of intermediate technologies, such as reedbeds for the treatment of effluent, may have considerable utility in many parts of the world. Work I have done with coffee growers in the uplands of Deccan India suggests that reedbed treatment systems may have significant utility in this warm climate for cleansing the various pollutants associated with coffee washings. This may help farmers with reuse of purified water, reduce harmful loads discharged to rivers or contaminating groundwater, and reduce abstraction from natural water resources with their associated climate change and low flow implications. I have also recommended reedbed systems as making a substantial contribution to attenuating some of the problems associated with industrial pollution on the Maharashtra/Gujarat border. These are areas of locally adapted technology that can make a major contribution to the more efficient and sustainable use of precious water resources.

Water in the built environment

Management of water flows through landscapes and the economy is critical for sustaining human well-being. These principles apply at all scales from the global to the smallest catchments, and also in urban as well as rural locations. Indeed, there is now an increasing awareness of the value of historically neglected ecosystems, including flows of water, in the built environment.

Significantly less dense and densely clustered human populations in the pre-industrial world enabled people to make more direct use of the diverse benefits provided by water systems in the landscape. Urbanization necessitated greater differentiation within society and also placed greater pressure on local natural resources, including river systems that often provided the food, water, power, transport and topography supporting settlements and their expansion.[39] This in turn led to an often-repeated pattern of increasing population density and urban sprawl progressively overriding the carrying capacity of local water resources, food production systems and other vital ecosystem services. Industrial-age cities and the industrial-scale agriculture and water management technologies that support them digested more of the surrounding landscape, including water-intense production along globalized supply chains.[40] Already, 50 per cent of the global population live in urban centres, and this proportion is predicted to increase,[41] so the trend of overlooking the value of functional aquatic ecosystems puts at risk further development.[42] Today, urbanization represents one of the most significant factors globally contributing to alterations of ecosystems.[43] Frequently, the extent of degradation is so great that urban rivers cease to provide the resources or services around which settlement and economies grew.[44] The traditional European approach to urban river management has been summarized as 'bury them, turn them into canals, line them with concrete and build upon the (now protected) floodplains',[45] producing networks of entirely or almost forgotten rivers buried in culverts under people's feet in long-established cities such as London.[46]

There is today emerging recognition of the value of freshwater ecosystems in urban areas, not merely for nature conservation but for a wide range of societal benefits that flow from functional ecosystems.[47]

Restoration of urban rivers to recover some of the multiple benefits they formerly provided is now occurring throughout the world. This includes, as just a few examples, tributaries of the River Thames in Greater London,[48] under the US EPA's Urban Rivers Restoration Initiative,[49] in South Korea,[50] a coordinated programme under the Australian River Restoration Centre[51] and around Johannesburg led by the NGO WET-Africa.[52] An evaluation of benefits in terms of ecosystem services stemming from restoration of the urban Mayes Brook and wider parkland regeneration in Mayesbrook Park in the east end of London[53] revealed significant benefits in terms of enhanced regulation of air and water quality, microclimate and flood risk, cultural services such as recreation, social cohesion and educational opportunities, and supporting services, particularly including nutrient cycling and habitat for wildlife. Restoration of another of London's 'lost' rivers, the River Quaggy in the south of the city, also provided a swathe of benefits forming a central element of urban regeneration. Allied to this is an economic study into the benefits of New York City's 592,130 street trees, which found that they produced a staggering $US122 million in annual benefits, including urban cooling, carbon storage, pollution removal, noise reduction and protection from flash flooding, in addition to their direct contribution to emotional and physical well-being. For water systems as for other ecosystems in both rural and urban environments, ecosystem-based solutions that work with natural processes rather than fighting against them tend to yield a greater range of benefits, addressing the perspectives and needs of more stakeholder groups, when compared to traditional, narrow-framed 'hard engineering' solutions.[54]

A range of novel approaches recognizing the value of ecosystems and their services are evolving in urban environments around the world, including, for example, 'Green Infrastructure',[55] sustainable urban drainage systems[56] (SuDS, also known as 'source control' in the USA), Community Forests,[57] the English Ecocities Initiative[58] and climate change commitments under the Nottingham Declaration,[59] as well as green roofs[60] and rain gardens.[61] In Australia and other nations such as Singapore, the term WSUD (water-sensitive urban design) is widely used as a land planning and engineering design approach which integrates storm water management, groundwater and waste water management and water supply into urban design to minimize environmental degradation and improve aesthetic and recreational appeal,[62] for example in the Sydney Metropolitan CMA's Water Sensitive Urban Design (WSUD) Program[63] assisting the transition to a 'Water Sensitive City'. WSUD is not exactly synonymous with SuDS, nor indeed is 'low-impact development' (LID) as promoted in some US cities, though it includes common principles of both SuDS and Green Infrastructure by working with natural processes. All of these 'green' technologies exploit or emulate natural processes to retain or restore a range of water-related and other ecosystem services, including flood regulation, groundwater recharge, pollution abatement, provision of 'green spaces', carbon sequestration and breaking down of urban 'heat islands'. The New York City 'Green Infrastructure Plan' records that the integration of green infrastructure into a mix of more traditional urban infrastructure saves the city approximately US$1.5 billion annually over a 'grey only' approach.[64] Incorporating the value of ecosystems into urban planning can also directly increase the value of real estate relative to denser development through the hedonic value of properties closer to water and green spaces, proximity to green spaces elevating house values by around 8 per cent,[65] as well as via better management of flood risk.[66]

Although these various urban initiatives often address a different set of target services, and their implementation is currently fragmented, all are inherently related through their focus on natural ecosystem processes. They may therefore be extended and better joined up to optimize the production of a wider range of ecosystem services of greater cumulative societal benefit.[67] As for the management of landscapes, catchments and economic activities, integral consideration of water flows through urban environments can make a substantial contribution to reversing historic destruction of supportive ecosystems, making a positive contribution to sustainable development and enhanced resilience.

As the world's urban areas expand, together with their pressures on natural resources across wider landscapes, there is increasing emphasis on the need to take account through smart design of their many impacts on ecosystem services,[68] significantly including those related to the water cycle.

Returning water into the environment

Concluding the previous chapter was a reminder that we have always to think at catchment scale, taking account of the many interconnected habitats and livelihoods that comprise catchment systems. It is timely to reiterate that perspective when considering the consumption and reuse of water. Efficient use is important in a resource-constrained world, and recycling water within society still does not automatically return it to the ecosystem. Water returning or left within underground and surface resources is not 'wasted', but will be doing important work for ecosystems and livelihood support locally and farther afield. The conservation of aquatic environments remains of paramount importance as the core resource underpinning human well-being and catchment integrity, so the return of water to the environment is as much a key to sustainability as its efficient use and reuse.

13 | Markets for water services

The marriage of ecosystems and economics has been bumpy. Natural capital and the viability of ecosystems have not been prominent features of the development of the market economy, which places value on the utility of products derived from ecosystems yet largely 'externalizes' the integrity and productivity of the resource base itself.

Valuing ecosystems

Awareness of the importance of linking economic systems with ecosystems emerged towards the middle of the twentieth century in the wake of numerous environmental 'shocks'. From deforestation and associated soil erosion to the drying of rivers and salinization of soils, acidification of forests from fall-out of aerial emissions, and the many human and ecological consequences of these and other unintended consequences, the roots of many of these problems were quite apparently embedded in the ways that nature was being over-exploited in commercial and development decisions.

The externalization of water systems and other critical natural resources is largely a legacy of the inherited yet anachronistic economic model that still pervades much of societal decision-making today. It is sadly true that if we ascribe no value to ecosystems, or rely on decision-makers to factor their 'inherent worth' into deliberations solely on an altruistic basis, they all too often are counted as of zero value in ensuing decisions. It is this reality which led to the founding and progressive evolution of environmental economics from the 1970s.[1] Many conservationists and philosophers express concern about putting a man-made value to that which transcends humanity and our parochial values. However, by ascribing a value, we at least bring the functions of organisms, habitats and ecosystems into the frame of contemporary decision-making, which remains largely economically based. Clearly, we need to do so cautiously to evade the trap of 'putting a price on nature' that may see it then traded off against short-term economic gain. However, the power of the economy to influence exploitation of the natural world, and the corresponding ongoing diminution of the natural world's capacity to sustain human well-being, makes it clear that the progressive inclusion of the wider values of nature into decision-support frameworks can constitute one of the most powerful levers available for its conservation.

While this is not the place to go into the complexities of the economy, one of the fundamental principles of its functioning is the trading of goods and services. Without trade, nothing has value. When the benefits of ecosystem exploitation accrue to a narrow sector of society involved in management decisions, for example in the production of crops or livestock, private markets are likely to work to maximize the production of these services, but generally at the expense of other non-traded ecosystem services flowing primarily to other people, as is the case for the public benefits of water purification, habitat for wildlife or climate regulation.[2] At global scale, the Millennium Ecosystem Assessment[3] demonstrated the scale of harm to global ecosystems arising from omission of the often irreplaceable value of their beneficial services from decision-making frameworks. At national scale, the UK's National Ecosystem Assessment (NEA) highlighted how

> Over the last 60 years the dramatic increases in provisioning services, including crops, livestock and trees, have been achieved both through using more land and through intensification, such that by 2000 the UK was able to produce more food and timber than at any time during the last century. However, the expansion of agriculture, forestry, and new settlements to meet the needs of the growing population, has come at the expense of non-provisioning services. For example, some key supporting services have been adversely affected, especially nutrient cycling, as well as regulating services, including soil quality, the control of pests and diseases, and pollination by insects. Also, cultural services may have deteriorated: for example, hedgerows have been lost from lowland landscapes.[4]

It is therefore essential that we proceed beyond valuation of ecological assets as an academic exercise, progressing towards the creation of markets in which different economic elements can be 'traded'. Some of these markets exist – for example, trading across the globe in water, timber and fish – but they are generally partial in that the catchment, forest and oceanic ecosystems that produce the traded goods are not generally part of the marketplace. A notable exception here are the various sophisticated water trading markets in Australia, initially based on extensive trading of physical volumes of water between farmers but now substantially diversified into the trading of water-based futures and derivative products.[5] The challenge remains to bring ecosystems themselves into the market, such that the many values they bestow upon society do not remain comprehensively externalized from exploitation and decision-taking.

Many conservation initiatives effectively create local markets, making priceless the habitat on designated sites and hence seeking their ongoing protection. However, this model of 'fortress conservation' is outmoded for many reasons. Unsympathetic environmental impacts outside of the designated conservation site inevitably erode the integrity of the conserved area. Designated reserves may simply be of an inadequate extent to sustain diverse ecosystems with their full genetic inheritance, conservation management often maintains these sites in a mid-succession state when the external forces driving habitat change are taken away, and climate change may exacerbate these effects and even make the conserved area non-viable for the species and habitats of concern. More important still is the fact that 'no-intervention' zones may merely implicitly sanction destructive practices across broader non-designated landscapes. A broader emphasis should rather be on modification of our mainstream farming, industrial and residential practices towards a more sustainable relationship with the ecosystems that support human well-being. The market, in short, needs to value the integrity and functionality of all ecosystems, embedding incentives to adapt our policies and practices towards increasingly greater sustainability. Achievement of this scale of long-term transition requires breaking out of narrow sectoral approaches which neglect potential relationships between environmental changes and policy dynamics in different sectors, including, for example, between energy, water and other scarce resources, and including socially induced scarcities.[6]

It is in this latter regard that ecosystem services are such a helpful tool, reflecting the things that ecosystems do that provide beneficial services to society and which in turn are amenable to valuation and negotiation between those sharing common and often formerly unvalued ecosystem assets. As an intriguing insight into what it is we are actually valuing, it is only when we value people – the breadth of society including future generations – that we can then recognize the value of the multiple services that ecosystems provide to support their diverse needs and aspirations.

Water and the economy

Aside from supporting diverse life forms, ecosystem services produced throughout river catchments support a diversity of human livelihoods. They sustain basic life support needs such as drinking and cooking, irrigation of crop and grazing lands and stock watering, materials for shelter and energy, fisheries and regeneration of soils, as well as providing a raw resource for industry, a convenient waste receptacle and other economic benefits, not to mention supporting cultural and spiritual dimensions of human well-being.

Water is inseparable from all of these human needs. Therefore, all of its associated utilities can be ascribed economic values if they are to be weighted in decision-making processes. However, a problem arises where there is no recognized market for these values, be they ecosystem services underpinning primary economic activities (such as water production in sparsely populated uplands flowing downstream to support often remote industry, land use and habitation) or where they relate to human activities outside the formal economy, such as traditional and subsistence lifestyles. Where these values are not reflected in management decisions, development options maximizing short-term and localized financial returns will tend to erode the many public benefits provided by water systems.

The crucial importance of addressing the economic value of water in catchment management is enshrined in the last of the four principles of the UN's 1992 'Dublin Statement on Water and Sustainable Development', which states that 'Water has an economic value in all its competing uses and should be recognized as an economic good'. This global consensus about the need to include the economic worth of water and other ecosystem resources is also central to the twelve principles of the 'ecosystem approach' advanced by the Convention on Biological Diversity[7] (see Box 13.1), which include: 'Recognizing potential gains from management, there is usually a need to understand and manage the ecosystem in an economic context. Any such ecosystem-management programme should: (a) Reduce those market distortions that adversely affect biological diversity; (b) Align incentives to promote biodiversity conservation and sustainable use; (c) Internalize costs and benefits in the given ecosystem to the extent feasible' (Principle 4); and also that 'The ecosystem approach should seek the appropriate balance between, and integration of, conservation and use of biological diversity' (Principle 10).

Paying for ecosystem services

'Paying for ecosystem services', or PES, is an emerging market-based approach reflecting the value of ecosystem services. The fundamental principle of PES is that those benefiting from ecosystem services pay those undertaking management (often land management) measures

Box 13.1 The 12 principles of the 'ecosystem approach' advanced by the Convention on Biological Diversity[8]

The Convention on Biological Diversity notes that the following twelve principles are complementary and interlinked.

Principle 1: The objectives of management of land, water and living resources are a matter of societal choices Different sectors of society view ecosystems in terms of their own economic, cultural and society needs. Indigenous peoples and other local communities living on the land are important stakeholders and their rights and interests should be recognized. Both cultural and biological diversity are central components of the ecosystem approach, and management should take this into account. Societal choices should be expressed as clearly as possible. Ecosystems should be managed for their intrinsic values and for the tangible or intangible benefits for humans, in a fair and equitable way.

Principle 2: Management should be decentralized to the lowest appropriate level Decentralized systems may lead to greater efficiency, effectiveness and equity. Management should involve all stakeholders and balance local interests with the wider public interest. The closer management is to the ecosystem, the greater the responsibility, ownership, accountability, participation, and use of local knowledge.

Principle 3: Ecosystem managers should consider the effects (actual or potential) of their activities on adjacent and other ecosystems Management interventions in ecosystems often have unknown or unpredictable effects on other ecosystems; therefore, possible impacts need careful consideration and analysis. This may require new arrangements or ways of organization for institutions involved in decision-making to make, if necessary, appropriate compromises.

Principle 4: Recognizing potential gains from management, there is usually a need to understand and manage the ecosystem in an economic context. Any such ecosystem-management programme should:

a. Reduce those market distortions that adversely affect biological diversity;

b. Align incentives to promote biodiversity conservation and sustainable use;
c. Internalize costs and benefits in the given ecosystem to the extent feasible.

The greatest threat to biological diversity lies in its replacement by alternative systems of land use. This often arises through market distortions, which undervalue natural systems and populations and provide perverse incentives and subsidies to favour the conversion of land to less diverse systems.

Often those who benefit from conservation do not pay the costs associated with conservation and, similarly, those who generate environmental costs (e.g. pollution) escape responsibility. Alignment of incentives allows those who control the resource to benefit and ensures that those who generate environmental costs will pay.

Principle 5: Conservation of ecosystem structure and functioning, in order to maintain ecosystem services, should be a priority target of the ecosystem approach Ecosystem functioning and resilience depends on a dynamic relationship within species, among species and between species and their abiotic environment, as well as the physical and chemical interactions within the environment. The conservation and, where appropriate, restoration of these interactions and processes is of greater significance for the long-term maintenance of biological diversity than simply protection of species.

Principle 6: Ecosystems must be managed within the limits of their functioning In considering the likelihood or ease of attaining the management objectives, attention should be given to the environmental conditions that limit natural productivity, ecosystem structure, functioning and diversity. The limits to ecosystem functioning may be affected to different degrees by temporary, unpredictable or artificially maintained conditions and, accordingly, management should be appropriately cautious.

Principle 7: The ecosystem approach should be undertaken at the appropriate spatial and temporal scales The approach should be bounded by spatial and temporal scales that are appropriate to the objectives. Boundaries for management will be defined operationally by users, managers, scientists and indigenous and local peoples. Connectivity between areas should be promoted where necessary. The ecosystem approach is based upon the hierarchical nature of biological diversity characterized by the interaction and integration of genes, species and ecosystems.

Principle 8: Recognizing the varying temporal scales and lag-effects that characterize ecosystem processes, objectives for ecosystem management should be set for the long term Ecosystem processes are characterized by varying temporal scales and lag-effects. This inherently conflicts with the tendency of humans to favour short-term gains and immediate benefits over future ones.

Principle 9: Management must recognize the change is inevitable Ecosystems change, including species composition and population abundance. Hence, management should adapt to the changes. Apart from their inherent dynamics of change, ecosystems are beset by a complex of uncertainties and potential 'surprises' in the human, biological and environmental realms. Traditional disturbance regimes may be important for ecosystem structure and functioning, and may need to be maintained or restored. The ecosystem approach must utilize adaptive management in order to anticipate and cater for such changes and events and should be cautious in making any decision that may foreclose options, but, at the same time, consider mitigating actions to cope with long-term changes such as climate change.

Principle 10: The ecosystem approach should seek the appropriate balance between, and integration of, conservation and use of biological diversity Biological diversity is critical both for its intrinsic value and because of the key role it plays in providing the ecosystem and other services upon which we all ultimately depend. There has been a tendency in the past to manage components of biological diversity either as protected or non-protected. There is a need for a shift to more flexible situations, where conservation and use are seen in context and the full range of measures is applied in a continuum from strictly protected to human-made ecosystems.

Principle 11: The ecosystem approach should consider all forms of relevant information, including scientific and indigenous and local knowledge, innovations and practices Information from all sources is critical to arriving at effective ecosystem management strategies. A much better knowledge of ecosystem functions and the impact of human use is desirable. All relevant information from any concerned area should be shared with all stakeholders and actors, taking into account, inter alia, any decision to be taken under Article 8(j) of the Convention on Biological Diversity. Assumptions behind proposed management decisions should be made explicit and checked against available knowledge and views of stakeholders.

Principle 12: The ecosystem approach should involve all relevant sectors of society and scientific disciplines Most problems of biological-diversity management are complex, with many interactions, side-effects and implications, and therefore should involve the necessary expertise and stakeholders at the local, national, regional and international level, as appropriate.

entailed in the protection or enhancement of these services.[9] Practical examples can be found in all continents wherein payments by water users (often mediated by water service companies representing the interest of large numbers of customers) are recirculated as grants or subsidies for environmentally sensitive farming which reduces pollutant loads, improves hydrology and so contributes to more reliable flows of water, requiring fewer 'downstream' treatment costs. PES schemes have also been developed around the world for other services, including carbon sequestration (the ecosystem service of climate regulation) and for protection of biodiversity. The OECD[10] estimated that some three hundred PES or PES-like schemes were operating around the world in 2010, and that number has since substantially escalated as the approach has entered the mainstream of political discourse and practice in some countries.[11]

The term 'PES' is often used loosely as an umbrella term for a variety of schemes in which the beneficiaries, or users, of ecosystem services provide payment to the stewards, or providers, of ecosystem services. However, there are some more precise definitions. Wunder[12] defined PES as a form of market for ecosystem services involving 'a voluntary, conditional agreement between at least one "seller" and one "buyer" over a well defined environmental service – or a land use presumed to produce that service'. In addition to these principles, a number of important concepts are also associated with PES schemes.[13] 'Additionality' is one such concept, such that the PES scheme results in benefits that would not otherwise occur and are also additional to statutory obligations; additionality to statutory demands also marks the switch-over point from where the 'polluter pays principle' gives way to the 'beneficiary pays/provider gets' principle. 'Leakage' is another important concept, as care must be taken to ensure that protective measures alleviating harm in one PES-subsidized area do not simply result in damage being transferred elsewhere. Another important concept is 'conditionality', referring to clarity about what the buyer is paying for in terms either of defined ecosystem service outputs (such as improvements in water quality and/or quantity) or else land use or other resource management measures likely to promote them (for example, implementation of an agreed level of deintensification, installation of riparian buffer zones or other water-sensitive land use practices).

The basic premise of a PES scheme is that, as for any economically valued service such as the buying or selling of food in a supermarket, those who provide ecosystem services should be rewarded or compensated for so doing. The simple underlying proposition is that individuals or communities are paid to undertake actions that increase levels of desired ecosystem services for individuals or groups,[14] although this simplicity may be hard to determine beneath the complexity of real-world operational schemes. In some cases, these payments may be made directly by beneficiaries to providers, as is the case with those paying for recreational access to an owned landscape.[15] More often, governments or other bodies (such as water service companies) may pay multiple providers on behalf of multiple beneficiaries. This is the case for agri-environment schemes, albeit that at present the service benefits are often poorly defined, limiting the value of many legacy schemes.

In practice, I have found that tedious debate about what precisely is or is not a 'true' PES is unproductive, and that it is more useful to apply a simple taxonomy of schemes creating markets that are: (1) one-to-one, as in the case of a dam owner and a large upland landowner from which water drains; (2) one-to-many, as in the case of an intensive water user paying (directly or indirectly) for sensitive land use by multiple farmers; (3) many-to-one, as in the case of many customers paying via charges for a water service company to subsidize sensitive, non-polluting land use on land owned by a large owner; or (4) many-to-many, as in the case of agri-environment subsidies.

Market-based approaches are increasingly seen as an important means to combat the degradation of biodiversity and its associated ecosystem services, explaining the rapid proliferation of PES schemes around the world.[16] PES is also perceived as one of the most effective levers of landscape-scale change, as PES schemes highlight the direct linkages between the benefits enjoyed by defined stakeholders and the ecosystems that they depend upon on the basis of the 'beneficiary pays' principle.[17]

A great deal more could be said about PES schemes, but that would stray from the purpose of this chapter, which is a broader consideration of how markets for water services could contribute to more sustainable management of water in the landscape. For those who want to know more, the 2010 OECD guide *Paying for Biodiversity*[18] is an excellent primer, supported by many case studies from around the world, some of which are also outlined in this book. A research project published by the English government department Defra, *Barriers and Opportunities to the Use of Payments for Ecosystem Services*,[19] also provides a comprehensive overview, including (as the title suggests) the opportunities and barriers to PES implementation both in broad principle and in an English context, and further guidance can be found in Defra's *Best Practice Guide for Payments for Ecosystem Services (PES)*.[20] The following five sub-sections of this chapter focus on examples of water-related PES schemes across the five major continents, collectively giving a flavour of the pervasion, diversity and efficacy of this approach.

Examples of water-related PES in Asia

China's Sloping Land Conversion Policy (SLCP) was initiated following devastating floods in the Yangtze river in 1998, signalling a significant change in the country's approach to ecosystem management. The Yangtze floods, which were partly attributed to massive deforestation in the watershed, killed 4,150 people, displaced more than eighteen million people and caused economic losses of 255 billion yuan (about US\$38 billion).[21] Of the 34 million hectares of farmland in the Yangtze and Yellow River basins, 4.25 million hectares is on slopes of greater than 25 degress, with average soil erosion levels on these slopes of 4,000 t km^{-2} a^{-1} (tons per square kilometre per year). With proper forest cover, erosion can be reduced by 80–90 per cent.[22] The SLCP aims to reduce soil erosion and flood risk and help alleviate poverty, and is set to run until 2018. Also known as Grain for Green, it is the largest land retirement and conversion programme in the developing world,[23] promoting the return of farmland on slopes over of 25 degrees to forest or grassland by providing compensation to farmers who plant trees and grass. Farmers receive annual compensation for loss of agricultural production of 100–175 kilograms of grain per mu (1 mu = 0.067 hectares), 20 yuan per mu to increase access to health and education, and 50 yuan per mu for seedlings or saplings planted (which are provided free in the first year).[24] The SLCP is currently being implemented in more than two thousand counties across 25 provinces, and involves tens of millions of rural households.[25] By the end of 2006, the SLCP had contributed to the conversion to forest of 9 million hectares of former cropland.[26] Between 1982 and 2012, China planted more than forty billion trees along the southern edge of the Gobi desert, and plans to cover a further 100 million acres by 2020, which will not only generate newly forested areas the size of Germany but also contribute to the re-emerging vitality of the Loess Plateau.[27]

A wide variety of issues have been raised in relation to the design and implementation of the SLCP. For example, the extent to which implementation reflects local circumstances is a key factor. The Forest and Grassland Taskforce of China argued that 'Implementation has not been tailored to local conditions, and there has been an over-emphasis on tree planting rather than restoring original vegetation cover. The SLCP does not give sufficient consideration to the ecological and economic functions of grasslands in semi-arid areas and the need to restore these ecosystems.'[28] Bennett and Xu argue that sanction mechanisms for non-compliance are not credible, indicating that the programme is not truly conditional. For example, survey results indicate that low survival rates for planted trees have not generally led to subsidies being withheld, with the main reason for this said to be the programme's dual goals of environmental amelioration and poverty reduction, which place local leaders in a dilemma.[29] In general, the SLCP has been designed with little scope for substantive differentiation across targeted areas and participants, such as, for example, bidding mechanisms or a more varied menu of contract choices,[30] and the short subsidy periods provided under the programme raise concerns about the permanence of ecosystem service provision. For example, although the five-year subsidy period might provide participants with sufficient time to establish sustainable orchards or plantations of trees with medicinal value, the eight-year period for 'ecological forests' (i.e. timber forests) is far too short.[31] Though there remains some contention about the role of forestry in catchment-scale hydrology, the emerging consensus is that trees can reduce run-off at the small catchment scale whereas, at larger scales, forests serve to intensify the recycling of water influencing climate systems and water storage as compared to deforested areas.[32] Trees then have a publicly beneficial role for water management as well as erosion risk, with adverse impacts expected where they are lost. Various suggestions for improving the SLCP have been proposed, including increasing local community input in design and implementation, clarifying the environmental services targeted, and verifying the measures needed to acquire these services.[33]

Many more PES schemes are being implemented across Asia. For example, in Nepal, an acute scarcity of water is driving a Payment for Watershed Services (PWS) initiative to allow communities to adapt to changing conditions. This Nepalese initiative spans both public payment schemes and self-organized deals, including a community water user association scheme in the area of Rupa Lake evolved through local, traditional mechanisms.[34] One of the most advanced PES schemes to date has been developed on the island of Lombok, Indonesia, where WWF is working to conserve the forests of Mount Rinjani.[35] These forests are vital to the $50 million per year agricultural sector of the region, and supply domestic water worth $14 million. Through the local regulations (Perda No. 4/2007), 75 per cent of the costs paid by the people who use the water services from PDAM Lombok are allocated to the people in the hills of Mount Rinjani as a payback mechanism to help look after the forests that sustain the living systems of this small island, including critical water resources.

Examples of water-related PES in Europe

SCaMP,[36] elaborated in Chapter 11, created a market linking the production of high-quality water with charges paid by remote users. Other well-advanced catchment-based markets between land managers and water service customers can be found on the River Tamar in south-west England under both 'Upstream Thinking'[37] and WEPES[38] initiatives, all mediated by the NGO the Westcountry Rivers Trust[39] (WRT).

'Upstream Thinking' deserves more detailed consideration, building as it does on a decade and a half of pioneering work by the WRT, which came into being largely in response to the frustrations of landowners on the Tamar and other river systems of south-west England about the lack of action to halt the decline of salmon stocks or the ravages of diffuse pollution. WRT did much to work with farm businesses in an integrated way, helping them save money on inappropriate pesticide and fertilizer usage, partitioning of clean roof water from dirty yard water, effective waste water treatment options, 'buffer zoning' wetlands and streams to help reduce stock foot disease and straying, loss of lambs, and a range of other self-beneficial measures simultaneously advantageous to river health. This emphasis on profitable means to secure river ecology has always been at the heart of Trust efforts. WRT was also successful in drawing in EU regional development funding and substantial grants from other sources. South West Water (SWW), the regional water utility, was quick to see the advantages of partnering with WRT as an effective means to broker farm improvements, diffuse pollution from agriculture being the greatest pollutant source and continuing threat to abstractions for public supply. 'Upstream Thinking' is the latest evolution of this close partnership between WRT and SWW, gaining government consent under the 2010–15 water industry investment cycle to recycle water customer investment through WRT to broker further farm improvements. From this, a 65:1 benefit-to-cost ratio is anticipated based on projected improvements to raw water quality and savings on treatment costs alone.

This is 'hard business', and government-sanctioned business at that, which should offer a better return to water service customers. Further ecosystem service benefits are 'stacked' free on top of the ecosystem improvements brought about by WRT actions, including fishery enhancement, improved biodiversity and amenity uses, reduced siltation, and anticipated hydrological improvements from wetland zone protection or rehabilitation. WRT today works with a wide range of other players, including the government-promoted Catchment Sensitive Farming (CSF) programme, as well as forestry and dredging interests, to better pool resources and target interventions where they can optimally contribute to multi-benefit outcomes. Thus the 'stacking' of services as add-on positive consequences is metamorphosing into a 'bundling' of different paid services achieved by promoting targeted interventions within catchments.

The early successes of WRT and its subsequent evolution in vision and scale are mirrored by similar initiatives operated by thriving British river trusts on the Rivers Wye, Usk, Tweed, Eden, Severn, Thames, Wandle, Bristol Avon and many others. Water companies have often been early and enthusiastic partners of fledgling rivers trusts, recognizing clear benefits arising from the work of these 'trusted brokers' in engaging with agricultural and other riparian businesses. As a further development, SWW has calculated that a big supply reservoir might cost it £90 million, with all the difficulties and delays of planning approval, but that it should in theory be possible to build the same water storage capacity into key south-western rivers for around £15 million by working through the WRT to encourage and provide incentives for land managers to restore wetland systems;[40] this could represent yet another substantial bundled PES market which would bring with it multiple additional stacked services.

Across Europe, project ALFA[41] ('Adaptive Land use for Flood Alleviation') is bringing together partners from Belgium, France, Germany, the United Kingdom and the Netherlands to explore and implement new ways of protecting people from flooding by creating new capacity for water storage or abatement of flooding peaks through land use, with an intent to explore the creation of markets between 'providers' and beneficiaries within catchments. The PES approach is also implicit in the intent of the UK's agri-environment schemes as reformed under the broader EU Common Agricultural Policy (as described in Chapter 11), as pubic money pays for outputs from the land beyond the mere production of commodities which generally provide private benefits for farmers. However, as discussed previously in this chapter, the vague definition of required ecosystem service outcomes in many legacy agri-environment payment schemes currently blunts their efficacy, yet it also highlights opportunities for their further evolution to deliver greater and clearer value for public investment.

A case study of the Vittel PES scheme published by Perrot-Maître[42] reviews the history, design and development of this French scheme to protect the valuable water source from which bottled water of the Vittel brand is obtained. Water marketed under the Vittel label is drawn from the 'Grande Source' ('Great Spring') located in the town of Vittel at the foot of the Vosges mountains in north-eastern France, naturally lifted from a 6,000-hectare aquifer some eighty metres underground. The water has been ascribed a range of beneficial properties since Gallo-Roman times, and has a value of many $US millions per annum. Maintenance of water quality is essential not only as contaminated water is disastrous to corporate reputation but also as, under French law, 'natural mineral water' is required to be bottled at source from a well-protected, specific underground supply of stable quality and with no further treatment other than the elimination of traces of potentially problematic metals. However, in the early 1980s, the then family owners of the Vittel brand recognized that intensification of agriculture in the Vittel catchment posed a risk to nitrate and pesticide levels in the Grande Source, and consequently to the Vittel brand, as traditional hay-based cattle ranching was becoming progressively replaced by intensive maize-based systems. The family owners therefore assessed five options to ensure water quality over the next fifty years:[43] (1) 'do nothing', which would result in the business closing down; (2) relocate to a new catchment, which would lose the valuable 'Vittel' brand; (3) purchase all the land in the spring catchment, which was infeasible and contrary to French law; (4) force farmers to change practices, for which there was no legal requirement; or (5) provide incentives for farmers to change their practices voluntarily. The fifth option was the only viable one, leading the family to instigate a patient process of negotiation in 1988, leading to a ten-year process to transform conflict between farming and bottling interests into a successful partnership. During this time, the Vittel brand and source were progressively taken over by the multinational Nestlé Waters company. The tale of the dialogue generating progressively greater mutual understanding between farmers and the spring owners is told elsewhere, but it is important to recall that through careful targeting, sound scientific analysis of risks, trust-building, understanding the diversity of farmers and their needs, the formation of a trusted broker organization, and the development of appropriate economic incentives over long timescales (eighteen- or thirty-year contracts), a critical majority of landowners (covering 92 per cent of the sub-basin area by 2004) reverted to extensive farming practices, securing the quality of the spring and the considerable revenue that it generates for the Vittel region as well as its owner. The main conclusion of the case study is that establishing PES is a complex undertaking requiring consideration not only of scientific information but also of social, economic, political, institutional and power relationships.

Success at Vittel was replicated for the Perrier brand, drawn from a spring of naturally carbonated water near Vergèze in the Gard *département* of France, which had also been bought by Nestlé Waters. This too resulted in mutually beneficial compensation schemes for landowners in watersheds upstream of the spring to retain forests, guaranteeing a clean and reliable water source.

Examples of water-related PES in the Americas

Development of the New York City water supply, discussed in Chapter 11, essentially comprised a negotiated agreement and market between urban water users and rural stewards of catchment land. It is perhaps the world's largest and most highly developed PES scheme, and in many ways an exemplar.

The US Conservation Reserve Program (CRP) is another large-scale

PES scheme. The CRP was initially instituted in 1985 as a means to avert soil erosion in cropland. However, it has since evolved to address a 'bundle' of connected ecosystem services, including water management and water quality, biodiversity and air quality protection. The CRP operates as a land set-aside programme under which the government, via the US Department of Agriculture (USDA), pays landowners incentives through ten- to fifteen-year contracts to change the use of specific lots of land for ecosystem service benefits.[44] The majority of lots are now let through 'inverse auctions' in which potential ecosystem service 'sellers' submit bids indicating the minimum payment they are willing to accept for the provision of an ecosystem service. Bids are prioritized by the USDA according to the potential environmental benefits associated with the proposal, which, calculated together with the proposed payment, derives an Environmental Benefit Index (EBI). Contracts are determined through the bidding process on the basis of the highest service benefit for the least cost. The benefits produced by the CRP are genuinely additional, as estimates suggest that 51 per cent of CRP land would be returned to crop production in the absence of CRP payments, with a corresponding decline in expenditure on outdoor recreation of as much as $300 million annually in rural areas.[45]

Rising concerns about nutrient enrichment in the economically and environmentally important Chesapeake Bay have also begun to be addressed by establishment of a PES approach, innovatively tackling water management problems where traditional regulation has failed.[46] In December 2010, the US EPA published a Chesapeake Bay Total Daily Maximum Load (TDML) defining the maximum allowable loads for nitrogen, phosphorus and fine sediment entering the bay. Load reductions expected from various sources are described in Watershed Implementation Plans (WIPs) for six states and Washington, DC. WIPs recognize that regulated point sources contribute only a fraction of the total load, so include programmes to limit diffuse and weather-dependent loads from agriculture and low-density suburban development. WIPs expect agricultural landowners to implement pre-approved best management practices (BMPs) in return for payments to offset a share of their costs for 'Bay-friendly' practices.

The Costa Rica Payments for Environmental Services (Pagos por Servicios Ambientales, PSA) is another PES scheme operational on the American continent since 1996. This scheme replaced an ineffective system of tax deductions with a national PES programme for services generated by forest and agro-forestry ecosystems. Participants entering this scheme are paid for four land use activities (protection of natural forest, establishment of timber plantations, natural forest regeneration, and establishment of agro-forestry systems) producing a bundle of ecosystem services, including carbon sequestration, water quality protection, biodiversity protection and the provision of scenic beauty.[47] The scheme is funded by reallocation of 3.5 per cent of the revenues from a fossil fuel sales tax into the National Fund for Forestry Financing (FONAFIFO), worth about US$3.5 million per year, on top of which the World Bank and other international aid donors also then contribute.[48] In addition, the programme allows individual beneficiaries (hydroelectric plants, breweries, irrigated farms and other organizations benefiting from ecosystem services) to pay FONAFIFO, through which they may negotiate contracts with service providers. This Costa Rican scheme was formerly poorly targeted, with money allocated on a 'first come, first served' basis[49] on a uniform per-hectare basis, taking little account of local conditions and making little contribution to deforestation.[50] A study has been undertaken to improve the efficiency of benefit production through spatial targeting and differentiation of payments.[51]

In Canada, recognizing the quantity of land in private hands and the thousands of kilometres of streams and rivers flowing through it, trials were launched in 2011 to pay farmers and ranchers in British Columbia to produce cleaner air, water and wildlife habitat alongside food.[52] By placing a monetary value on water purification through wetlands or preserved ecosystems on privately owned agricultural land, the intent of a consortium of government, academic and conservation groups is to pursue these beneficial environmental goals by compensating farmers for changing their practices and protecting sensitive lands. In its first phase, the project is being modelled on thirteen demonstration sheep and cattle ranches across British Columbia by the Ecological Services Initiative (ESI), a collaboration of farmers, academics and conservationists. Enhancements range from increasing the buffer zone between crops and waterways, livestock fencing around environmentally sensitive areas, replanting native plant species to encourage native wildlife, wetland protection or restoration, and reforestation to both capture carbon and shade salmon spawning streams. All of these measures are intended to enhance normal farming practices to co-produce ecological benefits. This represents good overall public value, with a return of these multiple beneficial services in return for compensation for loss of productive land as low as $100 per acre. This investment in restoring nature's capacity to produce these services is set against expenditure in the order of billions of dollars on projects, infrastructure and operating costs to clean air and water and to provide habitat for threatened species. Although there are as yet no formal markets for many of these publicly beneficial services, paying farmers from public funds for service delivery is seen as a means to overcome farmer reluctance to expand the current extent of protective buffers around sensitive areas which, once in place, are perceived as difficult to remove.

Another among many interesting American examples is the Florida Ranchlands Environmental Services Project (FRESP), designed as a cost-effective strategy to maintain water storage and reduce phosphorus loading in the northern Florida Everglades. FRESP is enacted via payments to ranchers for providing these environmental services, with payments simultaneously offering ranchers greater financial security and an incentive not to sell their land for urban development.[53]

These are just some among many PES schemes operating or under consideration across the Americas.

Examples of water-related PES in Australasia

Australia is the world's driest continent and, with nearly 62 per cent of its land area (some 473 million hectares) used for agriculture, there is a clear need for creative means to engage private landholders innovatively for effective nature conservation, water management and erosion control outcomes. The government of Australia regards economic incentives for landowners to take direct management action to protect or restore ecosystems as part of an effective policy mix, including subsidies as well as competitive market-based systems. A number of initiatives are already in place across Australia, enabling conservation-minded landholders to be funded for sensitive land management in a cost-effective manner. The state-government-run programme schemes include Nature Assist[54] in Queensland and Bush Tender[55] in Victoria state, both funding willing landholders to set aside part or all of their land as nature refuges, with greater rewards for setting aside the most environmentally significant areas. Funds are allocated through competitive tender systems to ensure the greatest public value for money in terms of ecosystem service benefits, with payments tied to the level of service provided. Although the primary focus of these two schemes is the protection or regeneration of native vegetation, wider contributions to biodiversity and the many services provided by protected land are increasingly being considered in scheme design, implementation and rewards.

Australia also operates the Hunter River Salinity Trading Scheme,[56] comprising a set of tradable or semi-tradable permit schemes to reduce salt, phosphorus and levels of other pollutants entering the Hunter river in New South Wales. This scheme involves eleven coal mines and two large power stations which, among them, are licensed to discharge a predetermined peak load of salt into the river or its tributaries. This is a classic 'cap and trade' scheme with an overall 'cap' set on discharge load, within which each firm is allocated discharge 'credits' which they are free to trade with other credit holders.

New Zealand too has implemented a range of PES schemes, significantly including protection of its forests. Interest in PES is taking root in some interesting contexts. While New Zealand undergoes a transition to a more urban-based economy, indigenous Maori landowners are expressing interest in markets for ecosystem services and nature conservation payments to help maintain their livelihood and culture in North Island.[57] A Maori conservation reserve programme called Nga Whenua Rahui already provides a mechanism enabling landowners to allow land to remain in, or revert to, native bush. Development of wider markets for ecosystem services covering biodiversity protection, watershed restoration and carbon sequestration may be essential to secure resources to feed and offset the impacts of New Zealand's rapidly urbanizing economy. Maori land is subject to a complex system of communal ownership, with decision-making authority for blocks of land vested in elected leaders. This creates some conflicts where there are opposing views on how land is best managed. Maori cultural values also mean there is a different relationship between the people and their land to that found in Western economies. However, these complexities do have the fortuitous consequence that environmental initiatives to prevent erosion, preserve water quality, restore forests and protect biodiversity resonate intuitively with traditional Maori resource management thinking. Indeed, *kaitiakitanga*, the Maori ethic of stewardship, demands a balanced approach to safeguarding the legacy of previous generations, the needs of current generations and opportunities for future generations; a fair articulation of what many of us understand by the term 'sustainability'. Ngati Porou Whenui Forests Limited (NPWFL) has been established as a tribal cooperative bringing together Maori landowners and Maori agencies to benefit from market opportunities for ecosystem services, including both government incentives for the management of erodible land and foreign investment. Some forest areas may also be eligible for funding for carbon sequestration services. These new markets for ecosystem services may potentially become a significant element of economic growth among Maori people.

Examples of water-related PES in Africa

We have already looked at the innovative application of ecosystem-services-based accounting to help shape more inclusive and sustainable decision-making in the Thukela catchment of KwaZulu-Natal, South Africa, and also in the nation's Working for Water (WfW) programme. The Thukela study and WfW are not the only groundbreaking initiatives bringing water and its multiple associated services into the frame of decision-making in South Africa, on the back of the visionary post-apartheid water laws.

South Africa's innovative water laws have enabled the development of some of the most advanced approaches to PES in the world. The Maloti Drakensberg Transfrontier Project,[58] initiated in 2007, explored hydrological and economic linkages between uplands that 'produce' water and the consumption of water lower down in selected river catchments, developing this into the design of market mechanisms for payment from consumers for the protection, restoration and management of upper catchment areas critical for dependable run-off of clean water. This potential market is founded upon the significant economic benefits to communities lower down catchments, particularly focused on heavy water users such as forestry, intensive agriculture such as sugar production, mining and industries such as paper and sugar mills potentially benefiting from investing in work to increase the water yield of the catchments upon which they depend. The marginal value of enhanced or protected flows, harnessed to convert water into economic products, is particularly significant in dry periods of the year. This Maloti-Drakensberg market model is favoured by the South African government as a replicable market means to embed the ecosystems approach as a basis for the equitable, sustainable and efficient provision of water.

Additional interest in investigation of the potential of PES is seen in remedies to current unsustainable land use practices yielding only poor economic returns on extensively farmed land in the Baviaanskloof and Tsitsikamma watersheds of KwaZulu-Natal.[59] Current land use practices are problematic for the sustainable supply of important eco-system services, including good veld condition, carbon sequestration and overall water security for downstream water users, among them farmers and the water-stressed urban areas of Port Elizabeth, Jeffery's Bay and Cape St Francis. PES appeared to offer a win-win opportunity by realigning the incentives available to farmers to deliver better for the needs of wider society. A legal review concludes that payment mechanisms can provide a basis for the equitable and sustainable management of South African catchments.[60]

Other PES initiatives are finding favour in the Lake Naivasha basin, Kenya, and in the Arc Mountains of Tanzania. There are also examples of international PES markets where rivers cross national borders, for example under the Lesotho Highlands Water Project,[61] a multibillion-rand water transfer and hydropower project implemented between the governments of Lesotho and South Africa under which South Africa pays Lesotho for the protection of the water resources flowing across the border and also for energy generation. The scheme represents an important source of foreign income for the poor upland nation of Lesotho, for which it has adopted a 'protected areas' approach to safeguarding the hydrology and quality of spring areas. The distribution of resources between the king, the government of Lesotho and local people disadvantaged by constraints on their farming methods has attracted considerable criticism, not least from international NGO International Rivers,[62] emphasizing the importance of robust and inclusive governance in these emerging markets.

Offshore in the ecologically unique island state of Madagascar, the WWF 'Watershed-Based Payments for Ecosystem Services in the Humid Forest of Madagascar' project[63] aims to identify and implement a system of PES schemes by watershed, connecting end users to upstream communities in order to reward them for the conservation and sustainable management of the watershed. The watershed in the humid Fandriana-Vondrozo forest corridor of Madagascar has been identified as a high-potential site, providing a range of ecosystem services including valuable water supply which may yield tangible economic, though as yet unrecognized and unrewarded, benefits for the services provided.

Wider links between water and the economy

Much of the text of this chapter has dealt with 'paying for ecosystem services' schemes precisely because they create real or surrogate markets linking the ecosystems that produce services beneficial to a wide variety of stakeholder groups. However, PES is just one of a range of market-based instruments being developed to recognize this interdependence between people and ecosystems, helping to bring it into mainstream management and policy.

Other relevant or potential market-based instruments, further detailed description of which is beyond the scope of this book, include various forms of charges (including fees for use of services such as access to recreational landscapes as well as taxes on use of services), subsidies to safeguard or promote service production, tradable permits, and eco-labelling to open up niche markets.

Tariffs on water consumption, ideally supported by quantitative metered use, may also have a role to play in suppressing water demand in both rural and urban contexts. For example, targeted tariffs may create incentives for a transition from spray irrigation to more water-efficient alternatives such as trickle irrigation or various in-field rainwater harvesting methods, as well as in urban and industrial processes and appliances. Conversely, as we have seen already in this book, inappropriate payment mechanisms can act perversely to promote inefficient use and so widen disparities between those with access to water and those without, for example in the case of free or subsidized energy to over-exploit aquifers in India or area-based rather than volume-based charging mechanisms.

Used appropriately, all of these economic instruments may have a role to play, along with such other forces as regulation, education and public activism, to develop a more sustainable relationship with biodiversity, sympathetic to both the workings of the market economy and also the value of the natural world. The incorporation of new market-based approaches to flood risk management, also as discussed in Chapter 11, redirects public investment into land, often formerly defended on an uneconomic basis for private gain, leading towards more natural floodwater storage and other water management regimes, as well as contributing to broader biodiversity, landscape, fish recruitment benefits and amenity. The use of markets for conservation biology increased substantially between 1996–98 and 2006–08, reflecting greater donor support for this approach and increasing recognition of the role of natural systems in supporting and stabilizing human well-being, where the contribution of nature conservation measures to wider dimensions of human well-being arising from ecosystem services is often unproven.[64] Nevertheless, PES offers a complementary tool to existing mechanisms such as regulation and consensual protocols.

Transition in markets, including the valuation of water resources, is today indicated by the sheer scale of investment in catchment-based protection. Globally, US$8.17 billion (£5.07 billion) was spent in 2011 on projects to protect areas that provide water supplies, with China the leading nation accounting for 91 per cent of the 2011 investment as water insecurity is perceived as probably 'the single biggest risk to the country's continued economic growth'.[65] Since 1973, US$66 billion of investment has been made globally in watershed projects in which individuals or communities have been paid to preserve or revive natural features such as wetlands, streams and forests that can store and filter freshwater supplies. This rapid growth has run against the trend of economic downturn in many parts of the world, highlighting the depth of change occurring with respect to valuation of water resources for future growth and security.

We live in challenging times, when the consequences of established natural resource use habits are conflicting with the escalating needs of the booming human population. The distribution of wealth too is a major challenge, with the $US240 billion (£150 billion) net income amassed in 2012 by the world's richest 100 billionaires sufficient to lift the world's poorest out of poverty four times over.[66] Disparities occur not merely between developed and developing countries. In the UK, 'inequality is rapidly returning to levels not seen since the time of Charles Dickens'; in China the top 10 per cent take home nearly 60 per cent of total income; and in the USA the top 1 per cent has doubled its income from 10 to 20 per cent of the national total since 1980. Meanwhile, the WHO/UNICEF Joint Monitoring Programme (JMP) for Water Supply and Sanitation finds that 783 million people do not use an 'improved source of drinking-water' and '2.5 billion people do not use improved sanitation', contributing to the preventable death of a child every twenty seconds,[67] well over four thousand per day, with the treatment of diarrhoea in sub-Saharan Africa consuming 12 per cent of the health budget.[68] By contrast, diseases of excessive consumption – including diabetes, heart diseases, various forms of cancer and the stresses induced by obesity – are escalating in the rich, developed world. We have to find another pathway of development that respects the fundamental importance of critical natural resources, but also the rights of all who share them. And, of course, climate change can only exacerbate the associated risks.

Societal transition is necessarily a long-term and iterative process of change. If sustainable change is to become mainstream, the market has to evolve to support it. Appropriate valuation of water is, as we have seen, explicit in both the Dublin Principles for IWRM and within the CBD's twelve principles of the 'ecosystem approach', to which most nations of the world have made explicit commitments. We are taking initial steps around the world towards internalizing into the market the ecosystems we rely upon to produce water and other crucial resources, but the road yet to be trodden remains long.

14 | Nature's water infrastructure

Most definitions of the term 'infrastructure' relate to basic physical and organizational structures necessary for the operation of society or of an enterprise or economy.[1] It is usual for this to relate to structural elements such as transport, communications, power, water conveyance and waste systems. However, it is far less common to see any serious consideration of natural infrastructure, notwithstanding its fundamental significance for basic life support, primary economic resources and future potential and security.

Recognition and appropriate valuation of ecosystems as a critical form of infrastructure are then long overdue. If we are to recognize and respond to the fundamental dependence of society upon natural resources and processes, it is essential to reconceive the term 'infrastructure' in this broader biospheric context, rather than singularly for what we build from and upon it.[2]

Recognizing nature's water infrastructure

The various chapters of Part 2 of this book address management of water through ecosystem processes at landscape and catchment scales, including accounting for water through society and the economy. Bringing nature's water infrastructure into the mainstream of national policy and practice is a significant challenge.

The Ramsar Convention, established in 1971, has long been a forum for innovation and advocacy to capture the value of wetlands, for example championing the inclusion of wetlands within river basin management plans.[3] From the late 1980s, Uganda has been among the first countries in the world to recognize the central importance of the multiple values provided by its wetland resource as integral to sustainable development, the National Wetland Programme[4] (NWP) constituting the first such national wetland strategy globally supported by knowledge exchange and innovative tools in collaboration with the developed world.[5]

Progress is being made or techniques rediscovered in various locations throughout the world to address locally appropriate technologies for local water capture to meet more directly a diversity of livelihood needs. In addition, the value of the natural functions and services of water systems is becoming increasingly recognized in the urban environment, as well as within economic instruments. We are also seeing clear policy signals, including both international protocols[6] and national-scale policy statements,[7] seeking progressively to bring the value of the natural world into the mainstream across society. The more integrated approach to water and land management, reflecting both natural and social 'landscape fit' as represented by Ireland's integrated constructed wetlands (ICWs) and by some initiatives such as progressive implementation of SuDS, Green Infrastructure and flood risk management, highlights modern innovations that work with natural processes to develop low-input solutions that produce multiple ecosystem service outcomes maximizing societal value. Green shoots of innovation are then clearly apparent, even if wholesale 'mainstreaming' of the value of water and other essential ecosystems has yet to shape business and governance, which still suffers the legacy of the industrial-era paradigm that treats ecosystems as a largely limitless, exploitable resource.

Part 2 of this book has essentially been about ecosystem-based solutions to water management, supply, use and reuse. 'Systemic solutions' that work with natural processes not only often have lower input requirements but can be optimized to deliver a wider range of ecosystem service outcomes, benefiting more sectors of society as compared to generally more narrowly framed, input-intensive 'hard engineering' solutions with their wider scope for unintended negative consequences.[8] However, there is greater uncertainty inherent in most ecosystem-based approaches as regards delivering specific targeted outcomes, such as the quantitative improvement of effluent quality guaranteed by traditional engineered solutions. Consequently, notwithstanding their inherently greater sustainability and cumulative societal benefit per unit of input, the challenge to established operational assumptions introduces significant 'regulatory lag' to the acceptance of multi-benefit, ecosystem-based solutions.[9]

Modification of governance structures and processes to create space for consideration of ecosystem-based, socially inclusive approaches in the mainstream of thinking, planning, investment and operational practice remains a pressing challenge.

THREE | **Rethinking water and people**

15 | Living within the water cycle

Narrow thinking about 'heavy engineering' of water has often resulted in a swathe of unintended consequences at broader spatial and temporal scales. Conversely, ecosystem-based solutions that work with natural processes and exploit 'natural infrastructure' have the potential for optimizing a wider set of benefits with lower associated inputs. However, it would be unwise, not to mention profoundly unhelpful, to fall into an over-simplistic 'engineering bad, ecosystem good' polarization.

Uncomfortable realities

The challenges facing the modern world are far more 'wicked' than that, as dwindling natural resources are met by a growing human population, compounded by a changing climate and an uneven distribution of resources both geographically and demographically. The challenge of human development is no longer about 'people versus nature', as it has often yet incorrectly been caricatured in the past.

The uncomfortable reality is that, in our complex, overpopulated world, the vision of a more benign, efficient and decentralized interaction with the water cycle exercised throughout Part 2 of this book is unlikely ever to form a complete alternative to 'heavy technology', including water transfers and dams. This parallels the better-exercised debate about whether environmentally friendly organic or other extensive food production systems alone could ever support the food demands of a burgeoning global population, given their lower productivity per unit area.[1] Add to the sheer size of the human population the fact that it is now clustered into dense urban centres, often enjoying profligate lifestyles, to serve both of which we are forced to manipulate ecosystems significantly to supply our booming demands for ecosystem services such as food, water and waste processing.

The only option, were we entirely committed to the ecological route alone, would be to depopulate our shared planet substantially and urgently, and for each of us, rich and poor alike, to simplify and reduce our consumption of water and other resources with immediate effect. These outcomes are as unlikely as they are practically unachievable, barring some mega-disaster that enforces this eventuality.

There may just be too many of us bipeds seeking to drink from the same well; polarization of natural versus engineered solutions is too over-simplistic for our over-complicated world. The hard reality is that our choice is not simply between entrainment of water by dams and other 'hard engineering' technology or, conversely, its management through 'soft' technologies sympathetic with ecosystem processes alone. The question, in the gritty reality of the real world, is how to mesh these two approaches – the 'heavy engineering' along with the ingenuity and innovation that create it, as addressed in Part 1, together with the more benign ecosystems-based thinking and management highlighted in Part 2 – in ways that are sustainable, equitable and efficient.

These thorny, multidisciplinary problems are sometimes referred to as 'wicked problems'[2] or 'messes'.[3] Regardless of the terms used to describe them, these are problems defined by complexly intertwining elements, conflicting interests and values between different organizations, a high degree of uncertainty, and continually changing conditions.[4] What is quite apparent is that these wicked problems evade historic, narrowly disciplinary management solutions, instead requiring a more systemic approach reflecting their inherent complexity. Whatever we call them, we are going to have to tackle them.

A synthesis of engineering and ecosystem management

Whatever their proponents may claim about the environmental consequences of dams and the success of mitigation measures, dams inevitably block flows of water, biota, energy sediment and solutes. This is what they are designed to do, so it would be disingenuous to deny the fundamental changes they bring about in whole river and catchment systems. Yet, by contrast, we may need heavy technologies to support both contemporary lifestyles and the needs of current and rising population levels. Dams of all scales and other alternative water technologies may have roles to play as locally context-dependent management options that best suit all people on an enduring basis by respecting the diversity of society and the systems that supply it with water. So it would be naive to posit heavy engineering and ecosystem management as automatically in conflict. Indeed, there is some merit in the sentiment expressed by the International Commission on Large Dams (ICOLD) that it may be immoral to block development where it may be enhanced by a dam. A wicked problem indeed: dammed if we do, damned if we don't!

The idealist in me is with ecosystem-centred approaches, inherently opposing an automatic presumption in favour of large dams with their profound perturbation of the flux of ecosystems services along catchment systems shared by many different human communities. As an ecosystems scientist who has worked extensively in both the developed and the developing worlds, I have seen too many times and at first hand the widespread adverse consequences wrought on human well-being and expectations by the unintended degradation of ecosystems and their supportive processes.

Conversely, the realist in me recognizes the difficulties of meeting basic water and energy needs for all people across the world, particularly where demands exceed natural resource flows. This is rendered far more complex by a human population which, owing to sheer numbers and a continuing upward trend with uneven geographical distribution and thirsty lifestyles, places demands vastly beyond nature's carrying capacity. And, of course, this is all amplified by the reality of a changing climate.

Fortunately, we can be guided by some established examples where synergistic ecological and engineered approaches have delivered benefits to people. In the UK, for example, catchment management approaches are being increasingly recognized as a means to prolong the asset life of dams and other 'heavy' water infrastructure by reducing the rate at which they silt up, their maintenance costs, and the levels of contaminants entering them, with implications for the intensity of treatment processes and associated costs. We have already seen in Chapter 13 the example of South West Water working with the Westcountry Rivers Trust to subsidize improvements in farm management under 'Upstream Thinking' and related programmes as a cheaper alternative to cleaning up polluted water abstracted downstream. We have also seen how opportunities for water storage, erosion control averting dredging costs, fishery enhancement and other potential novel markets are reinforcing the economic case for using multi-benefit natural catchment processes in place of, or as a means to increase the lifetime value of, heavy engineering technology fixes for discrete problems. Furthermore, ecosystem-centred arrangements that prolong and enhance the value of engineered infrastructure include alien species management effected through the Working for Water programme to enhance the longevity and value of South Africa's Skuifraam Dam and other water management infrastructure, as well as reforestation schemes to restore hydrology and control erosion in the upper Yangtze catchment that feeds China's vast Three Gorges Dam. Further synthesis of the engineering and ecological paradigms is seen in widespread recognition of the value of catchment management to downstream water treatment costs and the provision of more reliable flows in an increasing number of case studies addressed in all continents. Working with the grain of natural processes is also becoming complementary or indeed integral to the management of flood risk[5] and fisheries[6] as well as dredging,[7] as ecosystems thinking progressively permeates into mainstream policy.

As the World Commission on Dams concluded, 'The issues surrounding dams are the issues surrounding water, and how water-related decisions are made ... Conflicts over dams are more than conflicts over water. They are conflicts over human development and life itself.'[8] This book's independent analysis further endorses the principles derived by the WCD, but goes beyond them into the spectrum of options, different patterns of governance and, importantly, ways of thinking and engagement that can lead to bigger questions and more inclusive and sustainable solutions to water management.

Water management in a 'wicked world' is all about recognizing and enabling inclusive dialogue about human needs, and seeking to resolve problems optimally through an appropriate mix of technologies and agreements which respect the ecosystem processes that underwrite them. This is a radical, generational transition from the dominant industrial world model that shapes much contemporary thinking, legacy regulation and market forces, vested engineering interests and associated assumptions. So promotion of a new, connected management paradigm is also about immersion of tomorrow's decision-makers in the breadth of thinking, technologies and tools available to support current and emerging water needs, arming them not with a technical 'catchment repair manual' but with means to help real stakeholders address their real needs together.

Merging 'hard' and 'soft' technology approaches in practice

As Thayer Scudder put it in his 2005 book *The Future of Large Dams*,[9] large dams are 'a flawed yet still necessary development option'. We will certainly need heavy technology to help us span our current impasse of sustainability problems, and particularly so in arid regions in a climate-challenged world and in the face of population growth with its demands for water, energy, food and other essential resources. However, we cannot afford to be blinkered by today's particular range of technological options.

Fred Pearce observes in his 2004 book *Keepers of the Spring*[10] that water inequality can stem from technology choice as 'No one technology, or suite of technologies, can do the job alone, however. Ultimately, we may need to rethink our approach to water management. Among the hallmarks of the successful water projects of the past is that built on them is a water ethic, one that encourages the careful allocation and use of water as community property, property on which the survival of entire peoples depended.' If we remain focused solely upon the range of techniques available to us today, we ignore the astounding creativity of the human spirit which has driven our technological advancement out of limiting factors in the past, and can continue so to do into the future as we reframe the problem into one that is inclusive of all people and address the achievement of the full dimensions of sustainability. Our current technologies, ecosystem-centred and engineered, and our hesitant progress in merging them, are a good start; tomorrow's technologies are now required.

The way we think about water, our dependence upon and demand for it, and the means by which we plan to deliver it in ways that respect the capacity of ecosystems to continue to supply it indefinitely, are central to achievement of its sustainable and equitable management. Part 3 of this book turns attention to integrated thinking and practical tools to address that need.

16 | Governance of water systems

Sustainability is about people. The effects of degrading ecosystems are felt most immediately and acutely by people living closest to their limits in regions worst affected by drought, famine and other 'natural disasters', many of which are in reality human amplified. But, if the challenge of sustainable development is not grasped proportionately, declining opportunity is a reality even for those buffered by the happenchance of economic privilege.

Governance of water systems and other crucial resources cuts to the core of how the livelihoods of diverse citizens, the ecosystems that underpin their needs and indeed the future are conceived and respected by nations, regions, local communities and indeed entire economic ideologies. The integration of livelihoods, ecosystems and appropriate technologies is framed by governing political and economic paradigms; paradigms that can and must shift to better address the sustainable and equitable sharing of common resources.[1]

All people, including future generations, are as hard-wired to the adverse consequences of declining ecosystem integrity as they are integral to the pursuit of sustainable solutions. So, as noted in the Introduction of this book, 'Access to and management of water are therefore inescapably political. And of course all politics are personal, never more so than for those with insufficient water to enable their families to drink, cook and wash and whose crops are withering in the field.' All water management decisions, from those of villagers collaborating to dig a johad in Rajasthan through to national planning for construction of a major dam, are inevitably political regardless of their scale as all affect the welfare of the diverse people within interconnected socio-ecological systems.

Who decides?

We are used to hearing about environmental 'crises' of one kind or another, especially about the crisis of water.[2] Yet capitalism functions only on the basis of scarcity, common or unvalued resources traded cheaply or else freely with value increasing as resources become limited. Indeed, there are many examples of scarcity of organisms and natural resources creating desirability and hence escalating price, driving them to precipitous decline or even extinction.[3] On this basis, it is not clear who gains from these claims of crisis if not those best placed to profit from an increasingly lucrative trade in scarcity.[4] In truth, the causative factors of water shortages usually lie more in governance than in the resource itself, leading writers such as Joyeeta Gupta to note that 'The water crisis of the 21st century is in many ways a crisis of governance; a crisis of the failure of our institutions to manage our resources for the well-being of humans and ecosystems'.[5] Putting people at the centre of water management, and thinking of the world as an interconnected system in which all people have legitimate needs, impacts and a voice, is an absolute prerequisite for sustainable and equitable development.

Many examples in this book highlight the inevitability of future problems if we blinker ourselves and address only the demands of certain strata of society, or omit environmental functioning and carrying capacity from planning considerations. They also illustrate the consequences of treating established technological approaches and the ideologies they embody as panaceas, and how perverse regulatory and/or economic signals can enforce, favour or simply fail to exclude unsustainable behaviours. There is therefore a pressing need to reframe water management from a narrow technical challenge into an inclusive social process: what in the catchment should be the focus of management, and who should be involved in managing it?[6]

For much of early human history, decisions were taken at community level as small and largely nomadic assemblages of people determined strategies to meet their varying needs. This in all probability changed little when settled but predominantly small communities formed near more stable resources such as streams, forests, floodplains and wetlands. However, humanity is, by its very nature and evolutionary adaptations, a communicating and learning species capable of great advancement through joint innovation. As evidenced by the methods evolved in Mesopotamia to divert flows on to farmed land, and indeed by emerging farming methods and the subsequent differentiation of roles across society that seeded our first recorded civilization, successive human societies innovate solutions together to address their needs by manipulating available resources.

Inevitably, as civilizations emerged, expanded and grew ever larger and more complex, governance of community decisions had also to expand in scale, whether through democratic, autocratic or other decision-making processes. The evolution of New York City's water supply is an illustration of this transition from local use and informal governance of wells and smaller water bodies and watercourses by local residents, progressively replaced by a network of aqueducts and reservoirs and their collective management and higher-level governance as population boomed throughout the nineteenth century. This in turn led on to grand schemes to harvest water from the Catskill mountains and the more recent rural–urban market innovation to protect source quality across the whole Cat/Del system. The trend towards increasingly centralized governance systems pervades most of the developed world, from the national to the provincial and local or municipal, and has certainly achieved impressive outcomes that could not have arisen organically.

Municipal sewerage, water supply, transport and trade systems provide grand demonstrations of centralized planning to advance the common good of differentiated societies. In this regard, the United Kingdom has much for which to thank its industrial-era forebears, who, often as a matter of altruism and/or civic responsibility on the back of their elevated social status achieved through accumulation of unprecedented wealth, saw the need for and then instigated many of the municipal institutions that we take for granted today. These philanthropists were the champions of public education and healthcare, libraries and parks, town planning, sewerage systems, and many more social innovations besides. Centralized systems of governance have also expanded to multinational scale across the European Union, the North American Free Trade Agreement, the South Asian Association for Regional Cooperation (SAARC), the Arab League and other trading blocs around the globe. Further centralization of governance, trade and decision-making has occurred at global scale under bodies such as the United Nations, the World Trade Organization (WTO), the Organisation for Economic Co-operation and Development (OECD) and the 'G8' group of leading industrialized countries.

Centralized government serves a valuable role in terms of shaping and governing major infrastructure, development and transformation programmes at broader geographical scales – catchments, wider landscapes, regions, nations, continents and the entire global biosphere, as in the case of the Intergovernmental Panel on Climate Change (IPCC) – which may not automatically be served by the vision, resources and often competing interests of smaller structural units. Centralized planning is indeed essential for development of much major infrastructure, be that 'hard engineering' or ecosystems-based.

However, the power of centralized decision-makers has to be moderated, and where appropriate delegated, such that decisions benefit all people, and powerful interests do not annex such crucial resources as water to the detriment of the poor, the powerless and the integrity of supportive ecosystems. An overemphasis on centralized governance and its negative consequences for many of the people it purports to serve is exemplified by the collapse of fully centralized industrial, urban development, agricultural expansion and other areas of planning in Soviet-era Russia. As long ago as 1842, Frederick Engels had warned of the dangers of 'an aristocracy of locality' where 'the state overstepping its bounds, going beyond its essential nature' undertakes narrow application of a single set of doctrines framed solely by a ruling elite which serve only to centralize power and influence in a narrow oligarchy.[7]

In most nations today, hierarchical governance through elected and/or appointed decision-makers is the norm for most spheres of societal resource management, making use of expert judgement to develop proposals and make decisions. The assumption here is that the decision-making community possesses sufficient expertise and insight to make wise decisions on behalf of all in society, and that democratic processes appoint leaders with such vision and wisdom. However, understanding of politics and success in gaining the popular vote do not equip a person with expertise in all technical spheres of human endeavour, nor automatically apprise them of the perspectives of all in society whose interests they are charged with governing. As many examples throughout Part 1 of this book highlight, there is a serious risk of capture of decision-making, and associated technology choice, to favour the interests of influential, privileged strata of society. Furthermore, consultation processes about 'top-down' decisions often fail in practice to alter the fundamental assumptions and sunk financial and political investments behind them. As such, such expert-led decisions tend to be impervious to significant modification once announced. This has led to the branding of this model of imposed governance as 'decide-announce-defend', or DAD.

DAD-based processes may be initially cheaper and quicker, and may be appropriate for making many types of simple, non-contentious decisions for which there is democratic consensus and mandate, such as a municipal decision to repair a broken water service pipe. However, beyond simple, operational management decisions, most water management decisions are far from simple. Critically, DAD-based decision-making does not automatically engage or empower all potentially affected stakeholder groups in solutions development, nor does it account for their diversity of values, knowledge and needs. Consequently, the process of 'defending' decisions following announcement can introduce a raft of unanticipated challenges, delays and additional expenses. Some examples from Part 1 of these unforeseen yet substantial 'defensive' expenditures and delays following announcement include the consequences of involuntary settlement under the Ghazi Barotha hydropower project, disputes after construction of Brazil's Salto Caxias hydroelectric dam, emerging legal and regulatory revisions after completion of China's Shuikou hydroelectric dam, and massive economic liabilities arising decades after the lawsuit taken by First Nations people affected by the USA's Grand Coulee Dam.

This does not imply that centralized decision-making is necessarily either a bad or a good thing. Centralization certainly offers broader scope and reach to govern resources more sustainably and equitably. However, it requires controls to ensure that the needs of all and the long-term viability of supporting ecosystems remain critical to management outcomes. Indeed, this is the purpose of the safeguarding of the principle of subsidiarity in European Union legislation and in the enshrinement of public participation and delegated decision-making in such visionary national legislation as South Africa's National Water Act 1998.[8]

Taking account of the multiple value systems, types of knowledge and livelihood needs of all people potentially affected by water management options in the process of formulating decisions is inherently more likely to lead to equitable outcomes, and hence more robust and readily accepted decisions. This alternative 'engage-deliberate-decide', or EDD, process takes as its starting point the perspectives of various stakeholders, including but not dominated by the insight of experts, in thinking collectively about water management and other complex problems. Thereby, EDD processes tend to generate a broader range of potential solutions for achieving efficient and equitable outcomes, which can then be appraised by stakeholders in terms of how they serve the deduced needs of all constituencies. The EDD approach does not automatically result in consensus or universal acceptance of decisions. However, it is far more likely to produce a shared understanding of the perspectives of all stakeholders and the background to decision-making, more equitably accounting for diverse value systems and needs and resulting in resolution of many potential tensions prior to final decisions. Decisions stemming from participatory approaches thereby tend to better address a diversity of needs and to harness local perspectives and innovation.

DAD and EDD approaches clearly have different cost and benefit profiles, at least for complex and contentious schemes.[9] In particular, the engagement and deliberative phases of EDD processes have a higher initial timeline and associated cost. However, they may turn out cheaper in the long run as stakeholders contribute to rather than fight proposals.[10] In addition to the examples noted above (Ghazi Barotha, Salto Caxias, Shuikou and the Grand Coulee Dam), the rising costs of the Skuifraam dam exemplify the generally unanticipated and unplanned delays and cost escalations associated with 'defending' expert-led decisions, with dam costs rising by 226 per cent from an initial estimate of 620 million rand to R1.4 billion when the dam filled from 2006. By contrast, more consensual, harmonious and beneficial agreements resulted in management of the Eastmain 1A-Rupert diversion in Quebec, the Songwe River Transboundary Catchment Management project and in 'bottom-up participatory planning' in Vietnam.

As all complex water management issues inevitably touch upon many people, interests and organizations, methods to secure participatory decision-making are not only important but may be the only way of making durable management decisions. Effective stakeholder engagement is consequently increasingly required in legislation and protocols across the world, including, for example, the 1998 UNECE Aarhus Convention, the EU Water Framework Directive, the US approach to collaborative watershed planning, South Africa's National Water Act 1998 and China's emerging resettlement legal framework, as well as an explicit inclusion in the 'Dublin Principles' and the twelve principles of the ecosystem approach.

Transition to participatory decision-making is, however, far from complete or assured. Examples throughout this book highlight a spectrum of decision-making between DAD and EDD approaches, and hence practical progress up Sherry Arnstein's 'Ladder of Engagement',[11] which reflects the need for citizenry to effectively participate and positively influence processes enabling a redistribution of power away from centralized to localized levels. We have already looked at a range of DAD examples. South Africa's Skuifraam Dam and Thukela Water Project (TWP) are in fact halfway houses, with deliberative processes introduced post-announcement resulting in additional mitigation and ecosystem-centred catchment management in the former case and retrospective responses to stakeholder and legislative requirements in the latter. Relicensing of the Clark Fork project in the USA is another example of EDD-based stakeholder collaboration immediately post-decision, resulting in a 'Living License' to improve ongoing problem-solving, detailed licence provisions and funding of mitigation measures. Demonstrations of the EDD approach in practice include the prior examples of multi-stakeholder participation in integrated watershed management in the Adarsha Watershed, locally appropriate water management options generated in the Olifants River Water Resources Development project, the inclusion of 'physical' and 'emotional' characteristics in a vision for restoration of the upper River Tame, multi-criteria decision analysis in stakeholder engagement in the Sand river (South Africa), and the use of a range of modelling tools in Australia which also demonstrate to stakeholders the consequences of their suggestions.

Balancing centralization and decentralization in resource management

The permeation of renewable energy generation into developed-world energy distribution systems provides a graphic example of both potential conflicts and synergies of centralized versus decentralized management. Many renewable energy conversion technologies operate most efficiently within an energy mix as embedded, distributed and sometimes off-grid systems situated close to demand. This is at odds with the established model of centralized generation and distribution, the established infrastructure and institutions for which can present obstacles to connection of renewable energy sources. Conformance with various technical, legal and economic protocols, such as power grids and tariff structures, need not conflict. However, the vested interests of key players controlling the potentially outmoded centralized system can erect obstacles that make the planning process difficult and the costs of compliance unattractive or prohibitive for 'new entrant' interests in renewable energy.

The same juxtaposition of centralized and decentralized systems applies to computing systems, as indeed also their progressive integration. The dominant late twentieth-century model of mainframes servicing networks of 'dumb' terminals has now almost wholly been replaced by stand-alone personal computers and local area networks that can interact across the globe for purposes as diverse as financial transactions, weather forecasting, communications and shopping. While one benefit of centralization is the ease of maintaining accurately updated lists of data that can be easily accessed from all points, centralization's weaknesses in information technology terms pivot around the system's heavy reliance on a few central components; if the system's hubs are put out of operation, either accidentally or through hostile action, the system and its peripheral components are severely affected. By contrast, decentralized yet web-connected smart systems are more resilient and adaptive, though their operation still relies on a great deal of centralized protocols and planning. Computing is therefore an elegant example of centralized higher-level principles enabling decentralized operation and innovation, for example with open source internet protocols enabling access and participation by anyone with a PC, smart phone, tablet computer or other device, no matter by whom it is manufactured or for what purpose it is being used.

We are also experiencing transitions in terms of the emphasis of urban planning, moving from monolithic, top-down master plans based on zoning towards a more granular structure encouraging localized viable, mixed-use urban cells contributing to an overall more 'liveable city'.[12] There is also a transition in healthcare, from a prime focus on centralized treatment of disease to a greater emphasis on decentralized health protection through individual lifestyles as well as 'walk-in' centres and online advice. This principle of devolving decision-making to the lowest appropriate level found an elegant summation in the title of Fritz Schumacher's influential 1973 book *Small is Beautiful*,[13] in which he argued that 'One of the most fateful errors of our age is the belief that "the problem of production" has been solved', offering a powerful argument about the importance of preserving the environmental and social efficiencies in production systems worldwide that are deemed uneconomic by centralized industrial-scale thinking.

Water management across the world, from the USA to China, has often been implemented by the diktat of centralized, hierarchical institutional arrangements.[14] Big-scale planning to bring about 'economies of scale' and the degree of coverage required to ensure resilience in the supply of public goods necessitate a degree of centralized planning for delivery of universalized standards across society, providing rule-setting mechanisms for organizing relations between social groups.[15] However, rigid, inflexible and unresponsive state-centred frameworks and governments tend to handle difficult societal dilemmas and diverse local needs poorly, leading to a 'crisis of governance' through habitual inefficient water management practices, the blame for which rests at the doorstep of existing water institutions.[16]

By contrast, decentralized water management and service provision tackle problems at a different scale. Privatization of water services is often seen as a means to counteract service delivery inefficiencies by the state, including in the water sector,[17] though in reality privatized services merely implement the specifications of politically driven contracts. We have also to be wary about assumptions that market solutions automatically delegate decision-making to the lowest level appropriate for resource management, as emphasized by the 'ecosystem approach', the 'Dublin Principles' and the Global Water Partnership,[18] which adds that 'Water development and management should be based on a participatory approach, involving users, planners and policy-makers at all levels. States should devolve responsibility to the lowest appropriate level.' Whether privately or publicly operated, planning requires a significant degree of participation.

Participatory approaches challenge established power imbalances and dogmatically applied solutions.[19] However, by injecting local knowledge, promoting relevance to all beneficiaries and building on networks between organizations, public participation enhances the legitimacy and accountability of decision-makers.[20] However, the inherent value of stakeholder participation is reflected in various strands of water-related legislation across the world, including under the EU Water Framework Directive[21] (Article 14 contains provisions for Member States to 'encourage the active involvement of all interested parties in its implementation') and South Africa's National Water Act 1998, under which participation and the redistribution of rights across all in society are central threads. It is also recognized as of fundamental importance by the World Commission on Dams, the UNEP Dams and Development Programme (DDP) and by national policy shifts such as the UK's 'Big Society' concept launched in 2010.[22] However, participation is not an end in itself. Outcomes are tempered by the quality of the participatory processes used. There is always also a risk of the capture of participatory processes by historically powerful interest groups.[23]

'Self-organization' can also arise through effective cooperative partnerships forming without a dominant leading agency.[24] However, it is unsafe to assume that participation in decision-making will happen automatically in the absence of top-down management control, and especially when it is required to integrate across geographical scales. Governing principles need to be established centrally to prevent powerful vested interests or interest groups from dominating decentralized multi-stakeholder platforms. Some sort of enabling framework may also be required to avoid unwillingness to engage through either confusion about purpose or 'consultation fatigue' among participants. Furthermore, in addressing the complex ecosystems within which resource use and sharing occur, there is a need for different tiers of engagement. For example, it is unlikely that management addressing ecosystem processes at catchment scale would arise if decisions were taken only at village scale, from which village-to-village competition may dominate decisions. A macroscopic example here of the effective linkage of centralized intentions and decentralized implementation is seen in China's Sloping Land Conversion Policy (SLCP, addressed in Chapter 13), for which reforestation and reinstatement of other forms of vegetative cover was initiated to address devastating flooding and soil erosion problems across thousands of miles of the Yangtze river; centralization of vision, response and economic instruments was essential to identify and work practically to solve a catchment-scale problem, though solutions including reinstating tree and grass cover were undertaken at farm and field scale. At a wider scale still, the Intergovernmental Panel on Climate Change[25] is beginning to address climate management at a global scale, requiring a far bigger scale of collective thinking, planning, agreements and proportionate action, though locally and culturally appropriate actions themselves are delegated to nation-states.

The transition from imposed water management decisions to emergent and innovative solutions addressing local diversities of concerns, knowledge and values requires a different type of leadership. This new type of leadership has to deal with multiple layers of social, technological, economic, environmental and political complexity simultaneously, merging high-level principles with true participation. The true leader, then, is one who does not suggest that they know best, and does not impose 'solutions' upon others, but rather integrates many forms of knowledge to accommodate sustainable, equitable and efficient outcomes. As articulated by Max DePree, 'The first responsibility of a leader is to define reality. The last is to say thank you. In between, the leader is a servant.'[26] To support this, the state is called upon to create an 'enabling environment' to ensure optimal conditions for all actors to work together to deliver common objectives, as clearly defined roles and responsibilities are essential for effective interorganizational cooperation,[27] which also cannot work cooperatively in the absence of trust.[28]

The role of the state therefore does not diminish in an effective decentralized resource management system, but changes from a model of 'state as regulator' to 'state as facilitator'.[29] Knowing what we know now, it is clear that the quest for an equitable and sustainable future must entail a quite different trajectory of decisions and actions than have propelled us through the past two and a half centuries. Anthony Turton, a leading water scientist in South Africa, asked the question 'Can we solve tomorrow's problems with yesterday's experiences and today's science?',[30] underlining the need for new conceptual understanding and ways of making decisions. A learning approach will therefore be required, acknowledging that this will entail innovations that build upon the strengths yet reject the flaws in traditional assumptions and technologies. In addressing this transition in focus on water management, Falkenmark[31] notes insightfully that 'What stands out is the need for a new generation of water professionals, able to handle complexity and able to incorporate water implications of land use and ecosystem health in integrated water resources management'.

By whatever means, we need strong and insightful leadership to move to a catchment-scale level of awareness, and to use that perception to engage key stakeholders in those catchments in far-sighted and collective decisions about sharing and managing water together. The alternative is that we continue to undermine and impoverish ecological integrity, and consequently the health and wealth particularly of the least powerful in society. This will in many instances need to accommodate a hybrid approach making best use of the long-term legacy of existing water management infrastructure and the likely future need to integrate 'hard' with environmental engineering solutions. Dealing with this 'hard solutions' legacy remains important as, despite the years that have passed since the WCD report *Dams and Development*, there has been a substantial shortfall in research to address the governance of existing large dams and the specific nature of their associated infrastructure,[32] despite some novel adaptive approaches such as discharge modification at the Glen Canyon Dam in the USA.

Institutional development is not a value-free process, so the values and principles in higher tiers of government have to align with lower tiers for different scales of vision and cooperative action to thrive.[33] The (centralized) state has a clear duty to build capacity for local (decentralized) engagement, as low community awareness of institutional arrangements effectively excludes localized groups with an interest in water management from planning processes.[34] Lack of encouragement of community-level engagement is also commonly advanced as a reason for the slow pace of reform across Europe to implement not just the technical standards but the participatory principles of the Water Framework Directive.[35] Consequently, capacity-building support is one of the central threads of much aid flowing from the developed to the developing world, assisting local people, NGOs and government staff in recipient countries better to address their own needs and priorities. A great deal of patience and a steady approach to trust-building are essential to the establishment of functional institutional arrangements.[36] Skilled facilitation can also make a substantial contribution to overcoming conflicting interests across diverse groups, helping redress power imbalances, prolong and sustain interactions, and develop collective vision.[37]

There are also important issues associated with power and accountability, including how stakeholder groups are constituted and who is included or excluded and how the inevitable conflicting interests among diverse stakeholders are managed in decision-making processes.[38] Building an appropriate balance between expert and other forms of knowledge is also essential. For example, public participation was recognized as important to the process of restoring the longitudinal and lateral connectivity of the extensively regulated Murray river in Australia in order to share the scarce water between many strongly competing uses and values, recognizing that the river was more than just a water source but instead confers multiple benefits to society, so the 'stakes are high because the Murray is one of the Australian rivers of poetry, song and legend. The Murray is part of the national heritage.'[39] To attempt to achieve effective restoration, Australian governments at both commonwealth and state levels set up an independent expert reference panel on environmental flows, and holistic environmental flow assessment techniques were also developed better to inform a stakeholder panel representing a range of other river interests about river condition and flow requirements affecting their collective interests.[40] A similar technical advisory and wider stakeholder approach was also undertaken in addressing restoration of some of the former hydrological character in Australia's Snowy River, which had long been degraded by large-scale water diversions for the Snowy Mountains hydroelectric scheme. Stakeholder deliberation about future management of the Snowy River was supported by calculation of minimum environmental flow requirements and a composite river condition index based on metrics of hydraulic and physical habitats, water quality, barriers to fish passage and the condition of riparian vegetation as a very useful way to present and summarize information to non-specialist audiences, as well as a more robust evidence base for an expert panel process.[41] Some of these improvements were possible owing to the strength of the Australian economy, enabling the state to buy back water rights from farmers; this may not be the situation in many nations, though the principle of merging expert and local knowledge to co-create beneficial solutions remains robust.

From the Colorado river in the USA to the Yangtze in China, the Mekong in central Asia[42] and the Murray-Darling in Australia, across both the developed and the developing worlds, recognition of the need for greater participation in achieving sustainable outcomes is becoming increasingly recognized.[43] Indeed, there is growing acknowledgement that the transition from traditional top-down water management to more internally interactive multilevel governance requires a fundamentally bottom-up approach founded on strong societal self-organization at all levels.[44] The need for pragmatic tools to encourage participation in sustainable water management is therefore also becoming increasingly recognized,[45] even if the reins of power are not as yet being as rapidly and eagerly released by political elites. Analytical techniques (for example, technical knowledge and models) can effectively be combined with participatory and deliberative techniques (such as participatory modelling, multi-criteria analysis and deliberative monetary valuation), adding value to broader thinking and collective decision-making about the ramifications of proposed management actions for broader stakeholders without dominating the decision, and using the full breadth of the ecosystem approach, significantly emphasizing that ecosystem management is a matter of societal choice.[46]

Local need, catchment consciousness and global ecosystems

Integrating local needs and cultures with broader-scale continental socio-ecological systems and broad catchment processes poses major challenges. Beyond notable successes such as evolving agreements on a number of international rivers, we have much yet to achieve to attain the goal of connecting these scales and so addressing local need in the context of ecosystem processes spanning political boundaries. Yet the challenge of feeding and watering over seven billion people on the back of dwindling global resources of all kinds expands the scope of even wider challenges to be overcome, all of them compounded by instability in the global climate.

These challenges may be nowhere more acutely manifested than in mountain areas, themselves under ever-greater anthropogenic pressure,[47] from which water supplies for half the world population originate and which have profound impacts on climate and hydrologic cycles.[48] Their sustainable management, then, is not only an urgent priority but also a matter of global concern. Perhaps they are best regarded as 'critical natural capital', though governance of mountain regions is generally distributed on a national scale among those countries for which mountain ranges also serve as political boundaries. Meanwhile, the bulk of emissions affecting the global climate and water cycles, and so the capacity of mountain systems to retain critical water-related ecosystem services, may stem from remote nations with little or no mountain resources.

This level of truly integrated governance of water and the other habitats and other natural systems integral to its sustainable cycling, from the local to the national, international and biospheric, is not something that has yet been attempted other than through a few institutions such as the IPCC. Rather, interests at local and national scales still tend to dominate, with fragmentation of water governance addressing only poorly the larger scales at which these processes operate.[49] Perhaps the nascent Intergovernmental Science-Policy Platform on Biodiversity and Ecosystem Services[50] (IPBES), an 'IPCC for biodiversity',[51] will in time step up to address this connection of scales?

Tools to support sustainable water management

There is, then, no single, ubiquitously appropriate technology solution. All management situations are different, reflecting local hydrology and other natural variables, as well as the needs and aspirations of local people. To be blinkered about technological solutions, be they 'heavy engineering' or 'green', simply perpetuates a centralized 'expert view' which rarely embraces the needs of all in society, instead biasing decisions towards the interests of powerful economic and/or political elites. Decision-making processes that do not involve people will almost always result in people as net victims. However, it is also essential to reflect the primary importance of ecosystems as providers of water and other human benefits, rather than to posit them as competing consumers. In this regard, an ecosystem services view of the world is invaluable, providing an integrated tool to reflect the importance of conserving or restoring ecosystem structure and function as the primary resource underpinning many dimensions of human well-being.

The framework of ecosystem services, such as the classification scheme advanced by the Millennium Ecosystem Assessment,[52] serves as a valuable template with which to assess the breadth of human benefits provided by functional ecosystems. Furthermore, it also exposes deep biophysical, cultural, equitable and economic interdependencies, including how use of a resource by any individual or sector of society, including their technology choice, inevitably affects important ecological functions and so has inevitable consequences for other people both now and into the future. Ecosystem services then provide an insightful framework for integrated planning, deliberation and governance of complex socio-ecological systems.

The ecosystem services framework can also be applied as a screening mechanism for many existing environmental management tools to enhance their scope and insights, leading to more inclusive and sustainable outcomes. Practical examples of the kinds of tools that could be thus modified to provide greater insight include Environmental Impact Assessment (EIA), Strategic Environmental Assessment (SEA), identification and screening of wider impacts of measures proposed for implementation of the EU Water Framework Directive (WFD), pre-screening of spatial planning proposals, or other routine management tools facilitating innovations that optimize benefits and avert unintended consequences.[53] This would, without great innovation or the need for new primary legislation, bring the full ecosystem and its many beneficiaries and codependents across a range of scales into consideration in operational decision-making. This percolation of systemic considerations into operational tools can and must continue, overcoming established anachronistic habits and blinkered, discipline-specific views.

However, valuable as the integration of ecosystem functions and outputs with social benefits and economic implications may be within the ecosystem services framework, wider political and other governance considerations have to be considered in decision-making. One of the most useful approaches I have discovered for working with communities around their ecosystem interdependencies while connecting with governance mechanisms stems from a water reform capacity-building programme I co-ran in South Africa. I and a number of colleagues working at national and provincial government levels, and also with local stakeholders within target catchments, took an action learning approach.[54] Significantly, this centred around a systems articulation of the STEEP (Social, Technological, Economic, Environmental, Political) knowledge management framework. Devised initially as a strategic tool to support long-range business planning and to assess a range of global change issues,[55] STEEP provided a pedagogic tool and framework to orient much of our action learning programme, leading to deeper insight into problems and potential solutions by breaking them down into constituent but inherently interconnected categories. Therefore, rather than treating STEEP as a simple five-point checklist, we emphasized the systemic interconnections between the five constituent elements, including, for example, how technology choice has inevitable social, ecological and economic implications all affected by the political assumptions behind decisions to implement it.

We interpreted the 'social' dimension of STEEP as relating primarily to the 'sustainable livelihoods' approach, 'environmental' as pertaining to ecosystem services, and 'political' as wider governance mechanisms and not simply political processes. 'Economic' considerations related not merely to the dominant 'First World' market economy but to informal trading and other exchanges and valuation within the whole system. Each element is both integral to the whole and non-substitutable; no amount of money will compensate for a degraded water resource if no water is available to be purchased to compensate for the loss. This systemic interpretation of the STEEP model helped us think collectively with those with whom we were working about the interdependencies between constituent factors, and how these need to affect the decisions that we arrive at with others. This interpretation of the STEEP model and its graphic representation (see the figures below) proved to be powerful and readily grasped by the different groups with which we worked, ranging from central and provincial government to both large-scale white and small-scale black farmers, municipality workers, conservation interests and other diverse constituencies in catchment-level workshops, promoting understanding, visioning and collective planning.

One particular way in which we used this version of the STEEP model in our South African work was to help explore these diverse people's perceptions of their history, present and future through what we called a 'transition model'. This entailed drawing up the STEEP model on three different flip charts stuck to the wall of our meeting spaces. One flip chart represented historic water management under the influence of apartheid ten years prior to the exercise, the second represented the current situation, and the third provided a space to think about the desired future water management situation ten years hence. The first phase of this exercise involved all participants writing their thoughts about the historic water management situation on sticky notes, which they then stuck to the section of the STEEP model to which they felt they belonged. We repeated this with each group for the current and then the desired future scenarios. The next stage of the exercise involved people looking at what others had written then working together to cluster the thoughts, including moving the sticky notes around the STEEP model if a better association seemed appropriate. We then reflected together on what we had learned.

The first run of this exercise was during capacity-building with provincial staff of the Department of Water Affairs and Forestry (DWAF) and the proto-Catchment Management Agency (CMA) in KwaZulu-Natal. We repeated this exercise separately with a diverse group of catchment stakeholders (white farmers, industrialists, emerging black

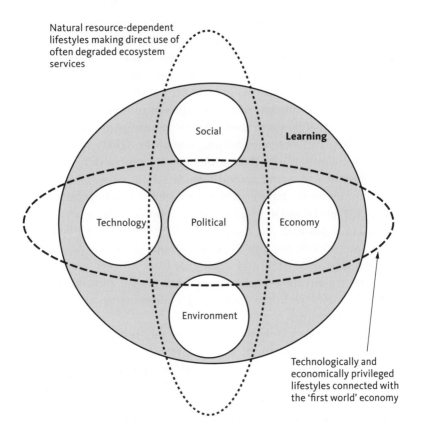

16.1 A society divided between the technologically and economically advantaged, and those living close to often degraded basic ecosystem resources

farmers, tribal leaders, tourism and conservation interests, etc.) with whom we were working to build a Water User Association (WUA) in the Mvoti catchment north of Durban, KwaZulu-Natal. The third running of this exercise was with senior national management of DWAF. Without any prior steerage, the learning outcomes arising from running the exercise at all three tiers – national government, provincial regulator and catchment-scale stakeholder group – were amazingly consistent, and proved revealing for all participants.

One piece of learning about the historic water management situation that was consistent with all groups, albeit replicated in different words and stories, was that there were two intersecting but otherwise disconnected axes through the STEEP model (Figure 16.1). The first of these was a distinct and concentrated axis from T(echnology) through

P(olitical) to E(conomic): a historic presumption in favour of applying 'heavy engineering' technologies, such as dams and water transfer schemes, to prioritize the advancement of a narrow, predominantly white stratum of society engaged in the 'First World' economic model. The second distinct axis through the model ran from S(ocial) through P(olitical) to E(nvironmental), reflecting the silent majority of people, mainly historically disadvantaged black people excluded from the 'first economy', whose livelihoods were based on access to an often impoverished or naturally less productive ecosystem resource. The dominant 'first economy' regime exerted control over technology to yield economic advantage by manipulation of ecosystem resources, often, as in the case of dams and water transfer schemes, benefiting disproportionately, with the associated costs either shared as a common or else entirely imposed upon less politically and economically powerful people dependent upon a degraded and depleting resource base. This is of course entirely consistent with prior observations in this book regarding how fantastic innovation and feats of engineering have diverted water to the 'first economy' powerhouse in Gauteng province, drawing resources from across the nation to favour a minority of (historically mainly white) people while coincidentally contributing to a highly uneven distribution of benefits and impacts on ecosystem services elsewhere. There is a very real risk that these inequities and vulnerabilities will become magnified as increasing climate instability exacerbates water stress. There are also strong parallels with the way factories, incinerators and conurbations pollute land, water and air, often to the detriment of the poorest in society,[56] another form of unsympathetic 'first economy' advancement that erodes ecosystems supporting the livelihoods of natural resource-dependent livelihoods. Consequently, those not engaging in the dominant economic model become increasingly marginalized and compromised in their capacity to meet their needs. Under this STEEP-based analysis of the then current situation of water management in South Africa, these two disconnected economies, one founded on hegemony and dominance and the other supplicant and subsistence-level, were found to coexist within the same socio-ecological system. The governance system is also divided, the powerful appropriating ecosystem resources for their economic advantage and the powerless struggling to address immediate subsistence needs from the remaining ecosystem capacity.

Those living the most directly 'natural resource-dependent lifestyles' often live close to subsistence without the aid of 'big technology' solutions or connection with the capitalist market economy, beyond some

Technologies better matched to a diversity of local needs, both within and outside the formal economy, and addressing ecosystem 'carrying capacity'

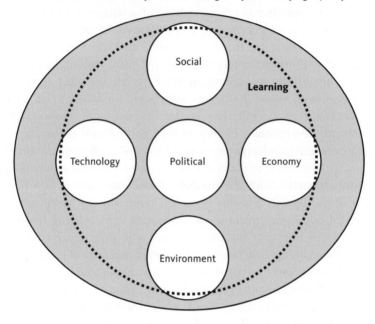

16.2 The future vision in which technology and the economy are governed to address diverse livelihood needs and the natural resources that support them

cash crop sales. This resource-dependent pattern may have been the norm in pre-industrial times. It remains so in non-industrialized regions of the world and in those places where sustainable communal management systems (i.e. locally adapted governance) have evolved, as evidenced by Asian terrace agriculture, village agreements about the sharing of water from wells, tanks and wetlands, taboos against certain practices that might compromise communal water resources, and so forth. However, this subsistence-level model runs into conflict with the industrialized, resource-appropriating world view.

This model of a divided society is not unique to apartheid-era South Africa. In my other work on river and lake systems in East Africa, I have witnessed how the long-established nomadic lifestyle of the Masai tribe naturally adapts to moving with the availability of grazing but runs into conflict when it interfaces with land appropriated and wired off into enclosures for horticulture and other production purposes feeding the privileged 'First World' economy. My work in India and China has also encountered continuing commitment to a 'large dam' ethos which ignores the potential for longer-term consequences for river ecosystems and the many livelihoods dependent upon them. The continental-scale diversion of the flow of the Yangtze river northwards to serve demands in the north China Plain, to the detriment of vast areas of the lower Yangtze river (the 0.8-million-square-kilometre catchment downstream of the Three Gorges Dam out of the Yangtze's total catchment area of 1.8 million square kilometres) and the ecosystems and livelihoods that it supports, are a dramatic example of this division of power and advantage. Such divisions in society result from often stark asymmetries of power, wealth, control of the most productive land, water and other natural resources, and the technologies chosen to control them. Across the world, technological solutions such as dams, armaments, irrigation and industrial production methods serve these narrower interests, yet often marginalize the needs of others and the integrity of the ecosystems that serve them. All of these examples reveal a similar pattern of an influential 'first economy', often advantaged by implementation of 'big engineering' solutions such as dams and inter-basin water transfer schemes, and a less formal 'second economy' struggling to subsist on remaining ecosystem capacity. Such stark divisions in society are hardly a formula for equity and harmony, let alone sustainability. I have also observed a similar pattern and technology bias in regulatory presumptions in Ireland, again also exposed using the STEEP model.[57] The 'divided society' model, which revealed itself so strikingly and consistently through our work on water sharing in South Africa, is therefore both widespread and inherently unstable, prone to conflict and hence inherently unsustainable.

Returning to our use of the STEEP systems model in our work in South Africa, consideration of a future approach to water management and sharing had implicit within it that the three primary driving principles of the National Water Act 1998 – equity, efficiency and sustainability – should be met in a balanced way. The sticky note, clustering and reflective learning phases of the exercise resulted in a more even narrative, acknowledging the need to consider technologies appropriate to meeting the diverse livelihood needs of all in society, both within and outside the formal economy, in ways that made use of natural processes without exceeding their finite carrying capacities (Figure 16.2). This integrated articulation of the roles of the economy and technology in meeting the livelihood needs of all sectors of society suggests a flexible approach to technology choice that addresses the legitimate needs of all in society, and which is sensitive to environmental limits and their equitable sharing. This is a very different model of governance, founded on dialogue, through which stakeholders are enabled to participate, innovate and co-create sustainable and equitable solutions.

Completing this account of the three-stage 'transition model' exercise, key learning about the (then) current situation of water management in South Africa was that it was chaotic. However, working through the 'transition model' helped people at national, provincial government and local levels recognize that this was understandable as they were in the midst of a process of profound transition, about which only the past and desired future were clear. This highlighted the need for practical tools to support enhanced participation, and the flexibility of an action learning approach acknowledging that the 'experts' do not have all the answers.

Adaptive management

In the spirit of adaptive management, there also needs to be recognition that getting it 'right first time', or at least stumbling upon perfect arrangements or sets of agreements, is an unlikely outcome given the novelty of devolved and inclusive decision-making processes, substantial uncertainties about the response of the water cycle, imperfect knowledge of stakeholder expectations, and of course a changing baseline due to climatic instability. Consequently, a collective learning approach needs to be woven into institutional frameworks, including in the relationships between holders of expert and local knowledge, as well as responsiveness to evidence of impacts on water and other shared resource systems.[58]

The value of harnessing collective intelligence and learning to inform better decision-making around complex problems in organizations is well established.[59] However, they remain generally only poorly reflected in practice.[60] The principle of building adaptation into management is nowhere more important than in complex systems such as the socio-ecological water cycle. And, as we saw in Chapter 10, it has led to recognition of the need for a paradigm of adaptive water resources management (AWRM), the essence of which is that human involvement and ownership are required from identification of optimal outcomes to modification of ensuing management regimes on the basis of experience and outcomes.

Continuous learning cycles and the monitoring of outcomes necessary to support adaptive management need to be built into governance processes and budgets. The EU Water Framework Directive process, for example, requires a six-year River Basin Management Planning cycle, while, in South Africa, CMA strategies are to be reviewed every five years. Learning at all scales must also be integrated if localized knowledge is not to be lost in planning processes which may, in its absence, revert to familiar top-down decision-making, losing the benefits of the participatory approach. A 'double loop learning' approach is necessary, going beyond the 'single loop' approach of assessing performance against set objectives, instead undertaking reflective and deeper analysis that questions the approaches that are used as well as the objectives set in previous planning rounds.[61] This thereby calls to account the effectiveness of water management practices and the processes put in place to administer them. Deeper applied learning also helps harmonize broader-scale aspirations, such as action on climate change or catchment integrity, with the needs of local people, to develop shared understanding and vision, which are essential enablers of integration across scales to support effective partnership working.

In summary, development of effective policy and practice is far more than a technical process; it is one that also demands active consideration of political and social factors when looking to include public organizations in water management. Evidence from the WCD, the DDP and various more recent case studies suggests that this remains remote in water management. Narrow presumptions about technical water management solutions divorced from specific catchment and local contexts are likely only to impose a particular world view on all affected people, conflicting with the ways in which they access water. The governance questions are often about who we involve in decision-making about provision of water and how we involve them in making and revising decisions that also respect the natural processes, and their limits, from which enduring societal benefits flow.[62] The problem may be far less technical than one of inclusive decision-making.

Governance models are as much in transition as the ways in which we understand the environment and water systems. Meanwhile, inertia and the influence of vested interests in maintaining a status quo continue to exert considerable power. We are in the midst of a 'live experiment' to find out how to make the bold transition from yesterday's assumptions to tomorrow's needs. What we have to ensure is that governance arrangements both respect those elements of water-sharing for which a 'higher-level view' is required, including, for example, maintaining a systemic perspective about the overall functioning of catchments, but also integrate the needs, wisdom and value systems of local people. The role of the regulator then changes from the developed-world norm of principal decision-maker towards a guardian of systemic perspectives and inclusive processes, protecting the rights of all in society against personal-interest decisions while delegating the deliberative process. Meanwhile, the market continues to evolve, as evidenced by various emerging examples (see Chapter 13) of the progressive integration of aspects of the natural environment, including critical ecosystem functions such as the generation of clean water.

It is then perhaps not surprising that, despite 5,000 years of global evolution of water law and policy, governance still has not reached stability but continues to evolve,[63] and with it the need for alternative institutional models to address the transnational and intergenerational values of water.[64]

17 | Towards a new hydropolitics

On our crowded planet, more of us will have to subsist on significantly degraded ecosystems which, given the momentum of current trends, will continue to degrade even if we can muster the courage to reverse the pressures we place upon them and to engage in their restoration as a matter of both self-interest and moral duty.

Yesterday's politics of water management, at least throughout the industrial age, has been of appropriation of water as just one of many natural resources, with little consideration of the finite limits of ecosystems and implications for those who share them. Tomorrow's hydropolitics will be different, shaped by knowledge of how ecosystems produce the many services supporting human prospects, the deep interdependencies between them and the many sectors of society who benefit from these services, and novel approaches to economics and governance that progressively recognize and internalize the value of water and other productive systems. Various of these principles are recognized in initiatives such as the World Commission on Dams, the 'Dublin Principles', the 'ecosystem approach' and are included in guidance such as TEEB for Policymakers.[1] While understanding these principles is essential, it is even more important that they are put into a practical action in the face of the gritty and uncomfortable realities of 'real world' water management decision-making. There is, let us remind ourselves, no 'right technology' choice, but there are means for thinking through technologies – whether 'hard engineering', ecosystems-based or more likely a hybrid of the two – that are appropriate in a catchment context for addressing the cultures and needs of the many stakeholders who share it.

Guidance for practical decision support

There are pedagogic and general-interest values in considering our 'heavy engineering' past (Part 1), ecosystems-based alternatives (Part 2) and emerging sustainable water management questions in an uncertain future (prior chapters in Part 3). However, it is above all important that guidance also emerges to support the practical decisions to be undertaken by those to whom this book is dedicated.

1 Develop common understandings of water systems

⇓

2 Acknowledge the central role of people at all scales

⇓

3 Develop or evolve institutions

⇓

4 Recognize the values, perspectives and uses of all stakeholders

⇓

5 Develop participatory and deliberative techniques

⇓

6 Develop a common vision of future water use and resource sharing

⇓

7 Deliberate on the basis of all views and ways in which water is used

⇓

8 Assess all options on a 'level playing field'

⇓

9 Factor the changing nature of natural systems into plans

⇓

10 Consider long-term ramifications

⇓

11 Develop or evolve practical tools

⇓

12 Assess the legislative baseline

⇓

13 Explore the role of markets

⇓

14 Consider how current infrastructure can be improved to mitigate damage

⇓

15 Resolve the needs of ecosystems with those of people

⇓

16 Monitor outcomes and adapt

17.1 Sixteen-point framework to guide deliberation and decisions for water management

This guidance emerges from lessons deduced from all of the issues addressed to date in this book, synthesized into a sixteen-point framework to guide deliberation and decisions for water management. The full guidance is articulated in the Annexe, 'Principles for sustainable water sharing', but is summarized in the figure above. This is obviously not a 'grand unified theory of decision-making' about water, as that language falls into the DAD-based trap of being excessively formulaic and squeezing out diverse human-scale perspectives and innovations. Rather, it is a checklist of things to consider. Each stage is substantiated in the Annexe, including how it relates to other published principles (CBD, The Economics of Ecosystems and Biodiversity – TEEB, 'Dublin Principles', etc.), how it is supported by case studies addressed in this book, and a 'key test' question to determine whether the stage has been addressed.

Why sixteen points, and why a new framework when we have the twelve principles of the CBD, the four 'Dublin Principles' and the six-point approach of TEEB for Policymakers? This is simply because, in supporting my own practical work with others to achieve sustainable water management decisions, I found some gaps, some overlaps but also a more practically useful flow of ideas. In other words, my sixteen-point framework is what I found worked in practice!

If this approach seems familiar to some readers, it is because I contributed the evolving ideas behind this chapter as the main content of a World Water Forum 6 (WWF6, Marseilles, March 2012) discussion paper. The key inputs were produced in summary form,[2] with a more complete discussion paper supporting debate about progressing WWF6 Theme 3.1.4: 'Bringing ecosystems into river basin management'. These concepts have thus been debated and tested by an international audience.

Continuous learning towards a new hydropolitics

We do not live in a sustainable world, at least not yet, but water management represents one of its mandatory building blocks. Neither do we start from a metaphorical 'clean sheet of paper' as we strive towards it. Rather, we face the reality of damaged ecosystems, deeply entrenched habits, inequities and vested interests, and a yawning lack of awareness of the gravity of our situation. In short, we remain far from achieving the goal so simply articulated by the three words 'sustainable water management'. The harsh reality is that we have to innovate, experiment, make mistakes and learn together as we adapt the principles exercised here to local situations. We also must address the fact that solutions to sustainable water management cannot be divorced from solutions to sustainability problems in other areas of societal interest, as the management of water is central to so many other facets of development, from food and land security to redistribution of power and wealth.[3]

It is important that these interlinked principles and steps are not 'cherry-picked' but that all are addressed as an integrated system. However, if any one element of the quest for sustainable water management stands above all others, it is simply the need to learn as we go.

Thus, the necessary new hydropolitics is characterized, above all, by humility. All of us need to acknowledge that no one uniquely has all the (DAD-based) answers. Rather, we are all part of the problem, but also integral to collaborative innovations in this deeply imperfect world.

The industrial-era 'one size fits all' solution of big dams and transfer schemes may have seemed a grand political gesture bringing water and wealth to all, much as it did (and in many places still does) for the supply of energy, food and other key societal services. It still remains a common assumption when water scarcity is called into question in many parts of the world, often enforced by strongly vested political, economic and other interests or just plain habit. However, we now know different, though also recognizing that 'heavy engineering' and ecosystem-based technologies both have a place in a mix of solutions necessary to water a burgeoning human population on a stressed planet.

Have we yet undertaken the political and economic innovations to recognize where thirty locally targeted £1 million schemes might do more net good than one £30 million scheme? Do we yet have the democratic infrastructure to encourage true participation in implementation of diverse schemes distributed across landscapes, designed to optimize human benefits while having lesser or no net cumulative consequences for hydrology and ecological viability? Undoubtedly, we have a considerable evolutionary journey in front of us if we are to attain the grail of sustainable, equitable and efficient water management.

However, let's be positive: we are at least waking up to the scale of the challenge facing us. We are also empowered by ever deeper knowledge of how ecosystems operate and how we interact with them. We are also a species imbued with an innate creativity that we have deployed constantly and innovatively throughout the last 100,000 years to find solutions – technical, social, economic, political or other – to the problems confronting us. We need now more than ever to work together to co-create a future that is fair to all and makes sustainable use of the world we inhabit.

Society in transition

A fascinating social breakthrough here is the 'Occupy' movement, originally launched anonymously as a Tumblr[4] blog page in late August 2011. Since then, it has taken root across many developed-world cities as a self-organizing civil movement protesting against social and economic inequality, with a primary goal of making society's economic structures and power relations fairer.[5] Local groups continue to arise, apparently spontaneously and often with different foci, but largely united by a prime concern that large corporations and global financial systems control the world in a way that disproportionately benefits a minority and undermines democracy, bringing with it the kind of inherent instabilities manifesting themselves in the global 'credit crunch'. One of the defining slogans under which 'Occupy' musters is 'We are the 99%', referring to the fact that developed-world societal rules and decisions are largely made by the advantaged 1 per cent of the population. As amply demonstrated by the outcomes of many major dam schemes throughout the world, decision-making tends to (using another 'Occupy' slogan) 'privatise gains, socialise losses'.

Another principle occupying this grassroots movement is insistence by spokespeople that they do not have all the answers, and this is inherent too in recognition of the need for social co-creation of solutions in the WCD, CBD and Dublin principles. Acknowledging that the problem is too big for any one individual or group to have all the answers may not be satisfying to the media, but it is refreshingly honest and politically courageous. Admission of imperfect knowledge and insight is indeed an essential starting point if we hope to achieve a systemic, adaptive approach to addressing 'wicked' problems involving the voices of all across society. Within this lies something of the humility but also the informed approach that we will need to orient ourselves collectively on to a pathway towards sustainability, without which our water-stressed, ever more populous, climate-changing and potentially more conflicted world will face rather more perilous consequences than non-violent viral civic action. Many Occupy camps have been forcibly dismantled around the world,[6] perhaps reflecting an unwillingness by authorities yet to engage in constructive dialogue with coexisting areas of cooperation and conflict that has proved so useful for innovation and eventual mutually beneficial collaboration under the 'soft power' approach. Whatever the politics and personal perspective of the Occupy movement itself, disparities of power and established norms of water management clearly need to be reassessed as part of a new, equitable and sustainable hydropolitics.

Indeed, whatever the mix of technologies that help us achieve it, a different type of hydropolitics is essential if we are to be adequately responsive, innovative, inclusive and informed, respecting the limits of the Earth's ecosystems and the rights of all who share them.

Annexe: Principles for sustainable water sharing

Throughout this book, we have encountered a range of overlapping principles and priorities for sustainable management and sharing of natural resources, including water and catchment ecosystem services. Significantly for water management, these include: the 'seven priorities' of the World Commission on Dams (WCD, covered in Chapter 5); four 'Dublin Principles' of IWRM (expanded in Chapter 10); and the CBD's twelve principles of the Ecosystem Approach (addressed in Chapter 13).

These are not the only relevant sets of guiding principles for natural resource management. For example, TEEB for Policymakers[1] proposes a six-point approach to: (1) specify and agree on the policy issue with stakeholders; (2) identify which services are most relevant; (3) define information needs and select appropriate methods; (4) have ecosystem services assessed; (5) identify and appraise policy options; and (6) assess distributional impacts. *Ramsar Handbook 9*[2] offers further specific targeted advice on integrating wetlands into IWRM. Indeed, for those exploring practical steps to address sustainable water sharing, the very diversity of alternative models can be bewildering.

As highlighted in Chapter 17, my own experiences of practical sustainable water resource management projects around the world have led me to distil the essence of the WCD, IWRM, CBD and TEEB approaches into an integrated framework for guiding deliberation and decisions for water management. This new synthesis of guidance, like the approaches upon which it is based, points not to a 'right technology' choice, but to means for thinking through technologies – whether engineered, ecosystem-based or hybrid – appropriate in a landscape context for addressing the cultures and needs of the many stakeholders who share it.

A framework for guiding deliberation and decisions for water management

Taking account of the synergies and, in two cases, the gaps in WCD, Dublin Principles, CBD and TEEB principles and priorities, an idealized sixteen-point framework of dialogic and decision-making (see the Figure 17.1, page 244) has been developed to guide the sustainable use, sharing and management of water.

The evolving ideas behind this framework for guiding deliberation and decisions for water management were published by the author in the form of a discussion paper for World Water Forum 6 in Marseilles (WWF6, Marseilles, March 2012). The key inputs were published in summary form,[3] but also as a more complete discussion paper supporting debate about progressing WWF6 Theme 3.1.4: 'Bringing ecosystems into river basin management'. This framework has thus been debated and tested by an international audience.

While sixteen stages may appear excessive, and there are arguments in favour of reducing them to, say, four, as in the 'Dublin Principles', or six, as in TEEB for Policymakers, this synthesis of approaches acknowledges three key 'real world' realities. First, it is necessary to make room for both 'hard' and 'natural' approaches to water management within the same dialogic approach. Secondly, as drawn particularly from the WCD approach, we have to consider not only new development but also the existence of long-lived assets already in place, management of which will need to be optimized. Thirdly, and most importantly, this guide is for 'real world' practitioners and therefore I have sought to be as explicit as possible in each step, rather than expecting practitioners to deconstruct the implications of a more condensed flow of concepts to apply at their local context.

Each of the sixteen stages is explained in the following set of sub-sections. For each, relevant WCD, Dublin, CBD or other wider principles are recorded, together with lessons from case studies overviewed previously in this book, finally posing a 'key test' question to help you assess whether this stage has been implemented. My overriding purpose here is to offer 'hands-on' guidance to those who I sincerely hope will use this book to guide practical water management and sharing challenges around the world.

Stage i) Develop common understandings of water systems

Water management is often frustrated by various forms of parochialism, both internationally and by local interests that do not take account of catchment-scale processes. This requires political courage to work on a cooperative basis to restore the functioning of water systems for collective rather than merely local benefits, and also support for relevant research to ensure that these processes are understood. This includes recognition of the many roles of water in the environment and of the ecosystems it supports, which in turn support diverse human interests, rejecting the narrow view of water as just an economic resource.

Related principles
- WCD Priority 4: Sustaining rivers and livelihoods
- Dublin Principle 1: Fresh water is a finite and vulnerable resource, essential to sustain life, development and the environment
- Ecosystem Approach Principle 1: The objectives of management of land, water and living resources are a matter of societal choices
- Ecosystem Approach Principle 5: Conservation of ecosystem structure and functioning, in order to maintain ecosystem services, should be a priority target of the ecosystem approach
- Ecosystem Approach Principle 6: Ecosystems must be managed within the limits of their functioning

Lessons from case studies
- The Australian Hunter River Salinity Trading Scheme and also the US Chesapeake Bay critical loads PES recognize the contribution of pollutants from multiple, often small sources across the catchment, and the need to balance overall loads
- The Okavango Delta Management Plan addressed village-level perspectives regarding different pressures on the system and its other users
- The Volta River Basin provided a common understanding of the river as a whole, regardless of political borders
- The Lake Tanganyika Basin, Mekong River Basin and Songwe River Transboundary Catchment Management project initiatives address the functioning and vulnerabilities of the lake and river systems and their catchments
- China's Sloping Land Conversion Programme is based on an understanding of erosion and downstream impacts at catchment scale
- The Vittel and Perrier PES schemes are founded on a scientific understanding of the functioning of the catchments
- The Lombok and WWF Madagascar PES schemes are based on an understanding of catchment dynamics and land uses that protect water sources
- The Upstream Thinking (SW Water) scheme is founded on understanding the functioning of catchments in the production of clean water, and their intimate interactions with land use practices and the economics of farming
- The Irish integrated constructed wetland initiative addresses

restoration of a range of interconnected ecosystems services across the catchment
- Pagos por Servicios Ambientales, the Nature Assist and Bush Tender programmes in Australia, and the Maloti Drakensberg Transfrontier Project address water resources, among a 'basket' of services, through forest catchment protection
- Indo-Bangladeshi negotiations over the Ganges, agreements between India and Pakistan over the waters of the Indus basin and the ZACPLAN provide examples of consideration of river basin functions beyond national borders

'Key test' question
- 'Is management being undertaken on the basis of how the water system functions as an integrated unit?'

Stage ii) Acknowledge the central role of people at all scales

This stage acknowledges the central role of people, poor and empowered and of all genders, both as beneficiaries and shapers of the water cycle, and at all scales, and how collaboration in water sharing can either build or erode social capital.

Related principles
- WCD Priority 7: Sharing rivers for peace, development and security
- Dublin Principle 1: Fresh water is a finite and vulnerable resource, essential to sustain life, development and the environment
- Dublin Principle 3: Women play a central part in the provision, management and safeguarding of water
- Ecosystem Approach Principle 1: The objectives of management of land, water and living resources are a matter of societal choices
- Ecosystem Approach Principle 7: The ecosystem approach should be undertaken at the appropriate spatial and temporal scales

Lessons from case studies
- The Hunter River Salinity Trading Scheme as well as the US Chesapeake Bay critical loads PES recognize the role of people in causing problems and of them trading to address solutions, though collective well-being of all stakeholders is reflected only in the critical loads of pollutants entering catchments
- The Okavango Delta Management Plan was based on views of all stakeholders at village level in preference to a top-down imposed solution
- The Lake Tanganyika Basin, Mekong River Basin and Songwe River

Transboundary Catchment Management project initiatives devolve actions to nation-states

- China's Sloping Land Conversion Programme recognizes that land conversion is an activity undertaken by people as a cause of and solution to problems
- The Vittel, Perrier, Lombok and WWF Madagascar PES schemes recognize that people's activities threaten or protect water in the springs and rivers
- The Upstream Thinking (SW Water) scheme addresses the need for working farms and local people as a basis of sustainable solutions to water pollution
- The Irish integrated constructed wetland initiative addresses 'fit' both with the natural and the working human landscape
- Pagos por Servicios Ambientales, the Nature Assist and Bush Tender programmes in Australia, and the Maloti Drakensberg Transfrontier Project address the needs of people to derive income from forest and grazing landscapes as part of sustainable management

'Key test' question
- 'Do proposed measures work for the people required to put them into practice?'

Stage iii) Develop or evolve institutions

There is frequently an over-reliance on unreconstructed regulations and unreformed institutions, rather than a recognition of the need to develop or evolve institutions, which can constrain progress towards systemic outcomes.

Related principles
- Dublin Principle 2: Water development and management should be based on a participatory approach, involving users, planners and policy-makers at all levels
- Ecosystem Approach Principle 2: Management should be decentralized to the lowest appropriate level
- Ecosystem Approach 3: Ecosystem managers should consider the effects (actual or potential) of their activities on adjacent and other ecosystems
- Ecosystem Approach Principle 7: The ecosystem approach should be undertaken at the appropriate spatial and temporal scales

Lessons from case studies
- The Okavango Delta Management Plan was founded on village-level experience, integrated into an overall plan

- The Volta River Basin example served as an institution with over-sight of the river system across political boundaries
- The Lake Tanganyika Basin, Mekong River Basin and Songwe River Transboundary Catchment Management project initiatives are forms of institutions providing an overview of the functioning of the lake and river catchments
- The Vittel and Perrier PES schemes both established trusted brokers between farmers and the water bottling businesses
- The Upstream Thinking (SW Water) scheme partners with the NGO the Westcountry Rivers Trust as a 'trusted intermediary'
- Pagos por Servicios Ambientales, the Nature Assist and Bush Tender programmes in Australia, and the Maloti Drakensberg Transfrontier Project establish brokerages for their PES mechanism
- Indo-Bangladeshi negotiations over the Ganges, agreements between India and Pakistan over the waters of the Indus basin and the ZACPLAN represent institutions established to provide overviews on international catchment-scale functioning, albeit with different degrees of success

'Key test' question
- 'Are current institutions fit for purpose for delivering systemic outcomes, and if not how should they be reformed?'

Stage iv) Recognize the values, perspectives and uses of all stakeholders

Retaining or merely paying lip-service to setting aside traditional DAD-based decision-making is still a common reason for failing to recognize the values, perspectives and uses of all stakeholders. Yet these perspectives are essential for sustainable water and other resource-related decisions at all scales, and all forms of knowledge from the technical to the tacit need to be integrated in far-sighted solutions.

Related principles
- WCD Priority 5: Recognizing entitlements and sharing benefits
- Dublin Principle 2: Water development and management should be based on a participatory approach, involving users, planners and policy-makers at all levels
- Dublin Principle 3: Women play a central part in the provision, management and safeguarding of water
- Ecosystem Approach Principle 1: The objectives of management of land, water and living resources are a matter of societal choices

- Ecosystem Approach Principle 2: Management should be decentralized to the lowest appropriate level
- Ecosystem Approach Principle 11: The ecosystem approach should consider all forms of relevant information, including scientific and indigenous and local knowledge, innovations and practices
- Ecosystem Approach Principle 12: The ecosystem approach should involve all relevant sectors of society and scientific disciplines

Lessons from case studies
- The Okavango Delta Management Plan addressed the perspectives of all stakeholders at village level
- The Lake Tanganyika Basin, Mekong River Basin and Songwe River Transboundary Catchment Management project initiatives connect the interests and impacts of all stakeholders within the lake and river catchment
- Patient stakeholder dialogue in the Vittel and Perrier PES schemes identified market mechanisms that worked for both sets of partners
- The Upstream Thinking (SW Water) scheme recognizes the need to establish PES schemes that work for people, benefiting both water service companies and their customers but also those whose land-use businesses affect catchment quality
- Value to multiple stakeholders across society is implicit in the Irish integrated constructed wetland initiative

'Key test' question
- 'Are consultative and other processes inclusive enough to ensure that the needs and perspective of all stakeholder groups are captured?'

Stage v) Develop participatory and deliberative techniques

This is necessary to engage representative stakeholders at each scale in significant management decisions, rather than relying on established methods.

Related principles
- WCD Priority 1: Gaining public acceptance
- Dublin Principle 2: Water development and management should be based on a participatory approach, involving users, planners and policy-makers at all levels
- Dublin Principle 3: Women play a central part in the provision, management and safeguarding of water
- Ecosystem Approach Principle 1: The objectives of management of land, water and living resources are a matter of societal choices

- Ecosystem Approach Principle 2: Management should be decentralized to the lowest appropriate level

Lessons from case studies
- The Okavango Delta Management Plan found means to collate the views of stakeholders at village level

'Key test' question
- 'What forms of techniques are required to integrate diverse views into deliberative processes?'

Stage vi) Develop a common vision of future water use and resource sharing

This sets a context against which to frame more localized decision-making. This may include recognition of regulatory and other obligations (including cross-border agreements on water sharing) but will consider means to achieve multiple societal benefits rather than the often narrow objectives of legacy obligations.

Related principles
- Collective visioning may be implicit in addressing other objectives but is not specified as an integral part of them. However, without a framing vision, there is a risk of fragmented action, so this stage also makes a contribution to integration across geographical scales. A map-based approach may be helpful here, not necessarily constrained by accurate spatial referencing but to capture the different perspectives held about water and its use by different stakeholder groups.

Lessons from case studies
- The Okavango Delta Management Plan was premised on a future management scenario that resolved conflicts between stakeholders
- The Volta River Basin example is founded on a vision of the river system in a healthy and functional state serving the needs of both countries
- The Lake Tanganyika Basin, Mekong River Basin and Songwe River Transboundary Catchment Management project initiatives are both founded on a vision of a protected and functional lake/river ecosystem
- The Lombok PES scheme addressed long-term security of clean water sources

'Key test' question
- 'Has a clear and consensual vision been established?'

Stage vii) Deliberate on the basis of all views and ways in which water is used

Politically and economically influential stakeholders still tend to dominate decision-making, so it is often essential to create and enforce open deliberation on the basis of all views and ways in which water is used. Co-creation by stakeholders of 'win-win' solutions around a shared vision (identified in the previous stage) provides opportunity for innovation and negotiation, before simple trade-offs are assumed and implemented.

Related principles
- WCD Priority 2: Comprehensive options assessment
- Dublin Principle 1: Water development and management should be based on a participatory approach, involving users, planners and policy-makers at all levels
- Ecosystem Approach Principle 1: The objectives of management of land, water and living resources are a matter of societal choices
- Ecosystem Approach Principle 2: Management should be decentralized to the lowest appropriate level

Lessons from case studies
- The Lake Tanganyika Basin, Mekong River Basin and Songwe River Transboundary Catchment Management project initiatives set a basis for more sensitive and integrated land and water management
- The Upstream Thinking (SW Water) scheme includes a 'reverse auctioning' mechanism to enable farmers to innovate solutions

'Key test' question
- 'What process has been established to provide space for co-created rather than imposed solutions?'

Stage viii) Assess all options on a 'level playing field'

There is historically often no objective and consensual basis established in order to assess all options on a 'level playing field'. The framework of ecosystem services is well suited to explore wider ramifications for ecosystems and people.

Related principles
- WCD Priority 2: Comprehensive options assessment

Lessons from case studies
- The Vittel and Perrier PES schemes addressed a range of options for source protection, and measures to achieve it

- The Upstream Thinking (SW Water) scheme 'reverse auctioning' approach enables all options to be considered on their merits
- Pagos por Servicios Ambientales, as well as the US Conservation Reserve Programme, provide evaluations of how proposed forest and catchment management can optimally contribute to increasing catchment functioning

'Key test' question
- 'Have outcomes for ecosystems and ecosystem service beneficiaries been tested on a standardized and transparent basis?'

Stage ix) Factor the changing nature of natural systems into plans

It still remains common practice to consider ecosystems on a steady-state basis rather than factor the changing nature of natural systems as well as human-induced change into plans.

Related principles
- Ecosystem Approach Principle 9: Management must recognize that change is inevitable

Lessons from case studies
- The Irish integrated constructed wetland initiative addresses ecosystem resilience, including maintaining functioning in the face of a changing climate

'Key test' question
- 'What is the baseline against which options are assessed, and is it acknowledged that this baseline will change over time?'

Stage x) Consider long-term ramifications

It is essential to plan for optimal benefits over longer time frames, not merely immediate benefits with (often) longer-term negative consequences.

Related principles
- Ecosystem Approach Principle 8: Recognizing the varying temporal scales and lag-effects that characterize ecosystem processes, objectives for ecosystem management should be set for the long term

Lessons from case studies
- Long-term sustainability of solutions was central to the Vittel, Perrier, Lombok and Madagascar PES scheme solutions
- The Upstream Thinking (SW Water) scheme seeks water management solutions that are workable and enduring

- The Irish integrated constructed wetland initiative is designed for low inputs and maintenance, reinstating natural wetland processes

'Key test' question
- 'Beyond the immediate benefits it will yield, what is the likely outcome of the decision being considered decades hence?'

Stage xi) Develop or evolve practical tools

Pragmatic operational tools are essential to support operational decision-making on a systems basis, including people and ecosystems. Without this, implementation of even the best policy ideals may be frustrated.

Related principles
- Not explicitly addressed by WCD, Dublin Principles or Ecosystem Approach, but important for facilitating decision-making

Lessons from case studies
- The simplified presentation of a 'traffic lights' system summarizing complex analyses in the 'Economic impacts on ecosystem services' for the Thukela Water Project makes transparent and operational decision-support informed by likely impacts for ecosystems and people
- The Hunter River Salinity Trading Scheme has devised a 'cap and trade' scheme to manage identified problems
- The Chesapeake Bay critical loads PES addresses maximum safe loads of pollutants entering the bay and means to address inputs
- The Lake Tanganyika Basin, Mekong River Basin and Songwe River Transboundary Catchment Management project initiatives delegate solutions to identified problems to nation-states

'Key test' question
- 'What tools will be required to deliver this policy choice, and how will they be put in place?'

Stage xii) Assess the legislative baseline

This includes both ensuring compliance with standards established for the protection of all in society but also reforming them where they obstruct sustainable outcomes. This therefore cautions against putting too much faith in existing legislation, often formed on the basis of outmoded world views or at least where narrow implementation may block sustainable practice.

Related principles
- WCD Priority 6: Ensuring compliance

Lessons from case studies
- Consideration of legally enforceable options was central to options identification in the Vittel and Perrier PES schemes
- The Sustainable Catchment Management Programme and the Upstream Thinking (SW Water) PES schemes were implemented within the UK's closely regulated AMP water investment programme
- Indo-Bangladeshi negotiations over the Ganges, agreements between India and Pakistan over the waters of the Indus basin and the ZACPLAN fix agreements about water allocation between countries; somewhat imperfect examples of integrated basin management
- Norwegian taxes and licence fee legislation was found to inhibit mechanisms ensuring benefit-sharing, as the tax system in Norway prevented municipalities with more hydropower installations raising more tax revenues

'Key test' question
- 'Have minimum legal obligations been observed, and where must these be reformed to achieve outcomes optimal for ecosystem functioning and those that benefit from it?'

Stage xiii) Explore the role of markets

Novel markets may be a useful means for connecting beneficiaries with providers, developing appropriate market-based instruments if they can support more sustainable use of catchments and water. This can include helping people better recognize the benefits that they provide as well as removing distortions from the market. Workable 'win-win' market solutions can also bring generally overlooked and undervalued ecosystem services into 'real world' markets, as well as proving workable where regulatory solutions are ineffective or block innovation.

Related principles
- Dublin Principle 4: Water has an economic value in all its competing uses and should be recognized as an economic good
- Ecosystem Approach Principle 4: Recognizing potential gains from management, there is usually a need to understand and manage the ecosystem in an economic context

Lessons from case studies
- The Hunter River Salinity Trading Scheme has established a 'cap and trade' scheme
- The Chesapeake Bay critical loads PES is a market mechanism to manage loads entering the bay
- China's Sloping Land Conversion Programme is based on incentives to revegetate sloping, erosion-prone soils
- The Vittel and Perrier PES schemes are market-based
- The Lombok and WWF Madagascar PES schemes are also market-based
- The Sustainable Catchment Management Programme and the Upstream Thinking (SW Water) PES schemes establish working markets
- Pagos por Servicios Ambientales is a PES scheme that recirculates levies of fossil fuel use to protect catchments, including carbon sequestration services

'Key test' question
- 'Is there a potential role for market-based instruments that is more effective than simple compulsion?'

Stage xiv) Consider how current infrastructure can be improved to mitigate damage

The need to consider how current infrastructure can be improved to mitigate damage recognizes that existing infrastructure may be suboptimal but that modified management practice can achieve more beneficial outcomes for all stakeholders based on agreed visions.

Related principles
- WCD Priority 3: Addressing existing dams

Lessons from case studies
- The Hunter River Salinity Trading Scheme builds upon existing emissions control measures
- The Vittel and Perrier PES schemes addressed changing farming infrastructure as well as practices to reduce nitrate and other inputs to groundwater
- The Upstream Thinking (SW Water) PES scheme works on the basis of improving farm infrastructure and management as well as a range of other measures
- Flow adjustments under the Glen Canyon Dam Adaptive Management Program, which seeks to emulate more natural variations in flow regimes, seek to combine water storage and hydropower

generation with the mitigation of at least some of the harm to the ecosystem (particularly addressing concerns about rare and diminishing species such as humpback chub), restoration river features such as sandbanks, and public enjoyment of the Colorado River

'Key test' question
- 'Can operation of existing infrastructure be modified to deliver better outcomes for ecosystems and the people that benefit from them?'

Stage xv) Resolve the needs of ecosystems with those of people

Sustainable outcomes resolve the needs of ecosystems and the people they support, including future generations.

Related principles
- Ecosystem Approach Principle 10: The ecosystem approach should seek the appropriate balance between, and integration of, conservation and use of biological diversity

Lessons from case studies
- The Hunter River Salinity Trading Scheme and the US Chesapeake Bay critical loads PES recognize that ecosystem health is important for collective well-being
- The Volta River Basin example addresses the functioning of the overall river system as a basis for serving the needs of the two countries that share it
- The Lake Tanganyika Basin, Mekong River Basin and Songwe River Transboundary Catchment Management project initiatives recognize that the well-being of the lake and river system and their beneficiaries are intimately interlinked
- China's Sloping Land Conversion Programme recognizes that halting catchment erosion is beneficial for the Yangtze river ecosystem and the benefits for which it is being managed
- The WWF Madagascar PES seeks to protect vital habitat for wildlife as a co-benefit of sustainable water management
- The Sustainable Catchment Management Programme and the Upstream Thinking (SW Water) PES schemes both address the benefits of measures to ecosystems, including rare species and fisheries, coincident with delivering better water resources
- The Irish integrated constructed wetland initiative rebuilds 'lost' ecosystem services beneficial to biodiversity, landscape, waste water treatment and a range of other benefits

- Pagos por Servicios Ambientales, the Nature Assist and Bush Tender programmes in Australia, the Maloti Drakensberg Transfrontier Project, as well as the US Conservation Reserve Programme, address coincident benefits for nature as well as the services that ecosystems provide for people

'Key test' question
- 'Have the full range of ecosystem dependencies of all stakeholder groups been identified and protected in identified options for water and catchment management?'

Stage xvi) Monitor outcomes and adapt

The shortfall of post-project appraisal has been long acknowledged, representing a failure to implement adaptive management practices. It is important to audit the outcomes of policies and practices for ecosystem and people, rather than assuming that they will automatically deliver intended outcomes. This then needs to be iterated back into review of policy and practice.

Related principles
- Interestingly, this is not explicit in any of the WCD, CBD and Dublin Principle guidance, though is perhaps implicit in:
- Ecosystem Approach Principle 8: Recognizing the varying temporal scales and lag-effects that characterize ecosystem processes, objectives for ecosystem management should be set for the long term

Lessons from case studies
- Time-limited PES agreements, for example under the US Conservation Reserve Programme and the UK Thinking Upstream, enable periodic revision of policy and subsidy to better target desired outcomes

'Key test' question
- 'What review cycle has been put in place and what parameters will be monitored to provide evidence for adaptive management?'

Notes

1 Replumbing the modern world

1 www.icold-cigb.org.
2 Ward (2002).
3 Wittfogel (1957).
4 World Commission on Dams (2000).
5 Reisner (1986).
6 Basson et al. (1997: 55).
7 www.ctgpc.com/.
8 See consideration of China's Sloping Lands Conversion Programme in Chapter 13.
9 www.iucnredlist.org.
10 McManus et al. (2010).
11 www.nagarjunasagar.com.
12 The India River Interlinking Project. (There is no specific home website, but many hits can be found, both pro- and anti-Project, using internet search engines.)
13 Pearce (2004).
14 Postel (1999).
15 Jackson et al. (2001).
16 Nilsson et al. (2005).

2 Temples of the modern world

1 W. Meyer, cited in Harris (2007).
2 National Inventory of Dams, February 2005, www.tec.army.mil/nid.
3 www.icold-cigb.org.
4 World Commission on Dams (2000).
5 www.unep.org/DAMS/.
6 water.worldbank.org/topics/hydropower, accessed 17 January 2013.
7 International Energy Agency (2006).
8 Barros et al. (2011).

3 Stemming the flow

1 Millennium Ecosystem Assessment (2005).
2 Malik and Negi (2007).
3 Hardin (1968).
4 Dietz et al. (2003).
5 Everard (2009a).
6 Harris (2007).
7 Bouguerra (2006).
8 National Rivers Authority (1990).
9 McCully (2001).
10 Roy (2002).
11 World Commission on Dams (2000).
12 Goldsmith and Hildyard (1984; 1986).
13 Everard (2005).
14 Bettey (1999).
15 Junk et al. (1989).
16 World Commission on Dams (2000).
17 For example, as addressed by Vaughan (2013).
18 Everard (2012a).
19 Johnson et al. (2008).
20 World Commission on Dams (2000).
21 Scudder (2005).
22 Pearce (1992); McCully (2001); Scudder (2005); Roy (2002); World Commission on Dams (2000).
23 World Commission on Dams (2000).
24 UNICEF (2008).
25 Cernea (2000); Termirski (2012).
26 World Bank (2007).
27 Kijne et al. (1998).
28 The World Commission on Dams (WCD) Knowledge Base,

www.unep.org/dams/Documents/
default.asp?DocumentID=356&
ArticleID=4207.

29 Postel (1999).

30 World Commission on Dams
(2000).

31 Carder (1945).

32 ICE (1981); Gupta (1992).

33 Pearce (2004).

34 Lima et al. (2007).

35 International Rivers (2007).

36 South Asian Network (2007).

37 Barros et al. (2011).

38 Provost (2012).

39 Mander (2003).

40 World Commission on Dams
(2000).

41 Morel et al. (1998).

42 D'itri and D'itri (1977).

43 Hopkins (1999).

44 Noel et al. (1998).

45 Hopkins (1999).

46 Mitchell (1993).

47 World Commission on Dams
(WCD) Knowledge Base.

48 National Library of Wales
(n.d.).

49 Thomas (2007).

50 BBC (2005).

4 A changing mindset

1 ICOLD (1981).

2 ICOLD (2008).

3 www.icold-cigb.net, accessed
September 2008.

4 Everard (2011).

5 NAS–NRC (1966: 60).

6 www.narmada.org.

7 Roy (2002).

8 www.friendsofganges.org.

9 Morse Commission (1992).

10 www.internationalrivers.org/
follow-money/manibeli-declaration.

11 World Bank (1994).

12 World Bank (2007).

13 Amazonwatch (2012).

14 Biello (2011).

15 McCarthy (2012).

16 Vaidyanathan (2011).

17 Watts (2010).

18 Survival International (2011).

19 www.gibe3.com.et/, accessed
1 July 2011.

20 East (2010).

21 Gleick (n.d.).

22 Alam et al. (2011).

5 World Commission on Dams

1 World Commission on Dams
(2000).

2 www.dams.org.

3 The World Commission on
Dams (WCD) Knowledge Base,
www.unep.org/dams/Documents/
default.asp?DocumentID=356&
ArticleID=4207.

4 Scudder (2005).

5 ICOLD (2000).

6 UNEP Dams and Development
Programme, www.unep.org/dams.

7 UNEP Dams and Development
Programme: Compendium on
Relevant Practices, www.unep.org/
dams/inventory/.

8 United Nations Environment
Programme (2007).

9 The Beijing Declaration on
Hydropower and Sustainable Development, www.un.org/esa/sustdev/
sdissues/energy/hydropower_sd_
beijingdeclaration.pdf.

10 www.water-alternatives.org.

11 Briscoe (2010).

12 Richter et al. (2010).

13 Mäkinen and Khan (2010).

6 The state of play

1 www.dams.org.

2 Hussey and Dovers (2007).

3 Simpungwe et al. (2007).

4 Scudder (2005).

5 Luger and Van Niekerk (2001).

6 DWAF (1994).

7 DWAF (1996).

8 DWAF (1997).

9 Wani et al. (2003).

10 Hoa and Tung (2008).

11 United Nations Environment Programme (2007).

12 Joubert and Pollard (2000).

13 Thukela river official web page. www.dwaf.gov.za/thukela/.

14 Croke et al. (2007).

15 www.bbc.co.uk/news/world-africa-12300285.

16 Hoa and Tung (2008).

17 World Commission on Dams (2000).

18 World Commission on Dams (2001).

19 International Rivers (2010).

20 International Rivers (2002).

21 World Commission on Dams (2001).

22 International Rivers Network, www.internationalrivers.org/en/africa/bujagali-dam-uganda.

23 Luger and Van Niekerk (2001).

24 Sahu (2008).

25 Petts (2006).

26 Jiggins et al. (2007).

27 Department of Environmental Affairs (2008).

28 ICOLD (2008: 42).

7 Dams and ecosystem services

1 Convention on Biological Diversity, www.cbd.int/ecosystem.

2 Millennium Ecosystem Assessment, www.millenniumassessment.org/en/index.aspx; Millennium Ecosystem Assessment (2005).

3 Annan (2001).

4 Millennium Ecosystem Assessment (2005).

5 Ibid.

6 Defra (2007). The scoring system is: ++ (potential significant positive effect), + (potential positive effect), o (negligible effect), – (potential negative effect), – – (potential significant negative effect) and ? (gaps in evidence/contention).

7 Costanza et al. (1997).

8 Balmford et al. (2002).

9 Millennium Ecosystem Assessment (2005).

10 UK National Ecosystem Assessment (2011).

11 United Nations Millennium Development Goals, www.un.org/millenniumgoals.

12 UNDP (2004).

13 Mander (2003).

14 Everard and Kataria (2010).

15 WBCSD (2011); Everard (2009a).

8 A new agenda

1 Turton (2003: 88).

2 Economist (2011).

3 Serageldin (2009).

4 United Nations Department of Public Information (2006).

5 www.unesco.org/water/wwap/pccp/.

6 Rowland (2012).

7 Turton (2005).

8 Phillips et al. (2006).

9 www.iucn.org/about/union/secretariat/offices/asia/regional_activities/mekong_water_dialogues__mwd_/.

10 Nye (1990, 2004).

11 Klark (2003: 182).

12 Zeitoun and Mirumachi (2008).

9 Water in the postmodern world

1 Beddington (2009).

2 Wilson (1978, 1998).

3 Roszak et al. (1995).

4 Suzuki and McConnell (1997).

5 Brown (2001).

6 Gleeson et al. (2012).

7 Brown (2001).

8 Reported in Everard (2009a).

9 Reported in United Nations (1997).

10 World Commission on Dams (2000).

11 UN Millennium Development

Goals, www.un.org/millennium goals.

12 Adamus (1983); Kusler and Riexinger (1986).

13 Finlayson et al. (2005).

14 EC (European Commission) Water Framework Directive (Directive 2000/60/EC of 23 October 2000 establishing a framework for Community action in the field of water policy).

15 Gleick (1993).

16 Calder (1999).

17 Pearce (2004).

18 Hunt (2004).

19 Everard (2009a, 2011).

20 Convention on Biological Diversity, www.cbd.int/ecosystem.

21 Gleick (1993).

22 Pearce (2008).

23 Everard (2011).

10 Managing water at landscape scale

1 Staddon (2010); Everard (2011).

2 Everard et al. (2012a).

3 Jie Liu et al. (2011).

4 Calder (1999).

5 Rahaman and Varis (2005).

6 www.wmo.int/pages/prog/hwrp/documents/english/icwedece.html.

7 ICWE (1992).

8 Global Water Partnership (2000).

9 Ison et al. (2007).

10 Global Water Partnership Toolbox, www.gwptoolbox.org/index.php?option=com_content&view=article&id=67&Itemid=65, accessed 21 January 2013.

11 Economist (2012).

12 Visscher et al. (1999).

13 Hill (2010).

14 Mostert (2006).

15 Holling (1978).

16 www.usbr.gov/uc/rm/amp/.

17 www.waterandnature.org/; www.waterandnature.org/en/results/wani-basins/volta.

18 lta.iwlearn.org/.

19 United Nations (2008).

20 Republic of South Africa (1998).

21 DWAF (2007).

22 Steenbergen et al. (2011).

23 Gordon et al. (2010); Everard (2011).

24 Maltby and Acreman (2011).

25 Cabot (1999); Stapleton et al. (2000).

26 Horwitz and Finlayson (2011); Purseglove (1988).

27 Bullock and Acreman (2003).

28 Gordon et al. (2010).

29 Finewood and Porter (2010); Turner et al. (2000).

30 Neal et al. (2006); Woods et al. (2007).

31 Wickham et al. (2010).

32 Nuttall et al. (1997); Vymazal (2011).

33 Fisher and Acreman (2004).

34 Morris et al. (2005); Wheater and Evans (2009).

35 Rebelo et al. (2010); Verhoeven and Setter (2010).

36 Erwin (2009).

37 Everard et al. (2012b).

38 Babatunde et al. (2008).

39 Carroll et al. (2005).

40 Culleton et al. (2005).

41 Doody et al. (2009).

42 Dunne et al. (2005); Harrington and McInnes (2009); Harrington and Scholz (2010); Mustafa et al. (2009); Scholz et al. (2007).

43 Becerra-Jurado et al. (2010).

44 Harrington and Ryder (2002); Scholz et al. (2007).

45 Everard et al. (2012b).

46 Department of the Environment, Heritage and Local Government (2010).

47 Royal Society (2009).

48 Harrington et al. (2011); Harrington and Ryder (2002); Scholz et al. (2007).

49 Everard and McInnes (forth-coming).

50 Acreman et al. (2009).

11 Catchment production and storage

1 Pitt (2007).

2 Hümann et al. (2011).

3 Reinhardt et al. (2011).

4 Joseph and Botha (2011).

5 Bouguerra (2006).

6 Wasson et al. (2010).

7 Parrott et al. (2009).

8 Macleod and Ferrier (2011).

9 Parrott et al. (2009).

10 Everard (2009a).

11 Dye and Jarmain (2004).

12 Seyfried and Wilcox (2006).

13 Doody and Benyon (2011).

14 agriculture.kzntl.gov.za/portal/Services/InvasiveAlienSpeciesPro-grammeIASP/tabid/237/Default.aspx.

15 Le Maitre et al. (2004); Marais et al. (2004).

16 Van Wilgen et al. (2007).

17 Central Ground Water Board (2007).

18 Tarun Bharat Sangh, www.tarunbharatsangh.org.

19 Ramon Magsaysay Award Foundation, www.rmaf.org.ph.

20 Balch (2012).

21 Murray-Darling Basin Ministerial Council (2001).

22 www.evergladesplan.org.

23 Everard (2011).

24 www.landcareaustralia.com.au.

25 As reviewed by Everard (2004).

26 Pearce (2004).

27 Theroux (1988).

28 Botha et al. (2007a, 2007b).

29 Vanclay et al. (2006).

30 Collyns (2012).

12 Water flows through society

1 Lee et al. (2011).

2 Codrington (2005).

3 Pearce (2004).

4 Ibid.

5 Envirowise (2008: 1).

6 Allan (1996).

7 Allan (2011).

8 Lawrence (2006).

9 Goldfarb (2012).

10 Allan (1998).

11 Calder (1999).

12 Wood and Van Halsema (2008).

13 Shiva (2008).

14 Gleeson et al. (2012).

15 Allan (1996).

16 For example, World Bank (2010).

17 Mehta et al. (2012).

18 Woodhouse (2012).

19 Williams et al. (2012).

20 Shiva (2008).

21 Hertzog et al. (2012).

22 Islar (2012).

23 Matthews (2012).

24 Sosa and Zwarteveen (2012).

25 Gasteyer et al. (2012).

26 Williams et al. (2012).

27 Ibid.

28 Shiva (2008).

29 Gasteyer et al. (2012).

30 peopleandplanet.net.

31 Hans (2001).

32 Everard (2005).

33 Curry (2002).

34 UK National Ecosystem Assessment (2011).

35 Millennium Ecosystem Assessment (2005).

36 Wood and Van Halsema (2008).

37 Ramsar Convention (2012).

38 Van Koppen et al. (2006).

39 Grimm et al. (2008).

40 Everard (2011).

41 UNFPA (2007).

42 Baron et al. (2002).

43 Pickett et al. (2001).

44 Groffman et al. (2003).

45 Eden and Tunstall (2006: 662).

46 Barton (1992).

47 Findlay and Taylor (2006);

Eigenbrod et al. (2009); Petts et al. (2001).

48 See many projects run by the Thames Rivers Restoration Trust, www.trrt.org.uk.

49 www.epa.gov/landreuse/urbanrivers/.

50 Nam-choon (2005).

51 www.australianriverrestorationcentre.com.au.

52 www.wet-africa.org.

53 Everard et al. (2011); www.trrt.org.uk.

54 Everard (2012b).

55 www.greeninfrastructure.co.uk/improve.html; Tzoulas et al. (2007).

56 Woods et al. (2007).

57 www.communityforest.org.uk/aboutenglandsforests.htm.

58 www.ecocitiesproject.org.uk/ecocities/index.aspx.

59 www.energysavingtrust.org.uk/nottingham/Nottingham-Declaration/The-Declaration/About-the-Declaration.

60 Gill et al. (2007).

61 Grant (2012).

62 www.wsud.org/.

63 www.sydney.cma.nsw.gov.au/our-projects/water-sensitive-urban-design-in-sydney-program-water-wsud.html.

64 NYC Green Infrastructure Plan, www.nyc.gov/html/dep/html/stormwater/nyc_green_infrastructure_plan.shtml.

65 CABE (2005).

66 Petts et al. (2001).

67 Everard and Moggridge (2012).

68 Eigenbrod et al. (2011).

13 Markets for water services

1 The evolution of environmental economics and the progressive inclusion of ecosystem services is extensively reviewed by Gómez-Baggethun et al. (2009).

2 Jack et al. (2008).

3 Millennium Ecosystem Assessment (2005).

4 UK National Ecosystem Assessment (2011).

5 Bushey (2007).

6 Teschner et al. (2012).

7 www.cbd.int.

8 www.cbd.int/ecosystem/principles.shtml.

9 Daily and Ellison (2002); Jenkins et al. (2004).

10 OECD (2010).

11 Defra (2011a).

12 Wunder (2005).

13 OECD (2010).

14 Engel et al. (2008).

15 Defra (2010).

16 Parker and Cranford (2010).

17 Baranzini et al. (n.d.); TEEB (2010a).

18 OECD (2010).

19 Defra (2011b).

20 Defra (forthcoming).

21 Embassy of the People's Republic of China in the United States of America (2010).

22 Xu et al. (2006).

23 Bennett and Xu (2005).

24 Weyerhaeuser et al. (2005).

25 Bennett and Xu (2005).

26 TEEB (2009).

27 Rowland (2012).

28 Forest and Grassland Taskforce of China (2003).

29 Bennett and Xu (2005).

30 Ibid.

31 Ibid.

32 Ellison et al. (2012).

33 Bennett (2008).

34 Pradhan et al. (2010).

35 www.wwf.or.id/en/about_wwf/whatwedo/freshwater/about_freshwater/.

36 www.unitedutilities.com/scamp.aspx.

37 southwestwater-cr-report.co.uk/pure-water/catchment-

management-upstream-thinking-developments/.

38 www.wrt.org.uk/projects/wepes/wepes.html.

39 www.wrt.org.uk.

40 Martin Ross, South West Water, personal communication.

41 www.alfa-project.eu/en/about/index.php?mod=login&sel=setcookie.

42 Perrot-Maître (2006).

43 Déprés et al. (2005).

44 OECD (2010).

45 Sullivan et al. (2004).

46 chesapeake.usgs.gov/coast/evaluate.html.

47 Wünscher et al. (2006).

48 OECD (2010).

49 Food and Agricultural Organization of the United Nations (2007).

50 Pfaff et al. (2007).

51 Wünscher et al. (2006).

52 Shore (2011).

53 Bohlen et al. (2009).

54 www.derm.qld.gov.au/wildlife-ecosystems/nature_refuges/natureassist/index.html.

55 www.dse.vic.gov.au/conservation-and-environment/biodiversity/rural-landscapes/bushtender.

56 waterinfo.nsw.gov.au/hunter/trading.shtml.

57 Funk (2006).

58 Maloti Drakensberg Transfrontier Project (2007).

59 Mander et al. (2010).

60 Quibell and Stein (2005).

61 www.lhwp.org.ls.

62 www.internationalrivers.org.

63 wwf.panda.org/who_we_are/wwf_offices/madagascar/?uProjectID=MG0921.

64 Ferraro (2011).

65 Bennett et al. (2013).

66 Oxfam (2013).

67 WHO/UNICEF Joint Monitoring Programme (JMP) for Water Supply and Sanitation, www.wssinfo.org/data-estimates/introduction/, accessed 20 January 2013.

68 Water Supply and Sanitation Collaborative Council, www.wsscc.org/, accessed 20 January 2013.

14 Nature's water infrastructure

1 For example: 'Infrastructure', *Online Compact Oxford English Dictionary*, www.askoxford.com/concise_oed/infrastructure, accessed 21 January 2013.

2 Shiva (2008).

3 Ramsar Convention Secretariat (2010).

4 www.foodnet.cgiar.org/scrip/docs&databases/ifpristudies_ug_nonscrip/pdfs/Nationa_Wetlands_Programme/index.htm.

5 Everard et al. (1995).

6 Convention on Biological Diversity, www.cbd.int.

7 Defra (2011a).

8 Everard and McInnes (forthcoming).

9 Everard et al. (2012b).

15 Living within the water cycle

1 ScienceDaily (2012).

2 Churchman (1967).

3 Ackoff (1973).

4 Rittel and Webber (1973).

5 Everard et al. (2009a).

6 Everard (forthcoming).

7 Everard (2009b).

8 World Commission on Dams (2000).

9 Scudder (2005).

10 Pearce (2004).

16 Governance of water systems

1 Everard et al. (2009b).

2 Barlow (2007); Bell (2009).

3 Milner-Gulland et al. (2001); Pomfret (2008); Johnson et al. (2010).

4 Bouguerra (2006).

5 Gupta (2011).

6 Wei et al. (2011).

7 Engels (1842).

8 Department of Water Affairs (1998).

9 Involve (2006); Carr Hill (2007); NICE (forthcoming).

10 Colbourne (2005, 2009).

11 Arnstein (1969).

12 Liveable cities, www.liveable cities.org.

13 Schumacher (1973).

14 Biswas et al. (2005).

15 Brett (2000).

16 UNDP (2006).

17 Mehrotra and Delamonica (2005).

18 Global Water Partnership (2005).

19 Cooke and Kothari (2001).

20 IAP2 (2008).

21 European Commission for Environment (2000).

22 UK Cabinet Office (2011).

23 Waalewijn (2005).

24 Harriss (2000).

25 www.ipcc.ch.

26 Dupree (2004).

27 Robinson (2000).

28 Harriss (2000).

29 Robinson (2000).

30 Turton (2007).

31 Falkenmark (2007).

32 Slinger et al. (2011).

33 Thomas (1996); Hirshmann (1999: 51).

34 Jonker et al. (2010).

35 Ibid.

36 Involve (2006).

37 Olsson and Galaz (2010).

38 Mayoux (2005).

39 Harris (2007).

40 Cottingham et al. (2002).

41 Young et al. (2004).

42 Hirsch (2006).

43 Bourblanc (2010).

44 Tonen (2011).

45 Jonsson (2005).

46 Fish et al. (2011).

47 Grêt-Regamey et al. (2012).

48 Garrido and Dinar (2008).

49 Wegerich and Warner (2010); Scheumann et al. (2008).

50 www.ipbes.net.

51 Nature (2010).

52 Millennium Ecosystem Assessment (2005).

53 Everard and Moggridge (2012).

54 Colvin et al. (2009).

55 Morrison and Wilson (1996).

56 Schlosberg (2007).

57 Everard et al. (2012b).

58 Hyatt and Kaplan (2006).

59 Isaac (1993).

60 Tippett et al. (2005).

61 Argyris and Schon (1978).

62 Everard et al. (2009b).

63 Dellapenna and Gupta (2009).

64 Conca (2005).

17 Towards a new hydropolitics

1 TEEB (2010b).

2 WWF6 (2012).

3 Lenton and Muller (2009).

4 www.tumblr.com.

5 For example, Karla Adam (2011); Walters (2011).

6 Bond (2011); Davies (2011); Burgis (2012).

Annexe

1 TEEB (2010b).

2 Ramsar Convention Secretariat (2010).

3 WWF6 (2012).

Bibliography

Ackoff, R. L. (1973) 'Science in the systems age: beyond IE, OR and MS', *Oper. Res.*, 21: 661–71.

Acreman, M. C., J. R. Blake, D. J. Booker, R. J. Harding, N. Reynard, J. O. Mountford and C. J. Stratford (2009) 'A simple framework for evaluating regional wetland ecohydrological response to climate change with case studies from Great Britain', *Ecohydrology*, 20: 1–17.

Adamus, P. R. (1983) 'FHWA Assessment method, v. 2 of Method for wetland functional assessment', Federal Highway Administration Report no. FHWA-IP-82-24, Washington, DC: US Department of Transportation.

Alam, U., O. Dione and P. Jeffrey (2011) 'Hydrology vs sovereignity: managing the hydrological interdependency of international rivers', *Water Policy*, 13(3): 425–42.

Allan, J. A. (1996) 'Policy responses to the closure of water resources: regional and global issues', in P. Howsam and R. Carter (eds), *Water Policy: Allocation and management in practice*, Proceedings of the International Conference on Water Policy, Cranfield University, 23/24 September, London: E. and F. N. Spon, pp. 3–12.

— (1998) 'Virtual water: a strategic resource. Global solutions to regional deficits', *Groundwater*, 36(4): 545–6.

— (2011) *Virtual Water*, London: I.B. Tauris.

Amazonwatch (2012) http://amazon-watch.org/work/belo-monte-dam.

Annan, K. (2001) *We the Peoples: The Role of the United Nations in the 21st Century*, United Nations, www.un.org/millennium/sg/report/full.htm.

Argyris, C. and D. Schon (1978) *Organisational Learning: a theory of action perspective*, Reading, MA: Addison Wesley.

Arnstein, S. (1969) 'A ladder of citizen participation', *Journal of the American Planning Association*, 35(4): 216–24.

Babatunde, A. O., Y. Q. Zhao, M. O'Neill and B. O'Sullivan (2008) 'Constructed wetlands for environmental pollution control: a review of developments, research and practice in Ireland', *Environment International*, 34(1): 116–26.

Balch, O. (2012) 'Mouth watering', Special edn, 'Water works', *Green Solutions for a Blue Planet*, October, pp. 22–3.

Balmford, A., A. Bruner, P. Cooper, R. Costanza, S. Farber, R. Green, M. Jenkins, P. Jefferiss, V. Jessamay, J. Madden, K. Munro, N. Myers, S. Naeem, J. Paavola, M. Rayment, S. Rosendo, J. Roughgarden, K. Trumper, and R. K. Turner (2002) 'Economic reasons for conserving wild nature', *Science*, 297: 950–3.

Baranzini, A., A. Faust and D. Huberman (n.d.) *Understanding the Private Demand for International Ecosystem Services – Public Attitudes and Preferences towards REDD*, online, cmsdata.iucn.org/downloads/ruig_ipes_final_report_0603_complet.pdf, accessed 27 April 2011.

Barlow, M. (2007) *Blue Covenant: The Global Water Crisis and the Coming Battle for the Right to Water*, New York: New Press.

Baron, J. S., N. L. Poff, P. L. Ammgermeier et al. (2002) 'Meeting ecological and societal needs for freshwater', *Ecol. Appl.*, 12(5): 1247–60.

Barros, N., J. J. Cole, L. J. Tranvik, Y. T. Prairie, D. Bastviken, V. L. M. Huszar, P. del Giorgio and F. Roland (2011) 'Carbon emission from hydroelectric reservoirs linked to reservoir age and latitude', *Nature Geoscience*, 4: 593–6, doi: 10.1038/ngeo1211.

Barton, N. J. (1992) *The Lost Rivers of London: A Study of Their Effects upon London and Londoners, and the Effects of London and Londoners on Them*, London: Historical Publications Ltd.

Basson, M. S., P. H. van Niekerk and J. A. van Rooyen (1997) *Overview of Water Resources Availability and Utilization in South Africa*, Pretoria: Department of Water Affairs and Forestry.

BBC (2005) 'Flooding apology', *Where I Live: Liverpool*, www.bbc.co.uk/liverpool/content/articles/2005/10/17/feature_welsh_reservoir_feature.shtml.

Becerra-Jurado, G., J. Johnson, H. Feeley, R. Harrington and M. Kelly-Quinn (2010) 'The potential of Integrated Constructed Wetlands (ICWs) to enhance macroinvertebrate diversity in agricultural landscapes', *Wetlands*, 30(3): 393–404.

Beddington, J. (2009) 'Food, energy, water and the climate: a perfect storm of global events?', Speech given as part of a trade mission to Thailand and Vietnam, 30 September, www.bis.gov.uk/go-science/news/speeches/the-perfect-storm.

Bell, A. (2009) *Peak Water: Civilisation and the world's water crisis*, Edinburgh: Luath Press Ltd.

Bennett, G., N. Carroll and K. Hamilton (2013) 'Charting new waters: state of watershed payments 2012', Forest Trends, Washington, DC, www.ecosystemmarketplace.com/reports/sowp2012, accessed 19 January 2013.

Bennett, M. T. (2008) 'China's sloping land conversion program: institutional innovation or business as usual?', *Ecological Economics*, 65(4): 699–711.

Bennett, M. T. and J. Xu (2005) *China's Sloping Land Conversion Program: Institutional Innovation or Business as Usual?*, Workshop on 'Payments for Environmental Services (PES) – methods and design in developing and developed countries', online, www.cifor.cgiar.org/pes/publications/pdf_files/China_paper.pdf, accessed 5 May 2011.

Bettey, J. (1999) 'The development of water meadows in the southern counties', in H. Cook and T. Williamson (eds), *Water Management in the English Landscape: Field, marsh and meadow*, Edinburgh: Edinburgh University Press, pp. 179–95.

Biello, D. (2011) 'World's largest river restoration project begins', *Scientific American*, 2 October, www.scientificamerican.com/podcast/

episode.cfm?id=worlds-largest-dam-removal-begins-11-10-02.

Biswas, A., O. Varis and C. Tortajada (2005) *Integrated Water Resources Management in South and South-East Asia*, Oxford: Oxford University Press.

Bohlen, P. J., S. Lynch, L. Shabman, M. Clark, S. Shukla and H. Swain (2009) 'Paying for environmental services from agricultural lands: an example from the northern Everglades', *Frontiers in Ecology and the Environment*, 7: 46–55, doi: 10.1890/080107.

Bond, S. (2011) 'Authorities move against Occupy protest', *Financial Times*, 15 November.

Botha, J. J., J. J. Anderson, D. C. Groenwald, N. Mdibe, M. N. Baiphethi, N. N. Nhlabatsi and T. B. Zere (2007a) *On-Farm Application of In-Field Rainwater Harvesting Techniques on Small Plots in the Central Region of South Africa*, vol. 1 of 2, TT313/07, Pretoria: Water Research Commission.

— (2007b) *On-Farm Application of In-Field Rainwater Harvesting Techniques on Small Plots in the Central Region of South Africa*, vol. 2 of 2: *Extension Manual*, TT314/07, Pretoria: Water Research Commission.

Bouguerra, L. (2006) *Water under Threat*, London: Zed Books.

Bourblanc, M. (2010) 'Social participation in water governance and management: critical and global perspectives', *International Journal of Water Resources Development*, 26(4): 709–13.

Brett, T. (2000) 'Understanding organisations and institutions', in D. Robinson, T. Hewitt and J. Harriss, *Managing Development: Understanding Inter-organisational Relationships*, London: Sage.

Briscoe, J. (2010) 'Viewpoint – overreach and response: the politics of the WCD and its aftermath', *Water Alternatives*, 3(2): 399–415.

Brown, L. R. (2001) *Eco-economy: Building an Economy for the Earth*, New York: W. W. Norton.

Bullock, A. and M. C. Acreman (2003) 'The role of wetlands in the hydrological cycle', *Hydrology and the Earth System Sciences*, 7(3): 358–89.

Burgis, T. (2012) 'Authorities clear St Paul's Occupy camp', *Financial Times*, 28 February.

Bushey, S. (2007) 'Australian water markets are growing up', *Ecosystem Marketplace*, 24 September, www.ecosystem-marketplace.com/pages/dynamic/article.page.php?page_id=5219&section=home&eod=1, accessed 18 January 2013.

CABE (2005) *Does Money Grow in Trees?*, London: Commission for Architecture and the Built Environment.

Cabot, D. (1999) *Ireland: A natural history*, London: HarperCollins.

Calder, I. R. (1999) *The Blue Revolution: Land Use and Integrated Water Resources Management*, London: Earthscan.

Carder, D. S. (1945) 'Seismicity investigations in the Boulder Dam area, 1940–44 and influence of reservoir loading on earthquake activity', *Bulletin of the Seismic Society of America*, 35: 175.

Carr Hill, R. (2007) *Cost Effectiveness in Community Engagement in Delivering Health Outcomes*, NICE Community Engagement Programme Development Group, June.

Carroll, P., R. Harrington, J. Keohane and C. Ryder (2005) 'Water treatment performance and environmental impact of integrated constructed wetlands in the Anne valley watershed, Ireland', in E. J. Dunne, K. R. Reddy and O. T. Carton (eds), *Nutrient Management in Agricultural Watersheds: A Wetlands Solution*, Wageningen: Wageningen Academic Publishers, pp. 207–17.

Central Ground Water Board (2007) 'Ground water scenario: Jaipur District, Rajasthan', Central Ground Water Board, Ministry of Water Resources, Government of India, cgwb.gov.in/District_Profile/Rajasthan/Jaipur.pdf, accessed 18 January 2013.

Cernea, M. (2000) 'Risks, safeguards and reconstruction: a model for population displacement and resettlement', in M. Cernea and C. Mcdowell (eds), *Risks and Reconstruction: Experiences of Resetttlers and Refugees*, Washington, DC: World Bank, pp. 11–56.

Churchman, C. W. (1967) 'Guest editorial: Wicked problems', *Management Science*, 14(4), December.

Codrington, S. (2005) *Planet Geography*, North Ryde, Australia: Solid Star Press.

Colbourne, L. (2005) *Literature Review of Public Participation and Communicating Flood Risk*, Lindsey Colbourne Associates for ComCoast/the Environment Agency.

— (2009) *Mainstreaming Collaboration with Communities and Stakeholders for FCERM*, Improving Institutional and Social Responses to Flooding, Joint Defra/Environment Agency Flood and Coastal Erosion Risk Management R&D Programme, Science Report: SC060019, Work Package 4, Bristol: Environment Agency, publications.environment-agency.gov.uk/pdf/SCHO0509BQBR-E-E.pdf.

Collyns, D. (2012) 'Peru's fog catchers net water supplies', *Guardian*, 19 September 2012, www.guardian.co.uk/global-development/2012/sep/19/peru-fog-catchers-water-supplies, accessed 18 January 2013.

Colvin, J. D., F. Ballim, S. Chimbuya, M. Everard, J. Goss, G. Klarenberg, S. Ndlovu, D. Ncala and D. Weston (2009) 'Building capacity for co-operative governance as a basis for integrated water resources managing in the Inkomati and Mvoti catchments, South Africa', *Water SA*, 34(6): 681–90.

Conca, K. (2005) *Governing Water: Contentious Transnational Politics and Global Institution Building*, Cambridge, MA: MIT Press.

Cooke, B. and U. Kothari (eds) (2001) *Participation: The New Tyranny?*, New York and London: Zed Books.

Costanza, R., R. d'Arge, R. de Groot, S. Farber, M. Grasso, B. Hannon, K. Limburg, S. Haeem, R. V. O'Neill, J. Paruelo, R. V. Raskin, P. Sutton and M. van den Belt (1997) 'The value of the world's ecosystem and natural capital', *Nature*, 387: 253–60.

Cottingham, P., M. C. Thoms and G. P. Quinn (2002) 'Scientific panels and their use in environmental flow assessment in Australia', *Australian Journal of Water Resources*, 5: 103–11.

Croke, B., J. Ticehurst, R. Letcher, J. Norton, L. Newham and A. Jakeman (2007) 'Integrated assessment of water resources: Australian experiences', *Water Resources Management*, 21: 351–73.

Culleton, N., E. Dunne, S. Regan,

T. Ryan, R. Harrington and C. Ryder (2005) 'Cost effective management of soiled water agricultural systems in Ireland', in E. J. Dunne, K. R. Reddy and O. T. Carton (eds), *Nutrient Management in Agricultural Watersheds: A Wetlands Solution*, Wageningen: Wageningen Academic Publishers, pp. 260–9.

Curry, D. (2002) *Future of Food and Farming*, London: Department for Environment, Food and Rural Affairs.

Daily, G. C. and K. Ellison (2002) *The New Economy of Nature and the Marketplace: The Quest to Make Conservation Profitable*, Washington, DC: Island Press.

Davies, E. (2011) 'Occupy movement: city-by-city police crackdowns so far', *Guardian*, 15 November, www. guardian.co.uk/world/blog/2011/ nov/15/occupy-movement-police-crackdowns?CMP=twt_gu, accessed 22 January 2013.

Defra (2007) 'Ecosystems approach action plan', London: Department for Environment, Food and Rural Affairs.

— (2010) *Payments for Ecosystem Services: A short introduction*, online, archive.defra.gov. uk/environment/policy/natural-environ/documents/payments-ecosystem.pdf, accessed 25 April 2011.

— (2011a) *The Natural Choice: Securing the Value of Nature*, London: The Stationery Office.

— (2011b) *Barriers and Opportunities to the Use of Payments for Ecosystem Services*, London: Department for Environment, Food and Rural Affairs.

— (forthcoming) *Best Practice Guide for Payments for Ecosystem Services (PES)*.

Dellapenna, J. W. and J. Gupta (2009) *The Evolution of the Law and Politics of Water*, Springer.

Department of Environmental Affairs (2008) *Okavango Delta Management Plan project: Okavango Delta Management Plan*, Department of Environmental Affairs, Botswana, January, www. ramsar.org/pdf/wurc/wurc_mgt-plan_botswana_okavango.pdf.

Department of the Environment, Heritage and Local Government (2010) *Integrated Constructed Wetlands: Guidance Document for Farmyard Soiled Water and Domestic Wastewater Applications*, www.environ.ie/en/Environment/ Water/WaterQuality/News/ MainBody,24926,en.htm.

Department of Water Affairs (1998) *National Water Act*, online, www.dwa.gov.za/Documents/ Legislature/nw_act/NWA.pdf, accessed 12 December 2010.

Déprés, C., G. Grolleau and N. Mzoughi (2005) 'Contracting for environmental property rights: the case of Vittel', Paper presented at the 99th Seminar of the European Association of Agricultural Economists, Copenhagen, Denmark, 24–27 August, www. eaae2005.dk/CONTRIBUTED_ PAPERS/S59_713_Mzoughi_etal. pdf#search=%22observatoire% 20environnement%202005%20 vittel%22.

Dietz, T., E. Ostrom and P. C. Stern (2003) 'The struggle to govern the commons', *Science*, 302: 1907–12.

D'itri, F. and P. D'itri (1977) *Mercury Contamination: A Human Tragedy*, New York: John Wiley and Sons.

Doody, D., R. Harrington, M. Johnson, O. Hofmann and D. McEntee (2009) 'Sewerage treatment in an integrated constructed wetland',

Proceedings of Civil Engineers, Municipal Engineer, 162(4): 199–205.

Doody, T. M. and R. G. Benyon (2011) 'Quantifying water savings from willow removal in Australian streams', *Journal of Environmental Management*, 92: 926–35.

Dunne, E. J., N. Culleton, G. O'Donovan, R. Harrington and A. E. Olsen (2005) 'An integrated constructed wetland to treat contaminants and nutrients from dairy farmyard dirty water', *Ecological Engineering*, 24: 221–34.

Dupree, M. (2004) *Leadership is an Art*, New York: Crown Business.

DWAF (1994) *Western Cape System Analysis: Main Report*, Department of Water Affairs and Forestry.

— (1996) *Skuifraam Feasibility Study: Environmental Impact assessment, Final*, Department of Water Affairs and Forestry.

— (1997) *Western Cape System Analysis: Evaluation of Options*, Department of Water Affairs and Forestry.

— (2007) *Catchment Management Strategy Guidelines*, Department of Water Affairs and Forestry, Pretoria.

Dye, P. and C. Jarmain (2004) 'Water use by black wattle (*Acacia mearnsii*): implications for the link between removal of invading trees and catchment streamflow response', *South African Journal of Science*, 100: 40–4.

East, R. (2010) 'Hydropower worth a dam?', *Green Futures*, January, p. 19.

Economist (2011) 'Unquenchable thirst', *The Economist*, 19 November, www.economist.com/node/21538687.

— (2012) 'Blooming horrible', *The Economist*, 23 June.

Eden, S. and S. Tunstall (2006) 'Ecological versus social restoration?', *Environ. Plan. C: Govt Policy*, 24: 661–80.

Eigenbrod, F., B. J. Anderson, P. R. Armsworth, A. Heinemeyer, S. F. Jackson, M. Parnell, C. D. Thomas and K. J. Gaston (2009) 'Ecosystem service benefits of contrasting conservation strategies in a human-dominated region', *P. Roy. Soc. B-Biol. Sci.*, 276(1669): 2903–11, doi: 10.1098/rspb.2009.0528. PMCID: PMC2817206.

Eigenbrod, V. F., A. Bell, H. N. Davies et al. (2011) 'The impact of projected increases in urbanization on ecosystem services', *Proceedings of the Royal Society B*, 278: 3201–8.

Ellison, D., M. N. Futter and K. Bishop (2012) 'On the forest cover-water yield debate: from demand- to supply-side thinking', *Global Change Biology*, 18: 806–20.

Embassy of the People's Republic of China in the United States of America (2010) 'Yangtze River flow set to exceed level of catastrophic 1998 floods', online, www.china-embassy.org/eng/gdxw/t718036.htm, accessed 5 May 2011.

Engel, S., S. Pagiola and S. Wunder (2008) 'Designing payments for environmental services in theory and practice: an overview of the issues', *Ecological Economics*, 65(4): 663–74.

Engels, F. (1842) 'Centralisation and freedom', Supplement to *Rheinische Zeitung*, 18 September.

Envirowise (2008) 'How much can you save?', *Envirowise Update*, Summer.

Erwin, K. L. (2009) 'Wetlands and global climate change: the role of wetland restoration in a changing world', *Wetlands Ecology and Management*, 17: 71–84.

European Commission for Environment (2000) 'DIRECTIVE 2000/60/EC of the European Parliament and of the Council of 23 October 2000 Establishing a Framework for Community Action in the Field of Water Policy', online, eur-lex.europa.eu/LexUriServ/LexUriServ.do?uri=OJ:L:2000:3 27:0001:0072:EN:PDF, accessed 4 January 2011.

Everard, M. (2004) 'Investing in sustainable catchments', *Science of the Total Environment*, 324(1–3): 1–24.

— (ed.) (2005) *Water Meadows: Living treasures in the English landscape*, Ceredigion: Forrest Text.

— (2009a) *The Business of Biodiversity*, Ashurst: WIT Press.

— (2009b) 'Ecosystem services case studies', Environment Agency Science Report SCHO0409BPVM-E-E, Environment Agency, Bristol, publications.environment-agency.gov.uk/pdf/SCHO0409BPVM-E-E.pdf.

— (2011) *Common Ground: The Sharing of Land and Landscapes for Sustainability*, London: Zed Books.

— (2012a) *Fantastic Fishes: A Feast of Fishy Facts and Fables*, Ellesmere: Medlar Press, Ltd.

— (2012b) 'What have rivers ever done for us? Ecosystem services and river systems', in P. J. Boon and P. J. Raven (eds), *River Conservation and Management*, Chichester: Wiley, pp. 313–24.

— (forthcoming) 'Freshwater fishery ecosystems and their services to society', Proceedings of the 42nd IFM Conference 'The rejuvenating role of urban fisheries in the Big Society', Oxford, 18–20 October 2011.

Everard, M. and G. Kataria (2010) 'The proposed Pancheshwar Dam, India/Nepal: a preliminary ecosystem services assessment of likely outcomes', IES research report, www.ies-uk.org.uk/resources/papers/pancheshwar_dam_report.pdf.

Everard, M. and McInnes, R. J. (forthcoming) 'Systemic solutions for integrated water and environmental management'.

Everard, M. and H. L. Moggridge (2012) 'Rediscovering the value of urban rivers', *Urban Ecosystems*, 15: 293–314.

Everard, M., P. Denny and C. Croucher (1995) 'SWAMP: A knowledge-based system for the dissemination of sustainable development expertise to the developing world', *Aquatic Conservation*, 5(4): 261–75.

Everard, M., L. Shuker and A. Gurnell (2011) *The Mayes Brook Restoration in Mayesbrook Park, East London: An ecosystem services assessment*, Environment Agency Evidence Report, Bristol: Environment Agency.

Everard, M., M. Bramley, K. Tatem, T. Appleby and W. Watts (2009a) 'Flood management: from defence to sustainability', *Environmental Liability*, 2: 35–49.

Everard, M., J. D. Colvin, M. Mander, C. Dickens and S. Chimbuya (2009b) 'Integrated catchment value systems', *Journal of Water Resource and Protection (JWARP)*, 3: 174–87.

Everard, M., T. Appleby, B. Pontin, E. Hayes, C. Staddon, J. Longhurst and J. Barnes (2012a) 'Air as a common good', *Environmental Policy and Management*.

Everard, M., R. Harrington and R. J. McInnes (2012b) 'Facilitating implementation of landscape-scale integrated water management: the integrated constructed wetland concept', *Ecosystem Services*, 2: 27–37, doi: 10.1016/j.ecoser.2012.08.001.

Falkenmark, M. (2007) 'Shift in thinking to address the 21st century hunger gap: moving focus from blue to green water management', *Water Resource Management*, 21: 3–18.

Ferraro, P. J. (2011) 'The future of payments for environmental services', *Conservation Biology*, 25(6): 1134–8.

Findlay, S. J. and M. P. Taylor (2006) 'Why rehabilitate urban river systems?', *Area*, 38(3): 312–25.

Finewood, M. H. and D. E. Porter (2010) 'Theorizing an alternative understanding of "disconnects" between science and management', *Southeastern Geographer*, 50(1): 130–46.

Finlayson, C. M., M. G. Bellio and J. B. Lowry (2005) 'A conceptual basis for the wise use of wetland in northern Australia – linking information needs, integrated analyses, drivers of change and human well-being', *Marine and Freshwater Research*, 56: 269–77.

Fish, R. et al. (2011) 'Participatory and deliberative techniques to embed an ecosystems approach into decision making: an introductory guide', Defra Project Code: NR0124, www.randd.defra.gov.uk/Document.aspx?Document=NR0124.pdf.

Fisher, J. and M. C. Acreman (2004) 'Wetland nutrient removal: a review of the evidence', *Hydrology and the Earth System Sciences*, 8(4): 673–85.

Food and Agricultural Organization of the United Nations (2007) *The State of Food and Agriculture 2007: Paying Farmers for Environmental Services*, online, ftp.fao.org/docrep/fao/010/a1200e/a1200e00.pdf, accessed 1 May 2011.

Forest and Grassland Taskforce of China (2003) 'In pursuit of a sustainable green west', Newsletter, January.

Funk, J. (2006) 'Maori farmers look to environmental markets in New Zealand', *Ecosystem Marketplace*, 24 January, www.ecosystemmarketplace.com/pages/dynamic/article.page.php?page_id=4097&section=home&eod=1.

Garrido, A. and A. Dinar (eds) (2008) *Managing Water Resources in a Time of Global Change: Contributions from the Rosenberg International Forum on Water Policy*, Routledge.

Gasteyer, S., J. Isaac, J. Hillal and S. Walsh (2012) 'Water grabbing in colonial perspective: land and water in Israel/Palestine', *Water Alternatives*, 5(2): 450–68.

Gill, S. E., J. F. Handley, A. R. Ennos and S. Pauleit (2007) 'Adapting cities for climate change: the role of the Green Infrastructure', *Built Environment*, 33(1): 122–3.

Gleeson, T., Y. Wada, M. F. P. Bierkens and L. P. H. van Beek (2012) 'Water balance of global aquifers revealed by groundwater footprint', *Nature*, 488: 197–200, doi: 10.1038/nature11295.

Gleick, P. H. (1993) *Water in Crisis: A Guide to the World's Fresh Water Resources*, Oxford: Oxford University Press.

— (n.d.) 'Zombie water projects (just when you thought they were really dead …)', www.forbes.com/sites/petergleick/2011/12/07/

zombie-water-projects-just-when-you-thought-they-were-really-dead/.

Global Water Partnership (2000) 'Integrated Water Resources Management', GWP Technical Committee Background Paper 4, Stockholm: GWP.

— (2005) *IWRM at a Glance*, online, www.gwp.org/Global/The%20 Challenge/Resource%20material/ IWRM%20at%20a%20glance.pdf, accessed 12 December 2010.

Goldfarb, B. (2012) 'Shifting streams', Special edn, 'Water works', *Green Solutions for a Blue Planet*, October, pp. 16–17.

Goldsmith, E. and N. Hildyard (eds) (1984) *Social and Environmental Effects of Large Dams*, vol. 1: *Overview*, vol. 2 (1986): *Case Studies*, Camelford, Cornwall: Wadebridge Ecological Centre.

Gómez-Baggethun, E., R. de Groot, P. L. Lomas and C. Montes (2009) 'The history of ecosystem services in economic theory and practice: from early notions to markets and payment schemes', *Ecological Economics*, 68(3): 643–53.

Gordon, L. J., C. M. Finlayson and M. Falkenmark (2010) 'Managing water in agriculture for food production and other ecosystem services', *Agricultural Water Management*, 97: 512–19.

Grant, G. (2012) *Ecosystem Services Come to Town: Greening cities by working with nature*, Chichester: Wiley.

Grêt-Regamey, A., S. H. Brunner and F. Kienast (2012) 'Mountain ecosystem services: who cares?', *Mountain Research and Development*, 32(S1): S23–S24.

Grimm, N. B., S. H. Faeth, N. E. Golubiewski, C. L. Redman, J. Wu, X. Bai and J. M. Briggs (2008)

'Global change and the ecology of cities', *Science*, 319: 756–60.

Groffman, P. M., D. J. Bain, L. E. Band et al. (2003) 'Down by the riverside: urban riparian ecology', *Front. Ecol. Environ.*, 1(6): 315–21.

Gupta, H. K. (1992) *Reservoir-Induced Earthquakes*, New York: Elsevier.

Gupta, J. (2011) 'An essay on global water governance and research challenges', in M. R. van der Valk and P. Keenan (eds), *Principles of Good Governance at Different Water Governance Levels*, UNESCO International Hydrological Programme (IHP), pp. 5–11.

Hans, A. (2001) 'Locating women's rights in the Blue Revolution', *Futures*, 33(8): 753–68.

Hardin, G. (1968) 'The tragedy of the commons', *Science*, 162: 1243–8.

Harrington, R. and R. J. McInnes (2009) 'Integrated Constructed Wetlands (ICW) for livestock wastewater management', *Bioresource Technology*, 100(22): 5498–505.

Harrington, R. and C. Ryder (2002) 'The use of integrated constructed wetlands in the management of farmyard runoff and waste water', *Proceedings of the National Hydrology Seminar on Water Resource Management: Sustainable Supply and Demand*, Irish National Committees of the International Hydrological Programme and International Commission on Irrigation and Drainage, Tullamore, Offaly, pp. 55–63.

Harrington, C. and M. Scholz (2010) 'Assessment of pre-digested piggery wastewater treatment operations with surface flow integrated constructed wetland systems', *Bioresource Technology*, 101(20): 7713–23.

Harrington, R., P. Carroll, S. Cook, C. Harrington, M. Scholz and R. J. McInnes (2011) 'Integrated constructed wetlands: water management as a land-use issue, implementing the "Ecosystem Approach"', *Water Science and Technology*, 63(12): 2929–37, doi: 10.2166/wst.2011.591.

Harris, G. (2007) *Seeking Sustainability in an Age of Complexity*, Cambridge: Cambridge University Press.

Harriss, J. (2000) 'Working together: the principles and practice of co-operation and partnership', in A. Thomas and G. Mohan, *Research Skills for Policy and Development: How to Find Out Fast*, London: Sage.

Hertzog, T., A. Adamczewski, F. Molle, J.-C. Poussin and J.-Y. Jamin (2012) 'Ostrich like strategies in Sahelian sands? Land and water grabbing in the Office du Niger, Mali', *Water Alternatives*, 5(2): 304–21.

Hill, M. (2010) 'Converging threats: assessing socio-economic and climate impacts on water governance', *International Journal of Climate Change Strategies and Management*, 2(3): 242–63.

Hirsch, P. (2006) 'Water governance reform and catchment management in the Mekong region', *Journal of Environment and Development*, 15(2): 184–201.

Hirshmann, D. (1999) 'Development management versus third world bureaucracies: a brief history of conflicting interests', in Open University, *TU870 Readings Part 1*, Wakefield: Charlesworth Group, Wakefield.

Hoa, T. and N. Tung (2008) 'Poverty reduction and Millennium Development Goal localisation: a case study of Ha Tinh Rural Development Project in Vietnam', in P. Steele, N. Fernando and M. Weddikkara (eds), *Poverty Reduction that Works: Experience of scaling up development success*, London: Earthscan, pp. 161–80.

Holling, C. S. (ed.) (1978) *Adaptive Environmental Management and Assessment*, Chichester: Wiley.

Hopkins, S. (1999) *A White Paper on Mercury*, New Mexico Environmental Department, 14 June.

Horwitz, P. and C. M. Finlayson (2011) 'Wetlands as settings: ecosystem services and health impact assessment for wetland and water resource management', *BioScience*, 61: 678–88.

Hümann, M., G. Schüler, C. Müller et al. (2011) 'Identification of runoff processes – the impact of different forest types and soil properties on runoff formation and floods', *Journal of Hydrology*, 409: 637–49.

Hunt, C. E. (2004) *Thirsty Planet: Strategies for Sustainable Water Management*, London: Zed Books.

Hussey, K. and S. Dovers (2007) *Managing Water for Australia: The Social and Institutional Challenges*, Collingwood, Australia: CSIRO Publishing.

Hyatt, J. and A. Kaplan (2006) 'Space for learning', in Open University, *TU872 Readings Parts 2 & 3*, Wakefield: Charlesworth Group.

IAP2 (International Association for Public Participation) (2008) *Core Values for the Practice of Public Participation*, online, www.iap2.org/displaycommon.cfm?an=4, accessed 15 December 2010.

ICE (1981) *Dams and Earthquake: Proceedings of a Conference at the Institution of Civil Engineers*, London: Thomas Telford Ltd.

ICOLD (1981) 'Dam projects and environmental success', *ICOLD Bulletin*, 37, International Commission on Large Dams, Paris.

— (2000) 'Response to the Final Report: ICOLD (International Commission on Large Dams)', Open letter to WCD chair, 30 November.

— (2008) *Dams and the World's Water: An Educational Book that Explains how Dams Help to Manage the World's Water*, Paris: ICOLD, www.icold-cigb.org.

ICWE (International Conference on Water and the Environment) (1992) *The Dublin statement on water and sustainable development*, Dublin: International Conference on Water and the Environment.

International Energy Agency (2006) *World Energy Outlook 2006*, Paris: IEA.

International Rivers (2002) 'The Nam Theun 2 Hydropower Project in Laos: another World Bank disaster in the making', International Rivers, Berkeley, CA, www.internationalrivers.org/files/attached-files/05.namtheun2.pdf, accessed 18 January 2013.

— (2007) '4% of global warming due to dams, says new research', Press release, International Rivers Network, 9 May, www.internationalrivers.org/node/1361.

— (2010) 'Nam Theun 2 hydropower project: the real cost of a controversial dam', International Rivers, Berkeley, CA, www.internationalrivers.org/files/attached-files/nt2_factsheet_dec10.pdf, accessed 18 January 2013.

Involve (2006) 'The trust costs of public participation', Involve.

Isaac, W. (1993) 'Taking flight: dialogue, collective thinking and organisational learning', in Open University, *TU872 Part 3 Readings*, Wakefield: Charlesworth Group.

Islar, M. (2012) 'Privatised hydropower development in Turkey: a case of water grabbing?', *Water Alternatives*, 5(2): 376–91.

Ison, R., N. Röling and D. Watson (2007) 'Challenges to science and society in the sustainable management and use of water: investigating the role of social learning', *Environmental Science and Policy*, 10: 499–511.

Jack, B. K., C. Kouskya and K. R. E. Simsa (2008) 'Designing payments for ecosystem services: lessons from previous experience with incentive-based mechanisms', *PNAS*, 105(28): 9465–70.

Jackson, R. B. et al. (2001) 'Water in a changing world', *Ecological Applications*, 11: 1027–45.

Jenkins, M., S. Scherr and M. Inbar (2004) 'Markets for biodiversity services', *Environment*, 46(6): 32–42.

Jie Liu, J., A. Dorjderem, J. Fu, X. Lei, H. Liu, D. Macer, O. Qiao, A. Sun, K. Tachiyama, L. Yu and Y. Zheng (2011) *Water Ethics and Water Resource Management*, Bangkok: UNESCO.

Jiggins, J., E. van Slobbe and N. Roling (2007) 'The organisation of social learning in response to the perception of crisis in the water sector of the Netherlands', *Environmental Science and Policy*, 10: 526–36.

Johnson, P. J., R. Kansky, A. J. Loveridge and D. W. Macdonald (2010) 'Size, rarity and charisma: valuing African wildlife trophies', *PLoS One*, 5(9), e12866.

Johnson, P. T. J., J. D. Olden and M. J. Vander Zanden (2008) 'Dam invaders: impoundments facilitate biological invasions into freshwaters', *Frontiers in Ecology and the Environment*, 6(7): 357–63.

Jonker, L. et al. (2010) *Exploring the Lowest Appropriate Level of Water Governance in South Africa*, online, www.wrc.org.za/, accessed 10 January 2011.

Jonsson, A. (2005) 'Public participation in water resource management: stakeholder voices on degree, scale, potential and methods', *Ambio*, 34(7): 495–500.

Joseph, L. F. and J. J. Botha (2011) 'Project tests mechanised soil moisture conservation techniques in heavy clay soils', *The Water Wheel*, March/April, pp. 36–7.

Joubert, A. and S. Pollard (2000) 'Using multi-criteria decision analysis in catchment manage-ment: a case study of the Sand River, Mpumulanga, South Africa', *African Journal of Aquatic Science*, 25: 238–42.

Junk, W. J., P. B. Bayley and R. E. Sparks (1989) 'The flood pulse concept in river–floodplain systems', *Canadian Special Pub-lication of Fisheries and Aquatic Sciences*, 106: 110–27.

Karla Adam, K. (2011) 'Occupy Wall Street protests continue worldwide', *Washington Post*, 16 October.

Kijne, J., S. A. Prathapar and M. C. S. Wopereis (1998) *How to Manage Salinity in Irrigated Lands: A Selec-tive Review with Particular Refer-ence to Irrigation in Developing Countries*, Sector-Wide Initiative for Water Management (SWIM).

Klark, W. K. (2003) *Winning Modern Wars: Iraq, Terrorism, and the American Empire*, New York: Public Affairs.

Kusler, J. A. and P. Riexinger (eds) (1986) *Proceedings*, National Wetland Assessment Symposium, Albany, NY.

Lawrence, J. (2006) 'The real cost of a bag of salad: you pay 99p. Africa pays 50 litres of fresh water', *Independent*, 29 April.

Le Maitre, D. C., D. M. Richardson and R. A. Chapman (2004) 'Alien plant invasions in South Africa: driving forces and the human dimension', *South African Journal of Science*, 100: 103–12.

Lee, M., B. Tansel and M. Balbin (2011) 'Influence of residential water use efficiency measures on household water demand: a four year longitudinal study', *Resources, Conservation and Recycling*, 56: 1–6.

Lenton, R. and M. Muller (2009) *Integrated Water Resource Manage-ment in Practice: Better Water Management for Development*, London: Earthscan.

Lima, I. B. T. et al. (2007) 'Methane emissions from large dams as renewable energy resources: a developing nation perspective', *Mitigation and Adaptation Strate-gies for Global Change*, published online, March.

Luger, M. and P. van Niekerk (2001) 'Experiences in applying the World Commission On Dams' guidelines to the proposed Skuifraam Dam, near Cape Town', Paper presented at the SANCOLD symposium on the World Commission on Dams Report, Midrand, 23/24 July.

Macleod, C. J. A. and R. C. Ferrier (2011) 'Temperate grasslands in catchment systems: the role of scale, connectivity and thresholds in the provision and regulation of water quality and quantity', ch. 24 in G. Lemaire, J. Hodgson and A. Chabbi (eds), *Grassland Productivity and Ecosystem: Services*, Wallingford: CAB International.

Mäkinen, K. and S. Khan (2010) 'Policy considerations for greenhouse gas emissions from freshwater reservoirs', *Water Alternatives*, 3(2): 91–105.

Malik, D. S. and K. S. Negi (2007) *Mahseer Fish Bionomics and Population: Barrage Impact on Fish Biology*, Daya Publishing House.

Maloti Drakensberg Transfrontier Project (2007) 'Payment for ecosystem services: developing an ecosystem services trading model for the Mnweni/Cathedral Peak and Eastern Cape Drakensberg areas', ed. M. Mander, INR Report IR281, Development Bank of Southern Africa, Department of Water Affairs and Forestry, Department of Environment Affairs and Tourism, Ezemvelo KZN Wildlife, South Africa.

Maltby, E. and M. C. Acreman (2011) 'Ecosystem services of wetlands: pathfinder for a new paradigm', *Hydrological Sciences Journal*, 56(8): 1341–59.

Mander, M. (2003) *Thukela Water Project: Reserve Determination Module*, Part 1: 'IFR scenarios in the Thukela River catchment: economic impacts on ecosystem services', Scottsville: Institute of Natural Resources.

Mander, M., J. Blignaut, M. van Niekirk, R. Cowling, M. Horan, D. Knoesen, A. Mills, M. Powell and R. Schulze (2010) 'Baviaanskloof and Tsitsikamma payment for ecosystem services: a feasibility study', FutureWorks, Everton, KwaZulu-Natal.

Marais, C., B. W. van Wilgen and D. Stevens (2004) 'The clearing of invasive alien plants in South Africa: a preliminary assessment of costs and progress', *South African Journal of Science*, 100: 97–103.

Matthews, N. (2012) 'Water grabbing in the Mekong basin – an analysis of the winners and losers of Thailand's hydropower development in Lao PDR', *Water Alternatives*, 5(2): 392–411.

Mayoux, L. (2005) 'Between tyranny and utopia: participatory evaluation for pro-poor development', in Open University, *TU870 Readings, Parts 2 & 3*, Wakefield: Charlesworth Group.

McCarthy, M. (2012) 'Betrayed by an act of despotism', *Independent*, 23 September, www.independent. co.uk/environment/nature/ nature_studies/nature-studies-by-michael-mccarthy-betrayed-by-an-act-of-despotism-2359240.html.

McCully, P. (2001) *Silenced Rivers: The Ecology and Politics of Large Dams*, enlarged and updated, London: Zed Books.

McManus, D. P., D. J. Gray, Y. Li, Z. Feng, G. M. Williams, D. Stewart, J. Rey-Ladino and A. G. Ross (2010) 'Schistosomiasis in the People's Republic of China: the era of the Three Gorges Dam', *Clinical Microbiological Review*, 23(2): 442–66, doi: 10.1128/ CMR.00044-09.

Mehrotra, S. and E. Delamonica (2005) 'The private sector and privatisation in social services, in Open University, *TU870 Reader Part 1*, Wakefield: Charlesworth Group.

Mehta, L., G. J. Veldwisch and J. Franco (2012) 'Introduction to the Special Issue: Water grabbing? Focus on the (re)appropriation of finite water resources', *Water Alternatives*, 5(2): 193–207.

Millennium Ecosystem Assessment (2005) *Ecosystems and Human Well-being: Wetlands and Water Synthesis*, Washington, DC: World Resources Institute.

Milner-Gulland, E. J., M. V. Kholodova, A. B. Bekenov, O. M. Bukreeva, I. A. Grachev, L. Amgalan and A. A. Lushchekina (2001) 'Dramatic declines in saiga antelope populations', *Oryx*, 35: 340–5.

Mitchell, J. (1993) 'James Bay: where two worlds collide', *National Geographic*, special edn, 'Water', 2 November, pp. 66–75.

Morel, F., A. Krepier and M. Amyot (1998) 'The chemical cycle and bioaccumulation of mercury', *Annual Review of Ecological Systems*, 29: 543–66.

Morris, J., T. M. Hess, D. G. Gowing, P. B. Leeds-Harrison, N. Bannister, R. M. N. Vivash and M. Wade (2005) 'A framework for integrating flood defence and biodiversity in Washlands in England', *International Journal River Basin Management, IAHR and INBO*, 3(2): 1–11.

Morrison, J. and I. Wilson (1996) 'The strategic management response to the challenge of global change', in H. Didsbury (ed.), *Future Vision, Ideas, Insights, and Strategies*, Bethesda, MD: Transaction Publishers.

Morse Commission (1992) *Sardar Sarovar: The report of the independent review*, Ottawa: Resources Future International.

Mostert, F. (2006) 'Participation for sustainable water management', in C. Giupponi, A. Jakeman, D. Karssenberg and M. Hare (eds), *Sustainable Management of Water Resources: An integrated approach*, Cheltenham: Edward Elgar, pp. 153–76.

Murray-Darling Basin Ministerial Council (2001) 'Integrated catchment management in the Murray-Darling basin 2001–2010: delivering a sustainable future', Murray-Darling Basin Ministerial Council, www2.mdbc.gov.au/__data/page/107/3624_ICM-PolStatement.pdf, accessed 18 January 2013.

Mustafa, A., M. Scholz, R. Harrington and P. Carroll (2009) 'Long-term performance of a representative integrated constructed wetland treating farmyard runoff', *Ecological Engineering*, 35(5): 779–90.

Nam-choon, K. (2005) 'Ecological restoration and revegetation works in Korea', *Landscape Ecol. Eng.*, 1: 77–83.

NAS–NRC (1966) *Alternatives in Water Management*, NAS–NRC publication 1408, US National Academy of Sciences–National Research Council (Committee on Water), Washington, DC.

National Library of Wales (n.d.), 'Celyn lake held a capacity of 71,200 mega litres of water, the biggest dam in Wales'.

National Rivers Authority (1990) 'Toxic blue-green algae' Water Quality Series, Bristol: National Rivers Authority.

Nature (2010) 'Wanted: an IPCC for biodiversity', *Nature*, 465: 525, doi: 10.1038/465525a.

Neal, K. V., D. A. Hepburn and R. J. Lunn (2006) 'Sediment management in sustainable urban drainage system ponds', *Water Science and Technology*, 53(10): 219–27.

NICE (National Institute for Health and Clinical Excellence) (forthcoming) *Public Health Guidance: Community engagement to improve health*, National Institute for

Health and Clinical Excellence, February 2008.

Nilsson, C. et al. (2005) 'Fragmentation and flow regulation of the world's large river systems', *Science*, 308: 405–8.

Noel, F., E. Rondecui and J. Sbeghen (1998) 'Communication of risks: organization of a methylmercury campaign in the Cree communities of James Bay, northern Québec, Canada', in R. Fortune and G. Coaway (eds), *Circumpolar Health*, 96, Anchorage: American Society for Circumpolar Health.

Nuttall, P. M., A. G. Boon and M. R. Rowell (1997) 'Review of the design and management of constructed wetlands', CIRIA Report 180, London.

Nye, J. (1990) *Bound to Lead: The Changing Nature of American Power*, New York: Basic Books.

— (2004) *Soft Power: The Means to Success in World Politics*, Cambridge, MA: Perseus Books Group.

OECD (2010) *Paying for Biodiversity: Enhancing the Cost-Effectiveness of Payments for Ecosystem Services*, OECD Publishing, doi: 10.1787/9789264090279-en.

Olsson, P. and V. Galaz (2010) 'Transitions to adaptive approaches to water management and governance in Sweden', in D. Huitema and S. Meijerink (eds), *A Research Companion to Water Transitions around the Globe*, London: Edward Elgar.

Oxfam (2013) 'The cost of inequality: how wealth and income extremes hurt us all', Oxfam, www.oxfam.org/en/pressroom/pressrelease/2013-01-19/annual-income-richest-100-people-enough-end-global-poverty-four-times, accessed 19 January 2013.

Parker, C. and M. Cranford (2010)

The Little Biodiversity Finance Book, online, www.globalcanopy.org/sites/default/files/LBFB_EN.pdf, accessed 25 April 2011.

Parrott, A., W. Brooks, O. Harmar and K. Pygott (2009) 'Role of rural land use management in flood and coastal risk management', *Journal of Flood Risk Management*, 2: 272–84.

Pearce, F. (1992) *The Dammed: Rivers, Dams, and the Coming World Water Crisis*, London: Bodley Head.

— (2004) *Keepers of the Spring: Reclaiming Our Water in an Age of Globalization*, Washington, DC: Island Press.

— (2008) 'Come the blue revolution', *Your Environment*, August–October, pp. 18–19.

peopleandplanet.net (2007) '"Blue revolution" needed to meet water needs', 9 August, www.peopleandplanet.net/doc.php?id=2819.

Perrot-Maître, D. (2006) *The Vittel Payments for Ecosystem Services: A 'perfect' PES case?*, London: International Institute for Environment and Development.

Petts, G., J. Heathcote and D. Martin (2001) *Urban Rivers: Our Inheritance and Future*, London: IWA Publishing.

Petts, J. (2006) 'Managing public engagement to optimise learning: reflections from urban river restoration', *Human Ecology Review*, 13: 172–81.

Pfaff, A., S. Kerr, L. Lipper, R. Cavatassi, B. Davis, J. Hendy and A. Sanchez (2007) 'Will buying tropical forest carbon benefit the poor? Evidence from Costa Rica', *Land Use Policy*, 24(3): 600–10.

Phillips, D., M. Daoudy, S. McCaffrey, J. Öjendal and A. Turton (2006) *Global Development Studies No. 4: Trans-boundary Water*

Co-operation as a Tool for Conflict Prevention and Broader Benefit Sharing, Ministry for Foreign Affairs, Sweden.

Pickett, S., M. Cadenasso and J. Grove (2001) 'Urban ecological systems: linking terrestrial ecological, physical, and socio-economic components of metropolitan areas', *Annu. Rev. Ecol. Syst.*, 32: 127–57.

Pitt, Sir M. (2007) *The Pitt Review: Lessons Learned from the 2007 Floods*, London: Cabinet Office, www.cabinetoffice.gov.uk/thepittreview/final_report.aspx.

Pomfret, J. (2008) 'Anglers let big cash bonanza get away', Reuters, www.reuters.com/article/2008/04/25/us-fish-odd-idUSHAR55771320080425.

Postel, S. (1999) *Pillars of Sand: Can the Irrigation Miracle Last?*, New York: W. W. Norton and Co.

Pradhan, N., I. Providoli, B. Regmi and G. Kafle (2010) 'Valuing water and its ecological services in rural landscapes: a case study from Nepal', *Mountain Forum Bulletin*, January, lib.icimod.org/record/14618/files/5475.pdf.

Provost, C. (2012) 'Energy companies pledge to measure impacts of large dam projects', guardian.co.uk, 19 March, www.guardian.co.uk/global-development/2012/mar/19/energy-companies-protocol-water-footprint.

Purseglove, J. (1988) *Taming the Flood: History and Natural History of Rivers and Wetlands*, Oxford: Oxford University Press.

Quibell, G. and R. Stein (2005) 'Can payments be used to manage South African watersheds sustainably and fairly? A legal review', Paper 2, South Africa Working Paper Series, July.

Rahaman, M. and O. Varis (2005) 'Integrated Water Resource Management: evolution, prospects and future challenges', *Sustainability: Science, Practice and Policy*, 1(1): 15–21.

Ramsar Convention (2012) 'Resolution XI.15: Agriculture–wetland interactions: rice paddy and pest control', 11th Meeting of the Conference of the Parties to the Convention on Wetlands (Ramsar, Iran, 1971): 'Wetlands: home and destination', Bucharest, Romania, 6–13 July, www.ramsar.org/pdf/cop11/res/cop11-res15-e.pdf, accessed 18 January 2013.

Ramsar Convention Secretariat (2010) *Handbook 9: Integrating wetland conservation and wise use into river basin management*, 4th edn, Ramsar Convention Secretariat, Gland, www.ramsar.org/pdf/lib/hbk4-09.pdf.

Rebelo, L.-M., M. P. McCartney and C. M. Finlayson (2010) 'Wetlands of sub-Saharan Africa: distribution and contribution of agriculture to livelihoods', *Wetlands Ecology and Management*, 18(5): 557–72.

Reinhardt, C., J. Bölscher, A. Schulte and R. Wenzel (2011) 'Decentralised water retention along the river channels in a mesoscale catchment in south-eastern Germany', *Physics and Chemistry of the Earth*, 36: 309–18.

Reisner, M. (1986) *Cadillac Desert: The American West and Its Disappearing Water*, New York: Viking Penguin.

Republic of South Africa (1998) National Water Act No. 36 of 1998, Pretoria, South Africa.

Richter, B. D., S. Postel, C. Revenga, T. Scudder, B. Lehner, A. Churchill and M. Chow

(2010) 'Lost in development's shadow: the downstream human consequences of dams', *Water Alternatives*, 3(2): 14–42.

Rittel, H. and M. Webber (1973) 'Dilemmas in a general theory of planning', *Policy Sciences*, 4: 155–9.

Robinson, D. (2000) 'Reforming the state: co-ordination, regulation and facilitation?', in D. Robinson, T. Hewitt and J. Harriss (2000) *Managing Development: Understanding Inter-organisational Relationships*, London: Sage.

Roszak, T., M. E. Gomes and A. D. Kanner (1995) *Ecopsychology: Restoring the Earth, Healing the Mind*, New York: Bantam Press.

Rowland, K. (2012) 'Recall of the wild', *Green Futures*, 86: 26–8.

Roy, A. (2002) *The Algebra of Infinite Justice*, London: Flamingo.

Royal Society (2009) *Reaping the Benefits: Science and the Sustainable Intensification of Global Agriculture*, London: Royal Society.

Sahu, B. K. (2008) 'Pani Panchayat in Orissa, India: the practice of participatory water management', *Development*, 51: 121–5.

SAMWU (1999) South African Municipal Workers' Union press statement opposing Skuifraam Dam, 16 July.

Scheumann, W., S. Neubert and S. Kipping (eds) (2008) *Water Politics and Development Cooperation: Local power plays and global governance*, New York: Springer.

Schlosberg, D. (2007) *Defining Environmental Justice: Theories, Movements, and Nature*, Oxford: Oxford University Press.

Scholz, M., R. Harrington, P. Carroll and A. Mustafa (2007) 'The Integrated Constructed Wetlands (ICW) concept', *Wetlands*, 27: 337–54.

Schumacher, E. F. (1973) *Small is beautiful*, London: Sphere Books.

ScienceDaily (2012) 'Can organic food feed the world? New study sheds light on debate over organic vs. conventional agriculture', *ScienceDaily*, 25 April, www.sciencedaily.com/releases/2012/04/120425140114.htm.

Scudder, T. (2005) *The Future of Large Dams: Dealing with Social, Environmental, Institutional and Political Costs*, London: Earthscan.

Serageldin, I. (2009) 'Water: conflicts set to arise within as well as between states', *Nature*, 459: 163.

Seyfried, M. S. and B. P. Wilcox (2006) 'Soil water storage and rooting depth: key factors controlling recharge on rangelands', *Hydrological Processes*, 20: 3261–75.

Shiva, V. (2008) *Soil Not Oil: Climate change, peak oil and food insecurity*, London: Zed Books.

Shore, R. (2011) 'Farmers to be paid to take a green approach', *Vancouver Sun*, 16 November, www.vancouversun.com/technology/Farmers+paid+take+green+approach/5718014/story.html.

Simpungwe, E., P. Waalewijn and B. Raven (2007) 'Multi-stakeholder dissonance in the South African water arena', in J. Warner (ed.), *Multi-Stakeholder Platforms for Integrated Water Management*, Farnham: Ashgate.

Slinger, J., L. Hermans, J. Gupta, P. van der Zaag, R. Ahlers and E. Mostert (2011) 'The governance of large dams: a new research area', in M. R. van der Valk and P. Keenan (eds), *Principles of Good Governance at Different Water Governance Levels*, UNESCO International Hydrological Programme (IHP), pp. 33–44.

Sosa, M. and M. Zwarteveen (2012) 'Exploring the politics of water grabbing: the case of large mining operations in the Peruvian Andes', *Water Alternatives*, 5(2): 360–75.

South Asian Network (2007) '19% of India's global warming emissions from large dams: myth of large hydro being clean shattered (again)', South Asian Network on Dams, Rivers and People, 18 May, www.sandrp.in/dams/India_Dams_Methane_Emissions_PR180507.

Staddon, C. (2010) *Managing Europe's Water Resources: Twenty-first Century Challenges*, Farnham: Ashgate.

Stapleton, L., M. Lehane and P. Toner (2000) *Ireland's Environment: A millennium report*, Wexford: Environmental Protection Agency.

Steenbergen, F. van, A. Tuinhof and L. Knoop (2011) *Transforming Lives Transforming Landscapes. The Business of Sustainable Water Buffer Management*, Wageningen, The Netherlands: 3R Water Secretariat.

Sullivan, P., D. Hellerstein, L. Hansen, R. Johansson, S. Koenig, R. Lubowski, R. McBride, D. McGranahan, M. Roberts, S. Vogel and S. Bucholtz (2004) 'The Conservation Reserve Program: economic implications for rural America', *Agricultural Economic Report*, 834, USDA Economic Research Service, online, www.ers.usda.gov/publications/aer834/aer834.pdf, accessed 2 May 2011.

Survival International (2011) 'World Water Day: global outrage over Ethiopia mega-dam', www.survivalinternational.org/news/7099, accessed 1 July 2011.

Suzuki, D. and A. McConnell (1997) *The Sacred Balance: Rediscovering Our Place in Nature*, Vancouver: Greystone Books.

TEEB (2009) *TEEB for Policy Makers – Summary: Responding to the Value of Nature*, online, www.teebweb.org/Portals/25/Documents/TEEB%20for%20National%20Policy%20Makers/TEEB%20for%20Policy%20exec%20English.pdf, accessed 5 May 2011.

— (2010a) *The Economics of Ecosystems and Biodiversity: Mainstreaming the Economics of Nature: A synthesis of the approach, conclusions and recommendations of TEEB*, online, www.teebweb.org/LinkClick.aspx?fileticket=bYh DohL_TuM%3d &tabid=924&mid=1813, accessed 25 April 2011.

— (2010b) *A Quick Guide to the Economics of Ecosystems and Biodiversity for Local and Regional Policy Makers*.

Terminski, B. (2012) 'Oil-induced displacement and resettlement: social problem and human rights issues', Simon Fraser University.

Teschner, N., A. McDonald, T. J. Foxon and J. Paavola (2012) 'Integrated transitions toward sustainability: the case of water and energy policies in Israel', *Technological Forecasting and Social Change*, 79(3): 457–68.

Theroux, P. (1988) *Riding the Iron Rooster: By train through China*, London: Penguin.

Thomas, A. (1996) 'What is development management?', in Open University, *TU872 Reader Part 1, Section 1 & 2*, Wakefield: Charlesworth Group.

Thomas, E. (2007) *Capel Celyn, Ten Years of Destruction: 1955–1965*, Cyhoeddiadau Barddas & Gwynedd Council.

Tippett, J. et al. (2005) 'Social learning in public participation in river basin management – early findings from HarmoniCOP European case studies', *Environmental Science and Policy*, 8: 287–99.

Tonen, T. (2011) 'The (changing) role of national government in multilevel (water) governance', in M. R. van der Valk and P. Keenan (eds), *Principles of Good Governance at Different Water Governance Levels*, UNESCO International Hydrological Programme (IHP), pp. 13–31.

Turner, R. K., C. J. M. van den Bergh, T. Soderqvist, A. Barendregt, J. van der Straaten, E. Maltby and E. C. van Ierland (2000) 'Ecological–economic analysis of wetlands: scientific integration for management and policy', *Ecological Economics*, 35: 7–23.

Turton, A. R. (2003) 'The hydropolitical dynamics of cooperation in Southern Africa: a strategic perspective on institutional development in international river basins', in A. R. Turton, P. Ashton and T. E. Cloete (eds), *Transboundary Rivers, Sovereignty and Development: Hydropolitical Drivers in the Okavango River Basin*, Pretoria and Geneva: AWIRU and Green Cross International, pp. 83–103.

— (2005) 'A critical assessment of the basins at risk in the southern African hydropolitical complex', Workshop on the Management of International Rivers and Lakes, Helsinki, Finland, 17–19 August.

— (2007) 'Can we solve tomorrow's problems with yesterday's experiences and today's science?', *CSIR*, September.

Tzoulas, K., K. Korpela, S. Venn, V. Yli-Pelkonen, A. Kaźmierczak, J. Niemela and P. James (2007) 'Promoting ecosystem and human health in urban areas using green infrastructure: a literature review', *Landscape Urban Plan*, 81(3): 167–78.

UK Cabinet Office (2011) 'Big Society', online, www.cabinetoffice.gov.uk/content/big-society-overview.

UK National Ecosystem Assessment (2011) *The UK National Ecosystem Assessment: Synthesis of the Key Findings*, Cambridge: UNEP-WCMC.

UNDP (2004) *Human Development Report 2004: Cultural Liberty in Today's Diverse World*, New York: United Nations Development Programme, hdr.undp.org/reports/global/2004/.

— (2006) *Human Development Report 2006: Beyond Scarcity: Power, Poverty and the Global Water Crisis*, New York: Palgrave Macmillan.

UNFPA (2007) *State of the World Population 2007: Unleashing the potential of urban growth*, New York: United Nations.

UNICEF (2008) *Our Climate, Our Children, Our Future Responsibility*, UNICEF, www.unicef.org.uk/campaigns/publications/pdf/climate-change.pdf.

United Nations (1997) *Nigeria Country Profile – implementation of Agenda 21: Review of Progress Made since the United Nations Conference on Environment and Development, 1992*, www.un.org/esa/earthsummit/nigeriac.htm.

— (2008) *The New Water Culture – Integrated Water Resources Management. Resolution of the World Conservation Congress, Barcelona, October 2008*, United Nations Resolution CGR4.MOT088.

United Nations Department of Public Information (2006) *Ten Stories the World Should Hear More*

About: From water wars to bridges of cooperation – exploring the peace-building potential of a shared resource, www.un.org/Pubs/chronicle/2006/issue2/0206p54.htm#Water.

United Nations Environment Programme (2007) *Dams and Development: Relevant Practices for Improved Decision Making*, DDP Secretariat, UNEP, Nairobi, www.Earthprint.com.

Vaidyanathan, G. (2011) 'Dam controversy: remaking the Mekong', *Nature*, 478: 305–7, doi: 10.1038/478305a.

Van Koppen, B., P. Moriarty and E. Boelee (2006) 'Multiple-use water services to advance the Millennium Development Goals', IWMI Research Report 98, International Water Management Institute, Colombo, Sri Lanka.

Van Wilgen, B. W., B. Reyers, D. C. Le Maitre, D. M. Richardson and L. Schonegevel (2007) 'A biome-scale assessment of the impact of invasive alien plants on ecosystem services in South Africa', *Journal of Environmental Management*, doi: 10.1016/j.jenvman.2007.06.015.

Vanclay, J., R. Prabhu and F. Sinclair (2006) *Realizing Community Futures: A Practical Guide to Harnessing Natural Resources*, London: Earthscan.

Vaughan, A. (2013) 'Severn barrage opponents dismiss wildlife-friendly claims as "guff": angling, wildlife and heritage groups dispute claims by developers that new proposal is environmentally friendly', *Guardian*, 10 January, www.guardian.co.uk/environment/2013/jan/10/severn-barrage-wildlife-claims-guff, accessed 18 January 2013.

Verhoeven, J. T. and A. T. L. Setter (2010) 'Agricultural use of wetlands: opportunities and limitations', *Annals of Botany*, 105: 155–63.

Visscher, J. T., P. Bury, T. Gould and P. Moriarty (1999) 'Integrated water resource management in water and sanitation projects: lessons from projects in Africa, Asia and South America', Occasional Paper 31, IRC, Delft, Netherlands.

Vymazal, J. (2011) 'Constructed wetlands for wastewater treatment: five decades of experience', *Environment Science and Technology*, 45: 61–9.

Waalewijn, P. (2005) 'Transforming river basin management in South Africa', *Water International*, 30(2): 184–96.

Walters, J. (2011) 'Occupy America: protests against Wall Street and inequality hit 70 cities', *Guardian*, 8 October, www.guardian.co.uk/world/2011/oct/08/occupy-america-protests-financial-crisis, accessed 22 January 2013.

Wani, S., H. Singh, T. Sreedevi, P. Pathak, T. Rego, B. Shiferaw and S. Iyer (2003) 'Farmer-participatory integrated watershed management: Adarsha Watershed, Kothapally India – an innovative and upscalable approach', Case 7 in R. Harwood and A. Kassam (eds), *Research towards Integrated Natural Resource Management: Examples of research problems, approaches and partnerships in action in the CGIAR*, pp. 123–47.

Ward, Diane Raines (2002) *Water Wars: Drought, Flood, Folly, and the Politics of Thirst*, New York: Riverhead Books.

Wasson, J. G., B. Villeneuve, A. Iital, J. Murray-Bligh, M. Dobiasova, S. Bacikova, H. Timm, H. Pella,

N. Mengin and A. Chandesris (2010) 'Large-scale relationships between basin and riparian land cover and the ecological status of European rivers', *Freshwater Biology*, 55: 1465–82.

Watts, J. (2010) 'Chinese engineers propose world's biggest hydro-electric project in Tibet', www.guardian.co.uk, 24 May, www.guardian.co.uk/environment/2010/may/24/chinese-hydroengineers-propose-tibet-dam, accessed 1 July 2011.

WBCSD (2011) *Guide to Corporate Ecosystem Valuation – a framework for improving corporate decision making*, World Business Council for Sustainable Development, www.wbcsd.org/work-program/ecosystems/cev.aspx.

Wegerich, K. and J. Warner (eds) (2010) *The Politics of Water: A Survey*, Routledge.

Wei, Y., R. Ison, J. D. Colvin and K. Collins (2011) 'Reframing water governance: a multi-perspective study of an over-engineered catchment in China', *Journal of Environmental Planning and Management*, doi: 10.1080/09640568.2011.597589.

Weyerhaeuser, H., A. Wilkes and F. Kahrl (2005) 'Local impacts and responses to regional forest conservation and rehabilitation programs in China's Northwest Yunnan Province', *Agricultural Systems*, 85: 234–53.

Wheater, H. and E. Evans (2009) 'Land use, water management and future flood risk', *Land Use Policy*, 265: 251–64.

Wickham, J. D., K. H. Riitters, T. G. Wade and P. Vogt (2010) 'A national assessment of green infrastructure and change for the conterminous United States using morphological image processing', *Landscape Urban Planning*, 94: 186–95.

Williams, T. O., B. Gyampoh, F. Kizito and R. Namara (2012) 'Water implications of large-scale land acquisitions in Ghana', *Water Alternatives*, 5(2): 243–65.

Wilson, Edward O. (1978) *On Human Nature*, New York: Bantam Books.

— (1998) *Consilience: The Unity of Knowledge*, New York: Alfred A. Knopf.

Wittfogel, Karl A. (1957) *Oriental Despotism: A Comparative Study of Total Power*, New Haven, CT: Yale University Press.

Wood, A. and G. E. van Halsema (2008) 'Scoping agriculture–wetland interactions: towards a sustainable multiple-response strategy', FAO Water Reports 33, Rome: Food and Agriculture Organization of the United Nations.

Woodhouse, P. (2012) 'Foreign agricultural land acquisition and the visibility of water resource impacts in sub-Saharan Africa', *Water Alternatives*, 5(2): 208–22.

Woods, B., R. Ballard et al. (2007) 'The SUDS manual', CIRIA Report C697, Construction Industry Research and Information Association, London.

World Bank (1994) *Resettlement and Development: The Bankwide Review of Projects Involving Involuntary Resettlement 1986–1993*, Environment Department, Washington, DC: World Bank.

— (2007) *World Development Report: Agriculture for Development*, Washington, DC: World Bank.

— (2010) 'Rising global interest in farmland: can it yield sustainable and equitable benefits?', Washington, DC: World Bank.

World Commission on Dams (2000) *Dams and Development: A New Framework for Better Decision-making*, London: Earthscan.

— (2001) 'Three "reality checks" of the WCD Report: economics and project development', *Dams* (the WCD newsletter), 9 March, www.dams.org/news_events/newsletter9266.htm.

Wunder, S. (2005) 'Payments for environmental services: some nuts and bolts', CIFOR Occasional Paper no. 42, Center for International Forestry Research, Bogor, Indonesia.

Wünscher, T., S. Engel and S. Wunder (2006) 'Payments for environmental services in Costa Rica: increasing efficiency through spatial differentiation', *Quarterly Journal of International Agriculture*, 45(4): 319–37.

WWF6 (2012) 'Target Session 3.1.4: Bringing ecosystems into river basin management', www.worldwaterforum6.org/uploads/tx_amswwf/Session_proposal_Target_3_1_4.pdf.

Xu, J., R. Yin, Z. Li and C. Liu (2006) 'China's ecological rehabilitation: unprecedented efforts, dramatic impacts, and requisite policies', *Ecological Economics*, 57: 595–607.

Young, W. J. et al. (2004) 'Improving expert panel assessments through the use of a composite river condition index – the case of the rivers affected by the Snowy Mountains Hydro-electric scheme, Australia', *River Research and Applications*, 20: 733–50.

Zeitoun, M. and N. Mirumachi (2008) 'Transboundary water interaction I: reconsidering conflict and cooperation', International Environmental Agreements, doi: 10.1007/s10784-008-9083-5.

Index

nature, perceived as villain, 155
Nature Assist programme (Australia), 204, 252–63 *passim*
navigation on river systems, 31
Nebuchadnezzar II, 8
Nehru, Jawarharlal, 22, 28, 61, 116, 122
Nepal, 113–14, 181; Medium Hydropower Screening and Ranking project, 89; mitigation project in, 94; National Hydropower Development Policy, 89; PES initiative in, 198
Nestlé Waters company, 201
Netherlands, 99, 200
New York City: evolution of water supply of, 221–2; Green Infrastructure Plan, 185; street trees in, 184; water management in, 158, 201
New Zealand, PES schemes in, 205
Nga Whenua Rahui programme (New Zealand), 205
Ngati Porou Whenui Forests Ltd (NPWFL), 205
Nigeria, 51, 129; dams in, 178
Nile river, 37, 97–8; silt transportation by, 19
nitrous oxide, 55
Nkrumah, Kwame, 59
non-governmental organizations (NGOs), 64–5, 66
Norfolk Island pine, moisture capture capacities of, 169
North American Water and Power Alliance (NAWAPA), 71
North China Plain, 128
Norway, taxation system in, 96
Nottingham Declaration, 185
Nubian sandstone aquifer, 129–30
nuclear power, failures of, 120
nutrient cycling, 110

Occupy movement, 246–7
Okavango Delta Management Plan, 100, 251–63 *passim*
Olifants River Water Resources Development Project (South Africa), 88, 226

open planning, 100
opposite-leaved pondweed (*Groenlandia densa*), 151
Orange river, 101
Organisaton for Economic Co-operation and Development (OECD), 222; *Paying for Biodiversity*, 196
overpumping of groundwater *see* groundwater, over-pumping of
overtopping: of dams, 21, 44, 108; of waterways, 52
oxygen, concentrations of, 44
Ozal, Turgut, 59

paddy system, 178
Pagos por Servicios Ambientales (PSA) *see* Costa Rica
Pakistan, 101; decision-making processes in, 95
Palestine, 176; water management in, 165
Pani Panchayat (India), 98–9
Papago Indians, water management techniques of, 173
Papua New Guinea, catchment management in, 139
participation, public, definition of, 140
participatory decision-making *see* decision-making, participatory
paying for ecosystem services (PES), 190–6; definition of, 195; use of term, 194; water-related (in Africa, 206–7; in Asia, 196–8; in Australasia, 204–5; in Costa Rica, 202–3; in Europe, 198–201; in the Americas, 201–4; involving Vittel company, 200–1)
Payment for Watershed Services (PWS), 198
Pearce, Fred, 26, 133–4; *Keepers of the Spring*, 165, 173, 218–19
peat harvesting, 148
Perrier company, 201; PES project, 251–63 *passim*
Peru, 118, 173, 176; fog-catchers in, 170
pest regulation, 108

About Zed Books

Zed Books is a critical and dynamic publisher, committed to increasing awareness of important international issues and to promoting diversity, alternative voices and progressive social change. We publish on politics, development, gender, the environment and economics for a global audience of students, academics, activists and general readers. Run as a co-operative, Zed Books aims to operate in an ethical and environmentally sustainable way.

Find out more at:

www.zedbooks.co.uk

For up-to-date news, articles, reviews and events information visit:

http://zed-books.blogspot.com

To subscribe to the monthly Zed Books e-newsletter, send an email headed 'subscribe' to:

marketing@zedbooks.net

We can also be found on **Facebook**, **ZNet**, **Twitter** and **Library Thing.**